Glossolalia and the Problem of Language

Glossolalia and the Problem of Language

NICHOLAS HARKNESS

The University of Chicago Press
Chicago and London

The University of Chicago Press, Chicago 60637
The University of Chicago Press, Ltd., London
© 2021 by The University of Chicago
All rights reserved. No part of this book may be used or reproduced in any manner whatsoever without written permission, except in the case of brief quotations in critical articles and reviews. For more information, contact the University of Chicago Press, 1427 E. 60th St., Chicago, IL 60637.
Published 2021
Printed in the United States of America

30 29 28 27 26 25 24 23 22 21   1 2 3 4 5

ISBN-13: 978-0-226-74938-9 (cloth)
ISBN-13: 978-0-226-74941-9 (paper)
ISBN-13: 978-0-226-74955-6 (e-book)
DOI: https://doi.org/10.7208/chicago/9780226749556.001.0001

Library of Congress Cataloging-in-Publication Data

Names: Harkness, Nicholas, author.
Title: Glossolalia and the problem of language / Nicholas Harkness.
Description: Chicago : University of Chicago Press, 2021. |
    Includes bibliographical references and index.
Identifiers: LCCN 2020035405 | ISBN 9780226749389 (cloth) |
    ISBN 9780226749419 (paperback) | ISBN 9780226749556 (ebook)
Subjects: LCSH: Glossolalia. | Language and languages—Religious aspects. |
    Evangelicalism.
Classification: LCC BT122.5 H37 2021 | DDC 234/.132—dc23
LC record available at https://lccn.loc.gov/2020035405

For my two ones

Contents

Note on Romanization and Translation ix

	Introduction	1
1	Abundance and the Ambivalent Gift	21
2	The Limits of Language	38
3	Feeling the Same Thing	65
4	Fusion and Force	89
5	Revelations	121
6	Deception	146
	Conclusion	167

Acknowledgments 171
Appendix: The Nineteenth-Century Invention of
Glossolalia; an Etymological Reconstruction 175
Notes 185
Bibliography 207
Index 225

Note on Romanization and Translation

I have mostly followed the McCune–Reischauer system of romanization for Korean. I did not make changes to the spelling of Korean names or proper nouns if quoted from a different publication or if circulated widely following a different romanization system (e.g., "Seoul"). In general, personal names appear in Korean order, with the surname followed by the given name, unless the person has specified a different order. However, for consistency, Korean names in the bibliography are styled with a comma between the surname and the given names, and in note citations they are styled with the given initials preceding the surname. I refer to the Republic of Korea as "Korea" or "South Korea" unless otherwise noted. Translations from Korean and German into English are mine unless otherwise noted.

Introduction

> Lorem ipsum dolor sit amet, consectetur adipiscing elit, sed do eiusmod tempor incididunt ut labore et dolore magna aliqua.

> Nae yaraba roshi lik'i yaraba na yaraba shik'u yaraba sat'a yaraba sannaribi. Nik'io lashi yaraba k'a na i i k'a na yŏrŏbŏ shi yaraba k'annari.

The two passages above are similar. Both are recomposed from the residual fragments of actual speech. They have been reassembled from elements of linguistic codes, but they do not follow the rules of assembly for those codes. On the left is *lorem ipsum*, a placeholder that graphic designers use to take up textual space prior to filling a nonlinguistic visual form with linguistic content (e.g., for the layout of a magazine or webpage). It is a syntactic and morphological jumbling of a first-century-BC Latin passage by Cicero.[1] Like the artificial mock speech that is used to parody whole populations of speakers, the patterns of the passage imply the presence of a specific, identifiable language (e.g., it seems to contain words like *dolor* and *magna* and suffixes like *-um*).[2] The jumble of forms produces a Latinate effect. But it is not Latin, and it can neither be translated as text nor abstracted as code. The success of this placeholder depends, crucially, on producing the intentionally limited effect of inscribed speech—writing—without the full functions of language.

The passage on the right is a transcription of glossolalia, which in English is also called "speaking in tongues." The glossolalia was produced by Cho Yonggi, founder and former head pastor of the Yoido Full Gospel Church in Seoul. Like *lorem ipsum*, it is a kind of placeholder, a verbal deferral that stands between everyday forms of interpretable speech (in this case, Korean) and spiritually elevated forms of speech, such as inspired prophecy or sacred utterances in ancient languages. Its phonotactics and segmentation suggest, for some listeners, that it is the materialization of a specific language with a specific grammar. The repetition of *yaraba*, for example, could be construed as a grammar pattern or even a word. Like *lorem ipsum*, glossolalia operates by the cultural logic of a container to be filled. How this logic looks depends on the semiotic lens one uses to look at it. For the linguist, the speech is untranslatable because, like *lorem ipsum*, it is semantically empty, devoid of meaning, a mere graphic-phonetic container without content. It is nonsense. For an evangelist of glossolalia like Cho Yonggi, the opposite is true—if glossolalic speech is uninterpretable and untranslatable, it is because it contains an abundance of meaning, a surplus of signification that coincides with the speaker's infilling of the Holy Spirit and exceeds normal human linguistic faculties.

Both passages produce the effect of language by undermining and suppressing one key function of language. Put another way, both passages are meaningful for the specific way in which they suppress one kind of meaning. This one kind of meaning is what makes language unique among other semiotic systems: denotation. It is the mode through which linguistic forms reliably correspond to classes of things. This correspondence depends on both a linguistic code or system that fuses those forms with concepts (a grammatico-syntactic precipitate called semantics), as well as repeated, historically situated, varied, practical instances of picking out and describing things in speech (called reference and predication). Denotation is commonly the most recognizable—often definitional—mode of language. It is the function of language that must usually be established to prove that something is, in fact, language. Both passages bear a paradoxical relation to language, because both produce an experience of language by suppressing this crucial function of language. The similarities are manifold, but the differences are profound.

The Problem of Language

This book is a study of glossolalia and its problematic relation to language. Using ethnographic data from South Korea, where Christians across Protestant denominations regularly speak in tongues, I aim to explain how and why an experience of language is produced through processes of its own negation. In contemporary Christian traditions of speaking in tongues, glossolalia is an explicitly linguistic type of involvement with the deity. Glossolalia is culturally intelligible as a kind of speech because its speech forms are unintelligible—*denotationally* unintelligible. Christian speech behavior becomes glossolalia when it suppresses the denotational function of language, targeting and rupturing the semantico-referential processes that link linguistic forms to denotata. The causes of glossolalia are complex, but its most obvious effect can be put simply. While many recognize glossolalia as an act of saying, few can answer the question, What is being said?

Practitioners of glossolalia worldwide take inspiration from a few passages from the New Testament that link denotational unintelligibility to the direct intervention of the Holy Spirit into human speech behavior. There have been extensive hermeneutical and theological debates regarding these passages.[3] Theologians and biblical historians puzzle over the differences between the accounts of Pentecost and Paul's First Epistle to the Corinthians, which provide the descriptive accounts as well as the Greek phrase *glossais lalein*, from which the modern invented term *glossolalia* was derived as a back-formed neologism in early nineteenth-century Germany.[4] They ask whether glossolalia was the miraculous production of earthly, unlearned languages (sometimes called xenolalia or xenoglossia) or a heavenly, spiritual language. They wonder if its practitioners were overcome by divine ecstasy or were sometimes agentively exercising a spiritual gift. They debate the necessity of interpreting tongues—of rendering denotational the nondenotational. Even more complicated are the possible social functions of New Testament glossolalia; namely, whether speaking in tongues was (and therefore should be) a true sign of the spirit, an instrument of missionization, or a medium for private devotion.

At the pinnacle of the problem is how these biblical interpretations should relate to, authorize, and guide present-day practice. From Acts of the Apostles to Corinthians, from the Montanists to the Camisards, Shakers, Irvingites, and the early Mormon Church, from the Pentecostals of Azusa Street to the multiple charismatic variations presently around the globe, Christian observers and producers of unintelligible utterances are confronted with the status and legitimacy of the behavior's relationship to language.[5] Real glossolalia—whatever that is taken to be—should ideally have a compounding effect on theology, because it is always characterized and practiced with reference to assertions about the gospel—the Word—and to the role of the Word in mediating social and spiritual relations. But the Word is fallible on these matters.

The Anglican cleric Frederic Farrar was early to herald the arrival of the word "glossolalia" from the German *die Glossolalie* into printed English. Recognizing the complexity of the problem, he wrote the following in his 1879 work, *The Life and Work of St. Paul*:

> Almost all the theories about the glossolalia are too partial. The true view can only be discovered by a combination of them. The belief that languages were used which were unknown, or only partially known, or which had only been previously known to the speaker; that the tongue was a mystic, exalted, poetic, unusual style of phraseology and utterance; that it was a dithyrambic outpouring of strange and rhythmic praise; that it was the impassioned use of ejaculatory words and sentences of Hebrew Scripture; that it was a

wild, unintelligible, inarticulate succession of sounds, which either conveyed no impression to the ordinary hearer, or could only be interpreted by one whose special gift it was to understand the rapt and ecstatic strain—none of these views is correct separately, all may have some elements of truth in their combination.[6]

Farrar criticized as partial those theories of glossolalia that project the salient from the selectively scriptural. The same criticism may be applied to nonreligious explanations. Some explanations tend toward theories of economic and educational deprivation. Others exaggerate the presence of ecstasy, trance, and dissociation. Others highlight the earthly politics of resistance and emancipation. Still others hold glossolalic utterances up to the semantico-referential capacities of known languages and find them, predictably, lacking. What unites these perspectives is a treatment of glossolalia as a deviation from a desirable modern disciplinary object, such as socioeconomic inclusion, lucid mental functions, participatory democracy, or standard speech. Whether viewed as creative or destructive, voluntary or compulsory, benign or malignant, glossolalia is frequently posited as a kind of exception, just as much as mainstream Christian theology tends to treat contemporary glossolalia as proceeding from an exceptional, even aberrant, interpretation of the New Testament.

In South Korea—now an economically powerful, highly educated, democratic, and increasingly multilingual society—glossolalia is practiced widely across denominations and congregations. Although Korean Pentecostal churches claim only approximately one million adherents, or roughly 10 percent of the total estimated Protestants, this stereotypically Pentecostal practice has penetrated nearly all denominations.[7] The vast majority of Presbyterians (by far the largest denomination, accounting for well over half of all Protestants), Methodists, and Baptists—let alone Pentecostals—in South Korea have personally encountered tongues in some way or another. Speaking in tongues was formally introduced in Korea in the late 1920s and '30s through Pentecostal missionary efforts but had little traction.[8] The practice began to spread in the 1960s with the rapid growth of one powerful church founded in 1958, eventually called the Yoido Full Gospel Church, led by Cho Yonggi and his mother-in-law, Choi Jashil. By the early 2000s and before a number of satellite churches became independent, the church claimed more than eight hundred thousand members. The church's expansion coincided with the rapid postwar growth of Protestantism in South Korea more generally—from around 3 percent in 1960 to 20 percent or more by the 1990s. By the 1980s glossolalia had become widespread across denominations.[9] Today, some churches promise the capacity of tongues for all. Others view it as an individual gift, widely but unevenly distributed across populations.[10] Still others criticize most of the glossolalia they observe as false. Whether people themselves practice it regularly, have tried to produce it, have been encouraged to produce it, or have prayed with someone who produced it, glossolalia is a ubiquitous genre of Christian speech.[11]

Anthropological objects are not given; they must be formulated. How, then, to formulate glossolalia as an anthropological object in South Korea? As frequently as South Korean Christians refer to scripture for guidance on New Testament glossolalia, they also confront and navigate glossolalia as a contemporary sociolinguistic reality. Their theological and doctrinal positions are themselves reflections of ideological positions on glossolalia's troubling relation to language—not an absolute one, but a malleable one with degrees of doubt and certainty. Across all instances of glossolalia and the debates that it instigates, one thing remains consistent: the problem of language.

The Korean term for *glossolalia* is not "speaking in tongues." While Koreans do talk about the tongue (*hyŏ*) as a practical instrument for generating glossolalia, Korean translations of the Bible do not explicitly appropriate the Greek metonym of the tongue-for-speech as do European-language translations. The term is *pangŏn* (usually combined with *kido*, "prayer"), a Sino-Korean compound that, outside of Christian contexts, refers to a regional dialect, what in "native" Korean is more commonly called *sat'uri*. Closer to the "other tongues," i.e., "other languages" (*tarŭn ŏnŏ*) of Acts 10:4, the Sinographs for *pangŏn* combine the characters for "place, direction, or region" (方) and "speech" (言).[12]

Pangŏn fits within a broader semantic field of Sino-Korean and native Korean terms for "speech" and "language." The term *mal* is the general unmarked lexeme corresponding to the nouns "language," "speech," "talk," "word," and "saying." *Malssŭm* is the general honorific variation and is also specifically used to refer to the Word of God in the context of church. Moreover, *mal* (and *malssŭm*) can be combined directly with the verb stem -*hada* (to do), to yield "to talk," "to say," "to speak," "to tell," and so forth. The Sino-Korean compound *ŏnŏ* (言語) has a different distribution. As a compound noun, it combines with other Sino-Korean lexical bases in scholarly and scientific registers dealing with language; e.g., *ŏnŏhak* (linguistics). In certain compounds, *ŏ* (語, words, language) can be exchanged with *mal*. For example, "Korean language" can be rendered as either *Han'guk mal* or *Han'gugŏ*, but the exchange is not possible for syntactically free uses of *mal*; e.g., "our language" is *uri mal* but not *uri ŏ*. *Ŏ* is also combined with other Sino-Korean lexemes to yield denotations related to linguistic units or types, such as *tanŏ* (vocabulary word), *yongŏ* (technical terms), and *sogŏ* (slang). *Ŏn* (言, words, talk) may be combined in a similar way to denote speech acts and genres, such as *choŏn* (counsel, advice), *ŏnjil* (pledge), or *yeŏn* (prophecy).[13]

It is important not to take the translation of the word *pangŏn* too literally. The central point is that *pangŏn*, as the Korean word referring to speaking in tongues, has a lexicalized relationship to a concept of language. Some Korean Christians, like early Pentecostals in the United States, do think of tongues as earthly languages acquired miraculously, often in missionary settings.[14] Although the utterance appears to the practitioner to be language-like enough, in many cases it should not appear so formally developed as to be investigated on linguistic grounds. At the same time, although it is semantically opaque, its religious legitimacy depends, fundamentally, on the promise of its interpretability and renderability as coherent denotational text. Most who engage in glossolalia treat tongues as an unintelligible spiritual language to be used for communicating directly and individually with God, even if the direction of communication (from the deity or to the deity) is not always clear. While practitioners do not always agree about the specific nature, purpose, or degree of supernatural involvement in glossolalia, they generally do agree that true glossolalia is the spoken manifestation of language, be it spiritual, ancient, transcendent, or simply foreign.

Like the scholars who study this phenomenon, Christians past and present struggle to discern which instances of glossolalia are real speech and which are merely speech-like. If it is not speech, then it is not real (glossolalia); if it is not real (glossolalia), then it is fakery, self-deception, or potentially heresy. In the last thorough analysis of glossolalia, published nearly fifty years ago, William Samarin dedicated a whole book to confirming one central point: "Glossolalia is indeed like language in some ways, but this is only because the speaker (unconsciously) wants it to be like language."[15] My book asks: Why do they want it to be like language? How do they make it so? What is glossolalia as a specifically linguistic medium? What is the significance of its linguisticality for practitioners? The point here is not to ask whether or not glossolalia is language; the point is to ask what it tells us about language—what people want and fear from language.

These questions cannot be answered by focusing solely on the forms that are produced or the theologies that explicitly evaluate its production. Glossolalia must be situated among an array of related communicative practices and the kinds of social relations they mediate. The approach of this book is to locate the communicative continuities and discontinuities, as well as the semiotic analogies and oppositions, that cluster around glossolalia, and to use these penumbral practices to illuminate the umbral center. This book proceeds as an expansive contextualization of glossolalia in South Korea, operating at different social scales, focusing on different cultural media, and pursuing different themes. The data come from fieldwork in Seoul from 2006 until 2018, with sustained research carried out in 2013 and 2014. The data consist of focused interviews; casual conversations; immersive observation and participation; analyses of internet and broadcast media; and readings of sermons, theological scholarship, and how-to guides for speaking in tongues. The methods and materials are as wide-ranging and variable as are the practices and practitioners. My ethnographic scope is the messy, heterogenous semiotic space where glossolalia is lived and debated. And the resulting depiction is of a kind of semiotic behavior that is not the obvious outcome of theological principles or existential contradictions, but rather is the historical precipitate of many different communicative processes.

This book makes three central assertions about glossolalia: empirical, analytical, and theoretical. The empirical assertion arises from the ethnography— Korean Protestants experience the ubiquitous presence of glossolalia as a sociolinguistic fact. I call it a sociolinguistic fact of Korean Protestant experience because its ubiquitous presence is socially coercive, and the most consistent characteristic of the practice across all instances of social variation is its problematic relationship to language, whatever other claims about its motivations or effects might be made. As I explain in chapter 1, glossolalia is a widespread but profoundly ambivalent practice among Protestants in South Korea. It is a semiotic tensor of numerous, often contradictory social forces, syncretic legacies, and spiritual desires that are condensed and amplified by Korea's specific historical encounter with Christianity.

The analytical assertion interprets these ethnographic facts through a dialectical formulation of the anthropological object: glossolalia should be conceptualized as cultural semiosis—sign behavior—that is said to contain, and therefore can be justified by, an ideological core of language, but in fact is produced at the ideological limits of language. An *ideological core* refers to the absolute necessary element that orients a cultural category (in this case, language), is prototypical or emblematic of the category, and is the conceptual focal point in terms of which other elements are assimilated to the category. The *ideological limit* refers to the threshold for assimilation to the category—the fuzzy boundary between what does and does not count. Traditions of glossolalia likely will differ on both the ideological limits and the ideological core of language, and this relation will shape how practitioners discern the nature of their contact and communication with the deity and with one another. In the present study, glossolalia both depends on and challenges assumptions about denotation and its role mediating social contact— crudely put, how social relations are managed through "words" for "things."

This cultural-semiotic treatment allows me to encompass the widest possible array of data and avoid the untenably narrow, purified definitions of glossolalia put forth by theological, psychological, or linguistic approaches.

The limits of language are internal and external, an imposed constraint and an extreme boundary. As I explain in chapter 2, glossolalia promises to break free from the restrictions of speech, to transcend what is possible with language, all the while depending on what is ideologically fundamental and essential about language.[16] It does so by severely restricting the linguistic elements available for speech. The co-occurrence of limited sound shapes can generate the effect of the spiritual outpouring of fluent speech with a language-specific character. From within, the formal elements of glossolalia seem to operate by a structural process that suppresses the forms to expand the functionality.[17] From without, it looks like a genre of radical heteroglossia, in which each relatively simple vocable is shot through with a profound multiplicity of potential semiotic histories and effects.[18] This inherently unstable model of speech to which glossolalists contribute phonically and orient sonically makes for a thrilling and malleable, but also fragile and often threatening phonosonic nexus of sociocultural activity.[19] By following Korean Protestant Christians as they regularly push speech to the limits of language, I explain how and why an expansive experience of language is produced, or at least promised, through processes of its own negation.

Finally, the theoretical assertion: the possibility of glossolalia's divine translation distracts from the pragmatics of its earthly creation. Glossolalia's capacity to suppress in practice the very ideological core it promises allows it to direct attention away from the social mediation that is necessary for, but potentially threatening to, the cosmology it supports. It is an equation of suspension, requiring both parts. The two parts—the narrow promise of denotation, which is absent, and the broad denial of social mediation, which is present—can magnify and reinforce each other, or one can undermine the other. Glossolalia will always fail the denotational test of language; it will carry the burden of denotation without delivery.

Glossolalia displays a curious relation between genre and register, two closely related, reflexive models of semiotic composition. By *genre*, I am referring to the typification of textuality, focusing attention on regularities of the internal structural cohesion of semiotic composition and its potential for extraction from context and circulation. Treated as a genre of speech, glossolalia promises to "say something." This "something" can then be reported as speech. By *register*, I am referring to the way some of the signs within a composition combine, i.e., "co-occur," to indicate "who" is behind the composition.

Enregistered signs point to context, especially to one specific dimension of context; namely, the social identities that are likely involved in the signs' production.[20] These identities can then be "voiced" (whether indicating a biographical individual or a general social persona). Treated as a register of speech, glossolalia promises that "someone" will say something to "someone." Paradoxically, as a genre, glossolalia depends on the nonreplicability of its uttered texts; glossolalic quotation is normally avoided, and its textuality is deferred and made explicit through related genres operating in the denotational mode, such as interpretation and testimony.[21] Ultimately, the emphasis on extreme spiritual individuation is assimilated to the heightened anticipation of the singular speaking voice of the deity, which is confirmed by these other genres. It is the register effects of glossolalia—the contextualizing indication of "who" is speaking or participating—and these related genres that legitimize it as having—in potential, at least—denotational textuality, and thus to be language.

Just as glossolalia must be oriented to the potential of denotation in order not to be viewed, linguistically, as nonsensical babble, it must also be oriented to the voice of the deity (or to an interaction with the deity) in order for it not to be viewed, sociologically, as mere undignified "self-talk."[22] In practice, however, interpretation is infrequent. Instead, the suppression of denotation has the more far-reaching but covert capacity to manage and avoid certain forms of social contact. In chapters 3 through 6, I demonstrate how glossolalia exposes the relations and ruptures between, on the one hand, traditions and doctrines of speech and spirituality, and, on the other, broader sociocultural concerns about the relation between speech and sociality. Specific topics include collectively shared feelings of the deity, global evangelical conduits of the gospel, gossip and the risks of intimacy, and the dangers of deception and isolation. On the whole, this study of glossolalia lays bare the aspirations for and anxieties about the linguistic mediation of socio-spiritual relations.

Observers of South Korean Christianity have remarked on the "fervent" (*kanjŏrhan*) quality of Protestantism that characterized the rapid church growth in the second half of the twentieth century. This ranges from the relatively mild attribution of an "evangelical ethos" to the stronger claim of a full "pentecostalization" across denominations.[23] This character emerged from a confluence of now well-documented sociological and historical factors. There is no easy answer to why Christianity emerged in the shape and magnitude that it did, but some important pieces of the puzzle include (1) pervasive, practical, popular, pantheistic spiritual traditions, including shamanism and lay Buddhism; (2) an early Protestant history identified with literacy, modern education and medicine, and national independence from Japanese imperial domination; (3) grinding postwar poverty and the desire for prosperity and healing; (4) a postcolonial, Cold War Christianity that identified spiritual forces of good (US, Europe) and evil (Japan, North Korea); (5) rapid urbanization and industrialization; (6) church growth organized around charismatic religious authority; (7) capitalist promises and failures within a developmental, authoritarian state; (8) the unequal distribution of spiritual labor along the lines of gender, class, and heredity; and (9) an aesthetics of sociality that encourages massive gatherings and institutions. The experience of glossolalia-as-language is caught up in all of these sociocultural processes, drawing them into the immediate facts of speech behavior and suffusing speech with concerns about class and distinction, spiritual contact and secrecy, mental health and personal sincerity, embodied affect and political authority, syncretic spirits and Christian modernity, pride and shame.

Across these multiple concerns, three prominent sociocultural forces shape the character of glossolalia as a kind of semiotic tensor. The first is the fundamental ambivalence of the spiritual gift. Glossolalia takes on different values in differently conceptualized economies of faith organized by the politics of church communities, revealing the uneven distribution of socio-spiritual power. For Christians in South Korea as elsewhere, a persistent question is the extent to which the gift of tongues, as a spiritual *charism* (in Korean, *ŭnsa*), is given to individuals and populations: its conceptualization and its value depend fundamentally on who can or should perform it and who cannot or should not. If the gift (*sŏnmul*) focuses attention on social relations and the commodity focuses attention on social distinctions, glossolalia is both desired and dangerous for its conceptualization in terms of both categories. Second is a preference for a sameness of feeling within social groups, where an explicit theory of the divine, i.e., "theology," is based on the desirable sensations of collective belonging through social contact. Whereas the ambivalent gift produces unevenness and distinction, the ethics of participation and communal feeling through glossolalia are designed to produce social integration, evenness, and a spiritual reality of a single source of spiritual authority. Spiritual abundance emerges as both a solution to and a problem for the radical democratization of glossolalia, because there is in principle enough to go around, but in practice it is never distributed equally. Finally, is the persistent pressure of speech placed on Christian communities in South Korea. Here, the culture of evangelism intersects with the institutional organization of hierarchy and intimacy. The obligation to receive the Word and pass the Word along turns glossolalia into a crucial social node through which control and agency, force and submission are negotiated, exploited, and expressed.

Other Anthropological Objects

One might object that I emphasize language too much in this study. I must be clear: the point is not to reduce glossolalia to language. Nor is it, in the manner of glossolalic interpretation, to render the nondenotational as denotational in order to explain its "meaning," when meaning (or signification) is understood through one narrow function of language; i.e., one that produces an intelligible message. The point is that glossolalia is best understood through the practical, ideological, and, to a limited extent, structural or formal problem of language. Only after one has dealt with the broad problem of language can one begin to make reliable assertions about other dimensions of the issue. The problem of language is the unavoidable first step before other claims can be made. William Samarin's *Tongues of Men and Angels*, published in 1972, makes a similar assertion: "You can't explain why people engage in unintelligible speech before you understand what it is they produce. This should be a perfectly obvious point of view, but it seems to have escaped most people."[24]

Samarin's book and related papers constitute the most sophisticated and systematic sociolinguistically oriented study of glossolalia to date. Many of his observations will be repeated in the pages that follow. However, when Samarin asserted that glossolalia is "meaningless but phonologically structured human utterance, believed by the speaker to be a real language but bearing no systematic resemblance to any natural language, living or dead," he was still, in the manner of twentieth-century linguistics, orienting to an understanding of language as primarily, rather than uniquely, denotational.[25] Since the publication of Samarin's book, denotation—or, more narrowly, the semantico-referential function of language—has been provincialized in anthropological analyses of speech and communication. Denotation is, on the one hand, what makes language unique among forms of cultural semiosis; it is a "true symbolic mode," in the idiom of Charles Peirce.[26] The symbolic mode of language is what Ferdinand de Saussure characterized as "arbitrary" about the relation between linguistic forms and their corresponding concepts, which established the foundations of modern linguistics.[27] On the other hand, denotation is not the only thing that goes on in speech, and it is often marginal to what is taking place through the other semiotic modes of what still falls, for speakers, into the cultural-conceptual category of language. There is a seeming paradox in denotation in our own scholarly conceptualization of language: denotation is at once analytically central and methodologically decentered, both essential and marginal. Denotation is analytically central because one must be able to recognize and explain it; it is methodologically marginal because one must be able to make good use of it and then move systematically beyond it.

Samarin's approach was self-consciously sociolinguistic at a time when sociolinguistics was still a young field. He viewed glossolalia in terms of a kind of sociolinguistic variation. Based on numerous interviews, surveys, recordings, and observations in North America, Europe, and the Caribbean, he concluded that glossolalia was best understood as anomalous speech behavior lacking a code (i.e., *langue*, the virtual scientific object posited by Saussure). Although this description is empirically unobjectionable—indeed, no account of glossolalia has been able to produce a grammar of its source language—it does little to explain the existence and practice of glossolalia. This is in large part because Samarin carried out his study prior to three important developments: (1) the theorization of language ideology as a constitutive dimension of the problematic anthropological object we call language; (2) the introduction and refinement of the tools of semiotic analysis that allow anthropologists to empirically and coherently examine a broader range of functions that fall into the cultural concept of "language"; and (3) the incorporation of these tools into an immersive ethnographic method—beyond metalinguistic interviews and surveys—that can address cultural semiosis as, in the words of Michael Silverstein, a "criss-crossing, frequently contradictory, ambiguous, and confusing set of pragmatic meanings of many kinds of behavior."[28]

Without the benefit of these three social-scientific developments, Samarin arrived at a view of glossolalia as the product of "regressive" speech, where the "speaker returns to processes that characterized his language learning in early childhood, at a time when he was first learning the part of language most obvious to a child—its phonetic representation."[29] He showed that purely formal analysis reveals quite clearly that the elements of glossolalic utterances are produced by "(1) echoism and (2) a tendency towards regularity of cadence . . . (3) a reduced inventory of sounds and (4) a preference for open syllables."[30] That is, he viewed glossolalia as returning to the combination of the sound shapes of speech prior to the acquisition of language.[31] For Samarin, glossolalia was a kind of linguistic mistake: a "façade" of language produced by a semiotic alchemy of prelinguistic elements.

In late nineteenth- and early twentieth-century Europe, various linguists (e.g., Victor Henry, Ferdinand de Saussure), psychologists (e.g., Théodore Flournoy), and psychoanalysts (e.g., Oskar Pfister) followed similar formalist pathways to interpret, apologize for, explain, or debunk glossolalia.[32] In the United States in 1895, William James encountered a glossolalist, a "literary man" he called Albert Le Baron, at a time when spiritualist mediums and seances were producing all sorts of examples of mystical "animation" for scientists and the public to puzzle over.³³ Le Baron produced unintelligible utterances that, the man asserted, carried "no subjective feeling of being due to his personal will" despite the fact that, as James put it, "his will could both start and arrest them, make them go fast or slow, and sing instead of speaking them." This man was "by no means willing to abandon the idea that his unintelligible vocal performances were involuntary reproductions of some ancient or remote tongue."³⁴ James and the psychical researcher Richard Hodgson observed Le Baron, transcribed his utterances, and corresponded with philologists on Le Baron's behalf. After considering all the evidence, James concluded that the "phonetic elements in his case again seemed English; and I tried to make him [Le Baron] believe (but all in vain) that the whole thing was a decidedly rudimentary form of motor automatism analogous to the scrawls and scribbles of an 'undeveloped' automatically-writing hand."³⁵ Ultimately James was able to temper Le Baron's convictions of the significance of his glossolalia, and even published Le Baron's autobiographical account in the *Proceedings of the Society for Psychical Research* (1896–97) while serving as the society's president.

It is now well known that the restricted phonetic inventory of glossolalia consists almost entirely of sounds from language systems with which the speaker is familiar. It may contain various indexes of otherness, such as exotic articulations, uncommon phonetic sequences, or the incorporation of ideologically nonlinguistic sounds like grunts, growls, or cries. It may emphasize or avoid shibboleths of familiarity—usually sound shapes that function as linguistic emblems of identifiable languages, such as nasality for French, velar fricatives for German, geminates for Italian, or tonal differentiation for Chinese languages. But on the whole, its phonetic materials are known to the speaker, even if they are made to sound strange.³⁶ Some amount of linguistic well-formedness—syntactic, prosodic, etc.—is certainly at issue, but it is not the only issue. Often, it is the least significant issue. To make the formal dimensions of glossolalia the central problem is to follow a methodological dead end, because it leads away from the cultural contextualization of the practice rather than illuminating it. It is unlikely that a purely formal, segmental analysis of glossolalia will reveal very much about the sociocultural dimensions of the problem, whether we are considering glossolalic forms specific to Korea or the various genres of phonetic, syntactic, or semantic unintelligibility and their oracular interpretation elsewhere. Such an analysis will provide clues but not an explanation. The question, rather, is how these fairly simple, formal, combinatoric patterns become privileged, priestly material; and, for Korean Christianity specifically, how a specialized, esoteric register becomes a democratic, exoteric channel of spiritual contact.

Glossolalists themselves often self-consciously appropriate formal simplicity as a way into the practice. A common approach to acquiring glossolalia is to allow oneself to talk like a baby and make oneself the verbal equivalent of a child before God. In South Korea, this is called "starter" or "elementary" tongues (ch'obangŏn). The effect of simplicity can be a feeling of improvisatory creativity and embodied expressivity—an abundance of spiritual signification that itself can generate celebratory theories of glossolalia as promising, even constituting, a "vocal utopia." Consider, for example, Michel de Certeau's account:

> As an invention of vocal space, glossolalia in fact multiplies the possibilities of speech. No determination of meaning constrains or restrains it. The decomposition of syllables and the combination of elementary sounds in games of alliteration create an indefinite space outside of the jurisdiction of a language. This vast space, artificial and entrancing, this virgin forest of the voice, is supposed to have "meaning" as a whole, as a totality, but one can circulate freely within it without encountering the limits that condition any articulation of meaning. Within this privileged space, within the ephemeral construction of this scene, the issue is no longer that of statements but of an opera composed only of the vocal modalizations that a statement might undergo. On the stage of a linguistic semblance, an enactment of language is replaced by a *vocalization of the subject*.[37]

Certeau's hopeful depiction of glossolalia as "jubilant indeterminacy" belongs to a more general category of "poetic noises" that he called "the linguistic analogue of an erection."[38] The surplus of signification beyond denotation—now an unremarkable, empirically researchable, straightforward semiotic fact of language—generated a whole post-structuralist scholarly industry composed of these sorts of emancipatory readings. Samarin and Certeau arrived at two different but equally predictable positions on glossolalia, both of which were outcomes of a theoretical preoccupation with denotation that reached its apex in the twentieth century. Whereas Samarin arrived from rich and wide-ranging data at a narrowly linguistic, unsatisfying conclusion of glossolalia as a mistake, a failure of language, Certeau arrived at the partial, selective, aspirational proposal of glossolalia as freedom, an emancipation from language.[39]

Samarin, however, was writing directly against the other major anthropological approach to glossolalia, which treated glossolalia as a trance phenomenon. In *Speaking in Tongues*, also published in 1972, Felicitas Goodman suggested that glossolalia was an "artifact of a hyper-aroused mental state"—a vocal result of extreme neurophysiological processes of dissociation and

INTRODUCTION 15

trance.⁴⁰ Goodman is one in a long line of scholars who have exaggerated the linkage between glossolalic behavior and extreme brain states. The most recent iteration of this can be found in neurophysiological studies, where neuroimages of cerebral activity of a handful of glossolalists of are exhibited and incredible conflations of empirical categories are made.⁴¹ Samarin wrote a scathing review of Goodman's book, which included a point-by-point refutation of Goodman's argument and a reanalysis of her data. Ultimately it came down to this:

> Let us say it clearly: G's treatment is erroneous, speculative, contradictory, and incredible, because of her relentless hold on an idée fixe. Yet her empirical base was simple enough: the vocalizations of Pentecostals who appeared to be in a state of dissociation. It was because she believed her hypothesis (on the causal relation between vocalization and dissociation) that she has gone to such extremes to prove it. A more careful person, working within the best scientific tradition, would have taken pains to DISPROVE it. If she had failed at that, she would have had more reason to believe the hypothesis.⁴²

Trance-like experiences are more aspirational than constitutive of the practice. Of course, it is tempting to imagine glossolalia—whether spiritually or neurophysiologically motivated—according to Farrar's most exciting description:

> Any one who fairly ponders these indications can hardly doubt that, when the consciousness of the new power came over the assembled disciples, they did not speak as men ordinarily speak. The voice they uttered was awful in its range, in its tone, in its modulations, in its startling, penetrating, almost appalling power; the words they spoke were exalted, intense, passionate, full of mystic significance; the language they used was not their ordinary and familiar tongue, but was Hebrew, or Greek, or Latin, or Aramaic, or Persian, or Arabic, as some overpowering and unconscious impulse of the moment might direct; the burden of their thoughts was the ejaculation of rapture, of amazement, of thanksgiving, of prayer, of empassioned psalm, of dithyrambic hymn; their utterances were addressed not to each other, but were like an inspired soliloquy of the soul with God. And among these strange sounds of many voices, all simultaneously raised in the accordance of ecstatic devotion, there were some which none could rightly interpret, which rang on the air like the voice of barbarous languages, and which, except to those who uttered them, and who in uttering them felt carried out of themselves, conveyed no definite significance beyond the fact that they were reverberations of one and the same ecstasy—echoes waked in different consciousnesses by the same immense emotion. Such—as we gather from the notices of St. Luke, St. Peter, and St. Paul—was the "Gift of Tongues." And thus regarded, its strict accordance

with the known laws of psychology furnishes us with a fresh proof of the truthfulness of the history, and shows us that no sign of the outpouring of the Holy Spirit could have been more natural, more evidential, or more intense.[43]

Spectacles of mass enthusiasm are readily on display in South Korea as elsewhere. However, there is enormous variability in how glossolalia is practiced beyond the extreme, albeit stereotypical, case of total possession by the spirit or Dionysian ecstasy. My interlocutors, like others elsewhere, did describe heightened feelings of various sorts during glossolalia, such as warmth, tightening, energy, or power in various parts of the body. They described states of extreme focus. They often characterized prayer as a cathartic form of therapy and emotional "release." They might even have felt the physical presence of the deity. But none of these feelings or states are unique to glossolalia. Moreover, very few of these people described regular occurrences of anything like trance or spirit possession. That is, they spoke in tongues far more often than they were taken over by the Holy Spirit. The hypothesis of glossolalia as primarily either producing trance or the product of trance is fundamentally flawed because it does not account for most of the instances in which glossolalia is said by practitioners to take place.

Practitioners did report experiencing various degrees of immersion, absorption, or what psychologists sometimes call "dissociation"—i.e., a focused awareness or concentration that is "detached" or directed away from the immediate context of activity. However, it was just as common for glossolalia to be described, even emphasized, in terms of group participation, practical necessity, or any other number of willed, self-conscious, self-aware, goal-directed, or socially oriented ways of acting. Utterances produced in this state can be completely conscious and intentional and yet still be considered glossolalia. Despite its local and familiarizing association with shamanic spirit possession, and the more global characterization of glossolalia as ecstatic, trance-like practice, it is by no means necessarily a consciousness-altering technique in South Korea, even if it may often appear so from the outside. Practitioners of glossolalia described a wide variety of experiences, with many degrees of agency, awareness, and arousal.

In many cases, glossolalia was positively banal. This was especially common for people who had been socialized to glossolalia as youths in the 1980s and '90s. For many of them, revivals, fervent group prayer, glossolalia, and other forms of socio-spiritual stimulation were routinized aspects of Protestant worship in South Korea. Even in cases where the glossolalist attributed their utterances to an agent apart from themselves, there was a blending or murky area of "will." Like Le Baron, they presented ambiguities with regard to personal agency when they admitted to maintaining some control over their utterances—if not the precise phonetic articulations, then, for example, the prosody, speed, or length of the utterance. It was also common for glossolalists to use speaking in tongues as a space of privacy, even secrecy, in which intentional thoughts and feelings could be communicated to the deity, in full but completely controlled verbal fluidity, without uttering anything publicly. By first establishing this communicative space through glossolalia, various feelings of spiritual contact could be generated, with varying degrees of intensity. In this way, glossolalia is continuous with other forms of communication with the deity, where thoughts, feelings, and utterances as well as other actions are thought to be motivated, at least partly, by some other force. But such feelings of a loss of agency through the external compulsion to act, in speech or otherwise, are not only attributable to the spiritual realm. People consistently reported feeling compelled to act, often against their will, simply by the overwhelming social pressures of everyday life. Despite the stereotype of a person filled with and under the control of the Holy Spirit, speaking fluently in an unknown language, in a state of altered consciousness, the practice is far more mundane and profane.

Glossolalia provokes the fundamental question rightfully asked of any utterance: Who is speaking?[44] In glossolalia, it is not always clear in which direction the communicative channel is flowing: from God to human (as in command or prophecy) or from human to God (as in confession or praise). The experience of glossolalia is idealized as fusional, but there is plenty of confusion and doubt, especially as one leaves the ritual centers and follows the practice to the peripheries. At the margins, questions about glossolalia's motivation—spiritual, psychological, social—are persistent and common. There, glossolalia is held up against two purified models of the Christian speaker, both of which are realized only under the most perfect of conditions. One is the model of modern Christian sincerity: the self-conscious, self-reflexive Christian, speaking biblically anchored denotational truth in one's own voice. The other is the overwhelming, authoritative, absolute voice of God. The anthropological object I am after resides in between.

Chapter Overview

This book contains six chapters—organized into three couplets—followed by a brief conclusion and an appendix. Chapters 1 and 2 develop the historical and ethnographic dimensions of the study, focusing on the foundational tensions that emerge out of glossolalic form and charting them across the ritual centers and peripheries of practice. Chapters 3 and 4 examine processes of circulation and mediation, looking closely at contending conceptualizations of the Word, as well as problems and solutions of evangelical translation and interpretation. Chapters 5 and 6 take a more intimate view of the individual, interactional, and institutional scope of glossolalia, the competing forces of enclosure and exposure that practitioners encounter, and the value of personal concealment in communities that are organized around promises of revelation.

Chapter 1 introduces the striking ubiquity of glossolalia in South Korea and its penetration into Korean Christian worship beginning in the second half of the twentieth century. It begins with an account of a Presbyterian informant who regularly speaks and even dreams in tongues, whose husband speaks in tongues against his will, whose mother longs to speak in tongues but cannot, and whose father never speaks in tongues but regularly prays with people who do. It then develops the sociohistorical context for the widespread emergence of glossolalia across denominations and congregations in South Korea. In particular, it looks at what informants self-consciously described as a general sociocultural predilection for stimulation in South Korea, which manifests in Christianity as seemingly syncretic elements in worship practices. It also demonstrates how the contemporary institutional dynamics of Korean Christianity—especially the megachurch—shape feelings of both social connection and competition, linking glossolalia to the political economy of gender, class, and commodification in Seoul. It concludes by focusing on the Yoido Full Gospel Church and its members during the postwar urbanization of South Korean Christianity to situate glossolalia within an array of spiritual gifts targeted at the suffering postwar masses.

Chapter 2 moves to the ritual epicenter of glossolalia in South Korea, the Yoido Full Gospel Church, to develop the analytical assertion of this book: glossolalia should be conceptualized as cultural semiosis that is said to contain, and therefore be justified by, an ideological core of language, but in fact is produced at the ideological limits of language. The analysis proceeds by looking at how the language-ideological features of glossolalia intersect in mass events of group prayer, where glossolalia and cacophony combine to impose limits on "normal" linguistic functions (namely, denotation, prosody, participant roles, and social indexicality) while reinforcing ideological commitments to language itself. However, the ritual teleology of these imposed limits generates an experience of virtual language that exceeds the limits of "normal" speech and produces the sensuous intensity of spiritual contact.

Chapter 3 investigates Korean Christian conceptualizations of "the Word" as something that seems to circulate—to "move"—in order to illuminate the ideological grounds for explaining the sense of a shared experience of the Holy Spirit. Focusing closely on the cultural conceptualization of the Word in contemporary South Korea, the chapter shows how theological assertions of two pastors who lead two of the largest churches in Seoul conceptualize in denominationally different ways (Presbyterian and Pentecostal) the relation of utterances to agents in order to make claims about the behavior of the Holy Spirit in Christian communities. The chapter shows how the logic of glossolalia is embedded in the more mainline Presbyterian model, and rises to the surface in the Pentecostal model, as emphasis shifts from the linguistic mediation of social contact in Christian fellowship to the linguistic mediation of contact with the Holy Spirit en masse.

Chapter 4 demonstrates how the logic of glossolalia is present in the Korean Christian emphasis on evangelism and revivalism. I analyze the final sermon of the American Evangelist Billy Graham's 1973 "crusade" in Seoul, South Korea, when he preached to a crowd estimated to have exceeded one million, the largest crowd ever amassed for a Graham event. Next to Graham at the pulpit was Jang Hwan "Billy" Kim, a Korean Baptist preacher who, in his capacity as interpreter, translated (and matched) Graham's sermon verbally and peri-verbally—utterance by utterance, tone by tone, gesture by gesture—for the Korean-speaking audience. For observers of this legendary event, one Christian's voice seemed to be filled with the speech of another, and both voices seemed to be fused together by the work of the Holy Spirit. The analysis reveals the dynamic pragmatics by which a verbal copy across linguistic codes became an evangelical conduit between Cold War polities, paving the way for the movement of the Word—and the Holy Spirit—from speaker to speaker, from code to code, from country to country, from heaven to earth. Although neither of the men engage in or encourage glossolalia, their collaborative manipulations of utterance and agency across domains of mutually unintelligible speech provide important clues for understanding the semiotic force of glossolalia in South Korea.

Chapter 5 investigates the value of glossolalia as a medium of intimacy, privacy, and secrecy for South Korean Christians. Informants often described glossolalia as a secret language with God or speech that allows the prayerful to share secrets with God. By speaking in tongues, Christians can confess and repent publicly without being heard—by friends and family, by strangers, or by the devil. The combination of socio-spiritual contact and verbal concealment afforded by glossolalia sits at the intersection of two competing models of semiotic circulation in the church. One, the gospel, fuses propositional truth with ideal social relations across contexts of action and interaction. The other, gossip, competes with the gospel by traveling through different routes of circulation, forging different kinds of social relations, and producing alternative truths. Whereas the gospel is supposed to be homogenizing and unifying, gossip is understood to be fracturing, heterogeneous, and divisive. This is why some insist that the gift to interpret glossolalia is given only to those who can keep a secret—i.e., those who speak only the gospel and do not gossip. As a moral system of secrecy, glossolalia regulates not merely what is or should be a secret, but also who may have access to it, how this access is achieved, the mechanisms by which access is controlled, and the routes and extent of circulation. In these highly determined complexes of secrecy, semiotic underdeterminacy is the very arena in which the capacity and privilege to speak privately to the deity is unevenly distributed.

Chapter 6 explains how the individuated, isolated spaces of spiritual intimacy, privacy, and secrecy afforded by glossolalia become—suddenly or gradually—spaces of deception and danger. As practitioners reflected on the process of speaking in tongues, they sometimes questioned the truth of their experiences. Their concerns emerged around three consistent objects of discernment: the forms, the feelings, and the forces. The glossolalic forms are empirically closest to the problem of speech itself. Many practitioners and aspirants experienced long periods of indeterminacy, when they were unsure whether they were "really" speaking in tongues. They also often noticed what appeared to be patterns of sociolinguistic variation among different groups, which, they surmised, might be a sign of earthly influence. The powerful feelings generated during glossolalia were at once the most indisputable and the most suspicious. Informants worried that their pleasure in glossolalia might be ghostly seduction, that their powerful experiences might be spiritually empty, or that their conviction might be mere self-deception. This led practitioners to ask what forces what could be behind or motivating glossolalia. Many Christians emphasized the need for careful spiritual "discernment" in glossolalia, lest Christians find themselves merely copying others or even speaking demonic tongues and ending up as "food for Satan." Ultimately, glossolalia became an object of doubt for the same reasons that it was an object of desire: the social and spiritual isolation that it is designed to produced.

Finally, the appendix is an etymological reconstruction of the invention of glossolalia through the exegetical debates of early nineteenth-century German theologians. It explains how the term *die Glossolalie* was coined through a Greek back-formation from the German nominalization of the phrase "speaking [in] tongues," *das Zungenreden*, borrowing from the key New Testament phrase, *glossais lalein*.

1

Abundance and the Ambivalent Gift

Glossolalic Dreams and Sociolinguistic Realities

Hyejin dreamed in tongues. She once dreamed she stood before a large audience of unknown faces. She opened her mouth to sing and heard her voice fill a vast hall. The hall was like a church but the size of a concert house. The sound, soft on her throat, rang brightly, powerfully. The music was operatic, an aria of some sort, but she could not make out the words. She realized she was not singing in any language she knew or recognized.

Heartbreak first led Hyejin to speak in tongues. As a high school girl in Seoul in the early 1990s, she fell in love with a boy from another school. When the boy did not return her affections, she cried and prayed in her room. She called out to God for help. She read the Bible. She recited Bible verses. She prayed through the night. At some point she began to speak in tongues. When she finished praying, she did not love the boy anymore.

Hyejin knew that her tongues involved the Holy Spirit, but she had not asked the Holy Spirit for tongues; nor did she think the Holy Spirit took over her speech entirely. She said it felt like the Holy Spirit was guiding her, giving her speech so that she could pray long and hard. She was not in a trance. She did not lose consciousness. It was like a well of speech from which she could draw, a spring from which she could drink. She simply opened her mouth and soothing unintelligible utterances came out. As an adult, she spoke in tongues both in private prayer and group prayer, softly and loudly, with fellow church members and with her music students at the universities where she worked, at home in Seoul and on mission trips abroad, in wakeful consciousness and in her dreams.

Hyejin's husband spoke in tongues against his will. In his rural childhood village near the city of Chŏnju in North Chŏlla province, his mother tried to raise him to speak in tongues. In the 1970s and '80s, before he moved to

Seoul, his mother took him to prayer meetings where it was practiced loudly, fervently, and sometimes ecstatically. He resisted. The glossolalia that surrounded him was frightening. It seemed to him more likely the product of shamanism, fakery, or self-deception than a true sign of the Holy Spirit.

He managed to avoid speaking in tongues for many years. He did not speak in tongues even when he worked as a musician at the largest megachurch in the world, the Yoido Full Gospel Church, while attending college in Seoul. He quit the church because he was bothered by its unorthodox theology and conservative politics, and its massive events of noisy, glossolalic prayer, where everyone was expected to participate. But some years later, while living as a foreign student in Germany, he spoke in tongues. While abroad he regularly worshipped and prayed with other Korean students. During one meeting of mostly Presbyterians, as others began praying in tongues, he suddenly lost control of his speech. Each time he tried to pray in Korean, strange sounds came out of his mouth. The strange speech poured forth quickly and rhythmically. He tried to suppress it, but the utterances kept flowing from his mouth like a faucet he could not turn off.

Hyejin's husband was never sure what spirit had taken over his speech that day. He described feeling a loss of control, but he was not yet ready to admit that it was the work of the Holy Spirit. He remained cautious of praying in groups, especially if others were praying in tongues, because his own speech would still sometimes break into unrecognizable patterns. And he avoided congregations where they encouraged tongues for fear that the same agent, whatever it was, might compel him to join.

Hyejin's mother wanted badly to speak in tongues, and everyone knew it. She heard her daughter praying in tongues loudly for hours at night. She heard other women speaking in tongues during their regular neighborhood prayer meetings. She even heard newcomers at the church praying in tongues. She envied them and doubted her own faith. As a senior deaconess, she managed her envy and doubt by participating even more fervently in church activities, donating even more money, and praying. She read instructional books and attended special seminars on glossolalia. Tongues never came to her.

Hyejin's father came from a Presbyterian family and had introduced her mother to Christianity. His wife converted to Christianity so that they could marry (they met on a bus). He neither spoke in tongues nor wanted to. Although he acknowledged the legitimacy of tongues and regularly prayed with others who spoke in tongues, he never desired the gift for himself. As an elder at their church, he was cautious of seeming too overcome by these kinds of uncontrollable spiritual matters. Although some elders did speak in tongues at the Friday-night prayer service, Hyejin's father did not.

Hyejin and her family were upper-middle-class, educated, urban Presbyterians, and they recognized glossolalia as a sociolinguistic fact of contemporary South Korean Protestant Christianity—unevenly practiced, clearly classed, vigorously debated, but seemingly ubiquitous.[1] Hyejin and her family thought of themselves as normal when it came to glossolalia. Given glossolalia's association with Pentecostals and the prejudice among her family against Pentecostal theology and worship as lower class or tainted by rural superstition, I was initially surprised when Hyejin first spoke of her own glossolalia. I had known her and her family for some years before learning that she spoke in tongues. Eventually I found that most Presbyterians and Methodists I asked, let alone Pentecostals, had spoken in tongues or had prayed with others who did. Many of them had initially encountered glossolalia as a foreign, unsettling practice even as they yearned for it, and they continued to treat it with caution even as they practiced it.

Korean Christians have become aware of glossolalia's striking ubiquity in Korean Protestant Christianity (as well as, in some cases, Catholicism). They often expressed wonder at how common it had become, pride at how spiritually advanced Korean Christians seemed, or dismay at how much social pressure they faced to produced it. And like theologians and church historians, everyday Korean Christians wondered about the nature and function of glossolalia as reported in the New Testament and in contemporary practice, and the relation between the two. For Hyejin, speaking in tongues was usually pleasurable, beautiful, arousing, and therapeutic. For Hyejin's husband, it was strange, suspicious, and potentially dangerous. For her mother, it was a sign of faith, evidence of God's love, but also a public site of competition, like wealth, education, fluency in English, or any other evidence of prosperity that could be linked with Christianity.[2] For her father, it was merely one more element of contemporary Korean Christianity that was all around him but not necessarily inside him. In frustration, competition, ambivalence, and compulsion—even in dreams—glossolalia was, like speech itself, an immersive space of socialization. So prevalent was the practice that a family like Hyejin's could see itself as completely average in this regard: each member was compelled to confront the sociolinguistic fact of glossolalia in some way or another, if not to reproduce it outright.

It is folk wisdom that dreaming in a foreign tongue is a sign of improving fluency and social immersion. This chapter proceeds from Hyejin's glossolalic dream to sketch an ethnographic picture of the sociolinguistic reality of glossolalia in South Korea. I look more closely at Hyejin's various explanations of her own glossolalia and that of her family members in order to highlight some of the ambivalent stances different Christians have on the perception that glossolalia is, on the one hand, ubiquitous, but on the other, unevenly distributed. Over the course of many conversations, it emerged that Hyejin saw the motivations of her husband, her mother, her father, and herself in different ways, each reflecting a different aspect of the glossolalia phenomenon in South Korea. Taken together, these different perspectives on glossolalia—as therapeutic practice, as communicative channel with the deity, as syncretic residue, as a site of competition and striving, on so on—highlighted a cultural complex of competing stances on glossolalia that oriented toward or away from an emanating institutional center. In the second half of the chapter, I turn toward this emanating center: the Yoido Full Gospel Church. I move from the ambivalences of a Presbyterian family like Hyejin's to the unequivocal stance on glossolalia held by a pastor and his wife from the Yoido Full Gospel Church. Theirs is a narrative of spiritual labor and divine inevitability, where glossolalia is an unambiguous practice that is central to the theology of their church and its founder, Cho Yonggi. It is in this ritual center that the tensions regarding glossolalia across its practical and ideological variations throughout Korean Protestant Christianity are resolved through a theology of spiritual "fullness."

Intimacy, Syncretism, and Class

Hyejin said that she could open her heart and reveal her secrets through glossolalia. Just as she had begun to pray in tongues decades earlier as a heartbroken high school student, as a middle-age wife and mother she could pray freely but with the security of privacy. The more she did so, the longer she did so, the more fervently she did so, the warmer she would feel, the more refreshed (*siwŏnhada*) she felt herself become. Hers was a familiar account of the emotionally heightened, sensuous embodiment of glossolalia.

Her glossolalia was also social. She often attended Friday-night prayer sessions at her Presbyterian church of a few thousand members in eastern Seoul. There, she would join others to pray in tongues throughout the evening. She spent many weeks abroad each year on musical mission trips, where she and others would pray together before their performances. Many of them spoke in tongues, sometimes becoming so engrossed in their prayers that they had to be drawn—carefully but persistently—out of their prayers by others. They had to remember not to exhaust their energies or their voices before the concert had begun. Hyejin and others at church would take up a prayer theme or goal and then distribute the act of prayer over each individual, taking turns at praying in sequence to form a "chain" of prayer. She said many of them found that praying in tongues allowed them to sustain these prayers for longer periods of time. Through glossolalia, they could focus on the topic without having to generate intelligible speech. Sometimes she prayed in tongues out of joy, and sometimes out of despair. Sometimes she sought out tongues, and sometimes she received them without asking. Sometimes she prayed in tongues out of social obligation when it was expected of her. Hyejin viewed her glossolalia as one of many dimensions of her Christian life, compatible with and comparable to Bible study, singing, service, listening to sermons, Sunday school, fellowship conversations over lunch, and so on. For her, it was one element in a multifaceted semiotic package of Christian worship and self-cultivation.

When I asked Hyejin and her husband why so many Korean Christians across denominations spoke in tongues, they responded: "Be careful" (*Chosim hae*). Hyejin warned that South Korea had a problem of spiritual abundance.[3] In her view, after the Korean War, in the depths of poverty and despair, Koreans had received the Holy Spirit too quickly. This had been a great blessing in the past, but it had become a challenge in the present. Rather than their having gradually gotten to know Jesus, learned to trust Jesus, adjusted to live with Jesus in their lives, the Holy Spirit had entered Koreans' lives swiftly and directly. Rather than reading the Bible, studying scripture, reflecting on the complexity of its teachings, they had taken the most rapid and direct route to becoming Christians. Like falling in love too quickly, Korean Christians quickly felt close to this new deity and felt dependent on the gifts they received from it. But, she emphasized, Koreans had not yet learned how to live normally with the deity. Their spirituality had become exaggerated in some areas, deficient in others. Suddenly their spiritual level, like their economic level, was as high as anywhere else in the world, in just a few decades. And this had introduced a host of new problems.

It was in this context that she echoed her husband's caution and suspicion. Since childhood, Hyejin's husband had been reluctant to join in the glossolalia of his village church because he was never sure exactly what was generating the unintelligible speech he heard around him. Although Hyejin spoke of her own glossolalic prayer as therapeutic, she and her husband both emphasized that one had to take caution, lest a person become too dependent on this kind of spiritual stimulation (*chagŭk*).[4] The problem, they repeated, was that many Korean Christians' first relationship with the deity was initially characterized by such spiritual stimulation, that they were constantly sensing and attempting to counter its dissipation. In an entirely critical tone, they explained that Koreans—and they included themselves in this group—had received the power of the Holy Spirit without the spiritual maturity to handle it. And so they returned, over and over again, crying and shouting (*ulgo pulgo*), repeating the same words, practicing the same actions, even chanting the same tones that they hoped would generate the feeling of that same initial contact they had had with the spirit. To Hyejin and her husband, the different churches were largely distinguishable both by how they appropriated this abundance and also by how they contained it, for it could be a dangerous force if not properly controlled. Immersed in tongues by their churches, compelled to speak in tongues by their peers, they were often isolated with their tongues as they sought to reestablish contact with their deity through a channel of extreme intimacy. In their isolation from one another, however, Christians could become spiritually confused. To Hyejin and her husband, like so many of the practitioners of glossolalia of I met, much of the glossolalia they observed around them seemed far too close to the shamanic practices of their ancestors and relatives in the countryside—what they perceived to be a dangerous syncretic residue that should be treated very carefully.

Hyejin recognized that her worries over a spirit that had come too fast paralleled the contradictions and even tragedies of South Korea's late but rapid economic rise in the postwar period.[5] In 1960, the annual GDP per capita was $155; by 1990, it was $6,153; in 2012, it was $22,590; and in 2018, it reached $30,000.[6] In 1960, South Korea was 28 percent urban; in 1990, nearly 75 percent. Between those years, the population grew from twenty-five million to nearly forty-four million, a 74 percent increase; and the urban population more than quadrupled, rising from seven million to just over thirty-two million.[7] In 2012, approximately 83.5 percent of the country lived in urban areas.[8] Currently, more than half of the population of approximately fifty million lives in or around Seoul.[9] During this major transformation of town and country, city and state, one of the most striking developments was the growth and persistence of Protestant Christianity, specifically the now-ubiquitous spectacle of the megachurch.[10] In 1960, Protestant Christians are estimated to have accounted for somewhere between 3 and 5 percent of South Korea's population; by the late 1990s, approximately 20 percent of the population reported themselves to be Protestants.[11] These days, it is regularly reported that many of the largest Protestant congregations in the world are in Seoul and that more than twenty thousand South Koreans are serving as missionaries abroad.[12]

Hyejin referred to this dramatic social, economic, and demographic change to describe her mother's relationship with tongues. To explain her mother, she downplayed the syncretic, spiritual, therapeutic elements of glossolalia and instead emphasized the social and economic dimensions of church growth in the postwar period. Hyejin said that the widespread practice of glossolalia among Korean Christians like her mother could not be understood without considering the particular growth and energy of South Korean churches after the war, which, moreover, could not be explained without considering two basic and widely acknowledged cultural facts of South Korean society: first, the enormous, pervasive, and overt social pressure to participate; second, the way participation was often organized around striving toward novelty—trends that exemplified participation in something conspicuously successful. This, she insisted, could explain the visible manifestation of evangelism in the form of evangelical crusades, the more permanent effects of evangelism in the form of the megachurch, and the mediating genres of Korean evangelical speech practices, including glossolalia.[13] She explained with a popular anecdote: when Koreans shopped for clothing, they did not in the first instance ask the sales staff for recommendations based on quality, price, or uniqueness. Instead, the most important question was always: "What is most popular?" or "What are most people buying these days?" In this view, the numbers justify the trend. This explicit, overt cultural orientation to popular trends, and equally explicit, overt cultural anxiety about being excluded from participation, expresses itself in consumer practices, fashion, speech, cosmetic surgery, child rearing, education, food, real estate, and so on. Hyejin's mother's orientation to glossolalia was not, she said cynically, in the first place to heal spiritually (in fact, she was a pretty happy person), or to submit to the Holy Spirit, or to fulfill a desire for intimacy with the deity. Rather, she was attracted to the cultural value of glossolalia, moved by the coercive pressure to practice it for anyone claiming to be a Christian in South Korea.[14]

Over many conversations, I tried to discern from Hyejin where she thought the source of glossolalia's cultural value lay. Denotational unintelligibility is by no means the sole property of glossolalia. Was it, like Church Latin or Koranic Arabic, coveted for its sacred, restricted character? Did it have the allure of a foreign language, an exotic argot, or a fashionable idiom? Was it more like a prestige register, wherein the farther one is from the authorized speakers and spaces, the more it is objectified as a register and is produced along a gradient of mimicry in the absence of mastery?[15] Did it have to do with Koreans' relation to Korean speech itself, given the decades of Japanese colonial rule (1910–45) followed by the ongoing presence of the US military, and an entire century of foreign, English-speaking missionaries and, more recently, English teachers?[16] Was its value associated with its unintelligibility, containing a necessary "coefficient of weirdness," "where obscurity is a virtue?"[17] Or was the unintelligible speech simply a form of exclusion serving to carefully maintain and control social boundaries, dividing in-group from out-group, an unnecessary jargon that serves merely to exclude by "its peculiarities of speech as a secret dialect?"[18] All of these influences seemed plausible to Hyejin when she considered people individually. But she maintained the more general theory that, within the competitive postwar environment of South Korea, emergent churches, new doctrines, new worship practices, and even new Messiahs seemed to pop up every day.[19] It was as if this particular spiritual gift, as an emblem of Christian social forms more generally, had all the features of the inevitable obsolescence of the conspicuous commodity in a society that felt the pressure to participate in success and was anxiously on the lookout for something new. This was the ambivalence of abundance: although it was assumed that God had a limitless supply for his people, access to this supply at any given moment could be severely limited.

To Hyejin, congregational membership in a Protestant church was practiced explicitly as a kind of neotribal identity.[20] One very literally belonged to a church. She joked that when Korean Christians went to church—called *kyohoe* in Korean—some went for the *kyo* (教, instruction or teaching; religion) and others went for *hoe* (會, social meeting or gathering). Her father went for the *kyo*; her mother went for the *hoe*. Like a corporation or a school, churches become a site of institutional reproduction through identification and explicit social relations. After the Korean War, when millions of South Koreans left the countryside to move to Seoul, these sites of social incorporation were important social and financial replacements for, or enhancements to, what they had left behind. As the city expanded, churches also expanded, in many cases beginning as small outposts at the urban frontier and growing rapidly into megachurches with tens of thousands of members.[21]

Hyejin, like many people, emphasized the cultural value placed on having an institutional position of seniority, such as a teacher, manager, or leader.[22] In this view, the attractiveness of Protestant Christianity was not only membership within an expanding group or the expression of success through association with prosperity, but also the institutional status and authority that were linked to evangelism itself. Hyejin specifically used familiar social stereotypes to explain: within the church, the nagging aunt giving beauty tips could become a church deaconess, the pedantic father waxing on about important principles could become a church elder, and the model student tutoring for the university entrance exam could become the Bible study leader. Even the mediocre student could become a missionary, just as the failed entrepreneur could become a pastor.[23] In some circles, to have the gift of tongues was to catapult oneself into a position of authority, for glossolalia was easily construed as a persuasive sign of faith, spiritual industriousness, and God's favor. By learning one could teach, by joining one could lead, by receiving the Word one was authorized to pass the Word along to someone else. The Word itself was not just a means of transitioning from scriptural propositions to spiritual contact with the divine, but, as the speech of God appropriated discursively by humans, also a very medium of socialization and social positioning that ambitious Christians could manipulate within an expansive social network.

When it came to her father, Hyejin emphasized his restraint. It was his character to be reserved. But she also suspected that her father was put off by another contaminant, which he usually avoided mentioning: the lower-class origins of the practice in South Korea. Her father came from a Presbyterian family and had introduced her mother to Christianity. He was a Christian before the rapid growth of Christianity, and certainly before the popularization of glossolalia. He had lived through the early days of the growth of Pentecostalism in Seoul, and he had seen how it emerged at the fringes to influence more mainstream Presbyterians.[24] Although he was supportive of his daughter's spiritual fluency and understanding of his wife's desire to pray like the others at church, he himself was "not interested" (*kwansim ŏpta*). He tended to suspect various non-Christian forces at work in the practice, whether the scent of shamanism, the appearance of striving, the attraction to a trend, or the conspicuous, exaggerated performance of spiritual labor. And so in his quiet, reserved way, he let others pray as they wished, but he himself did not catch the fire. Although the fire was supposed to be sanitizing and purifying, to him it seemed unclean.[25]

Spiritual abundance and imbalance, spiritual gifts and the contradictions of postwar prosperity, social striving and evangelism, the scent of shamanism and the contamination of class—to Hyejin and her family, these all seemed immanent in glossolalia as a sociolinguistic reality, despite its promise of transcendence. Different categories of personhood led Hyejin and others to form different assumptions—or suspicions—about the agents of influence. Her family's very ambivalence over glossolalic practice, however, was a sign of their classed, urban, Christian modernity.[26] Likewise, although glossolalia was regularly practiced at her church, it was carefully regulated, carried out at a remove from the Sunday worship service or any other event where it might seem, at best, out of place, or at worst, terrifying. This careful combination of acceptance and distance, appropriation and suppression, submission and caution, formed a calculated position against the sources and influences of glossolalia's emanation in South Korea, both spiritual and sociological. If the gift (*sŏnmul*) focuses attention on social relations and the commodity focuses attention on social distinctions, glossolalia is both desired and dangerous for its conceptualization and value attribution in terms of both categories. I turn now to the ritual and institutional center of glossolalia, where spiritual gifts (ŭnsa) and capitalist prosperity are united in the promises of a single church doctrine.

A Theology of Fullness

During one research trip to Seoul, I stayed in the apartment of the head pastor of a satellite branch of the Yoido Full Gospel Church. Pastor K had worked for many years as a journalist for the church-affiliated newspaper, the *Kukmin Ilbo* (*Kungmin Ilbo*), until he felt the calling to preach. He admitted that he was grateful for this calling because his job as a pastor was more lucrative than it had been as a journalist. North of the Han River in the Sŏdaemun district of Seoul, the apartment I stayed in was formerly the residence of K and his family, who by then had moved to a newer, larger apartment nearby. The Sŏdaemun apartment is on the top floor of a five-floor apartment building; Pastor K owned the entire building. Pastor K had received the new apartment (which I did not visit) as part of his compensation from the church, which owned extensive real estate in Seoul. At that time, the family was using the older Sŏdaemun apartment mostly for storage. I noticed that it contained multiples of nearly everything of which one would normally need fewer: four televisions, three refrigerators, two microwaves, and so on. Pastor K's wife, whom I addressed respectfully with the old-fashioned appellation *samonim*, told me to eat anything I wanted in the refrigerator, because all of it had come from God. She and her husband received gifts (*sŏnmul*) such as food from the congregants at nearly every church service. Indeed, the three refrigerators were fully stocked.

One evening, after Samonim had sliced a few apples and pears for us to share, she explained to me that Korean Christians were worried about America. She said that America used to be the source of Christian values—after all, it was largely North American Christians who had dedicated their lives to bringing the gospel to Korea. According to her, the Holy Spirit had led these missionaries to Korea and thereby transformed the country. But now the United States was growing distant from the Holy Spirit, and it was up to Korean Christians to bring the gospel back to the United States, as they were doing for the rest of the world. South Korea was to be the new Christian leader of the world.[27] And her church, the Yoido Full Gospel Church, was at the center of this effort. The problem was that the United States had grown too comfortable in its prosperity. She worried that South Korea also was growing too comfortable, as exemplified by the numerous churches throughout the city that claimed to be Christian but did not exhibit the power and presence of the Holy Spirit. They were quiet, calm, even scholarly, but did not manifest the spiritual gifts (ŭnsa, i.e., charism) that come through faith. Even if they did cultivate the Holy Spirit, they often seemed embarrassed to do so. When the Holy Spirit was present, she said, there was no way to remain quiet and calm. A person could not control the Holy Spirit. One had to surrender to the spirit and pray fervently, with all of one's heart. Indeed, pastors at the Yoido Full Gospel Church preached that, despite the blessing of prosperity, Christians should beware of growing too comfortable, because that is when Satan appears.

Samonim discussed the awful poverty experienced by her parents and grandparents, who had moved to Seoul from the rural south, where they visited shamans and worshipped idols. At that time, she told me, South Korea was "as poor as India."[28] There were homeless people throughout the city, living in the most informal and uncomfortable dwellings. People simply did not have enough to eat. Now that South Korea was rich, she said, it was South Korea's time to help, and she mentioned the medical student from India who occupied one of the rooms in her building and whom she enthusiastically was trying to convert.

Samonim spoke about the Korean Peninsula as if it were an axis mundi, linking heaven and earth. And at the center of this axis was the church—specifically, for her, the Yoido Full Gospel Church, which presents itself as a leader in the evangelicalization of South Korean Christianity and of the development of the nation through the direct intervention of the Holy Spirit. The kind of prosperity that Samonim had described in her apartment as "gifts" (sŏnmul) given to them by congregants, ultimately coming from God, was directly linked to this large-scale socioeconomic transformation of the country and its visible manifestation in the city of Seoul. And the socioeconomic transformation was possible because of the manifestation of the spiritual "gifts" (ŭnsa), such as glossolalia, that could be realized through the "full" or "pure" (sun) gospel teachings of their church.

In the years following the Korean War, the Yoido Full Gospel Church emerged with an effective contextual theology that targeted South Koreans' very specific material conditions and spiritual traditions. It is often referred to as the largest Protestant congregation in the world, once boasting more than eight hundred thousand members before a number of satellite churches outside of Korea became independent. However, its origins were humble. In 1958, after graduating from the Full Gospel Seminary, Cho Yonggi and Choi Jashil (Cho's future mother-in-law) established the church next to Choi's house in a slum in Taejodong in the northwest of Seoul. During the first decades of

Seoul's rapid postwar urbanization, shantytowns sprang up throughout the city. So widespread were shantytowns that some have estimated that as much as 20 to 30 percent of the South Korean population lived in slums and squatter settlements in the 1960s and '70s.[29] These settlements emerged quickly, but most were eventually destroyed as the city government carried out plans for development and beautification.[30]

Perfectly in line with the functionalist theory of Pentecostalism's emergence through social marginalization and economic deprivation, the church's mission and its evangelical message related explicitly to the conditions of its impoverished congregants—people who represented a large portion of the country's population.[31] In a dissertation sympathetic with Full Gospel theology, Kim Sin Ho summarized the scene of postwar "devastation when most people despaired in emptiness and frustration":

> [Yonggi] Cho recognized that residents around his church needed not only spiritual salvation but also material blessings, including food and healing. He boldly proclaimed Pentecostal faith with emphasis on the baptism of the Holy Spirit and the subsequent signs like speaking in tongues with divine healing and blessings based on his threefold gospel: spiritual blessing, divine healing, and blessing. His message of the holistic salvation of Christ in both spirit and body gave enormous comfort and hope to the poverty stricken people who were suffering under absolute poverty and disease. How he began to preach a fivefold gospel and the threefold blessing was deeply based on his unique contextualization of the gospel in the context of his ministry in 1958. Soon six hundred congregants who were poor, sick, and uneducated gathered in the church in 1960. In 1961, the church membership reached to 1,000 and the regular worship attendants were 600, which was more than the total number of people living in the village. The tent became too small and had to be enlarged.[32]

The Taejodong congregation grew to such a size that construction on a new church with a fifteen-hundred-seat chapel began in 1961. This church was in a historical area of Seoul named after the old west gate, Sŏdaemun, and opened in 1962 on the site of a revival that had taken place in 1961. According to the church, by 1964 it had three thousand members, and although the building was soon expanded to seat twenty-five hundred, by 1968 the church had to offer three services on Sundays to accommodate its membership of eight thousand.[33] The Sŏdaemun church, like Seoul itself, was overcrowded.

In August 1973, as the general superintendent of the Assemblies of God of Korea, Cho announced in a full-page advertisement in the *Pentecostal Evangel* that the 10th Pentecostal World Conference would be held in Seoul, September 18–23 of that same year (figure 1.1).[34] The advertisement counterposed

PRAY FOR KOREA

Prayer requests for Korea

☐ The 10th Pentecostal World Conference will be held in Seoul, September 18-23. Pray that many outpourings of the Holy Spirit in Korea will result.

☐ A 10-city pioneer church program is underway. Pray that each of these large cities will be open to the full-gospel message.

☐ Full Gospel Bible Institute is in the process of relocating and upgrading to offer a degree program. Pray that these objectives shall be accomplished.

☐ The old revival center in downtown Seoul is being used for a multipurpose ministry center. Pray for the programs of evangelism literature, International Correspondence Institute, youth work, deaf ministries, and child evangelism emanating here.

☐ The Korean church is catching the vision of a missionary program to other parts of Asia. Pray that this will become an increasing challenge.

☐ Diplomatic talks are continuing between North and South Korea. Pray that the door may be opened for ministry in North Korea.

☐ Teen Challenge plans to launch a much-needed ministry to the American military in Korea as well as to the Korean youth. Pray that this work will be effective.

WONDERFUL MIRACLES of the Holy Spirit are continuing to happen in Korea. Recently more than a million people crowded into the last rally of the Billy Graham crusade, and 30,000 surrendered their lives to Christ. Without the almighty power of the Holy Spirit of God, such miracles could never be.

The Korean Assemblies of God has made rapid progress. Full Gospel Central Church in Seoul now has a membership of 18,000 and is completing a new building which will seat 10,000. This church will host the 10th Pentecostal World Conference to be held September 18-23 this year. I firmly believe this will be the biggest convention ever recorded in Pentecostal history.

Korean churches need God's blessing for revival and to encourage them to further their missionary enterprises. It is my conviction that through a miracle of the power of God they will grow to be the largest churches in Asia within one generation.

It is with deep appreciation for all world brethren who pray for Korean churches that I look forward to seeing all of you at the 10th World Pentecostal Conference in Seoul.

—CHO YONGGI
*General Superintendent
Assemblies of God in Korea*

FIGURE 1.1. Advertisement, Cho Yonggi and the 10th Pentecostal World Conference in Seoul, 1973

an image of a bearded Korean man, dressed in traditional clothing white clothing and horsehair hat, holding a long pipe, with another Korean man, Cho Yonggi, dressed in a Western suit.[35] The headline for the advertisement, "Pray for Korea," was written in uppercase "oriental script" and was followed by a list of "prayer requests for Korea" and a personal message from Cho.[36]

In the advertisement, Cho announced that his church had grown to eighteen thousand members in a mere fifteen years and that it was completing a new building that would seat ten thousand, where the conference would be held. He added, "I firmly believe this will be the biggest convention ever recorded in Pentecostal history." Cho had good reason to express this confidence. Earlier that year, as he also announced, Cho had witnessed more than one million people gather just steps from his new church building for a crusade led by Billy Graham (see chapter 4). The new Full Gospel Church building was constructed on the island of Yoido, an empty, sandy strip of land in the Han River that earlier had served as an airstrip for the Japanese colonial government. In that same announcement, Cho predicted, correctly, that South Korean churches would grow to be the largest churches in Asia within one generation.[37]

The Yoido Full Gospel Church mirrors with great precision the story of the South Korean population overall, with the urban migration of peasants from the provinces and those made homeless by the war, and from absolute, dire poverty and suffering to relative wealth and stability. And it, like other giant churches, is ridden with scandal and corruption.[38] Coinciding with the years of urbanization and economic growth under a Cold War military regime, such accounts fit within a broader conceptualization of Christianity in South Korea as directly related to, emerging out of, and confronting the relationship between a specifically Korean narrative of suffering and the salvation that manifests as physical and psychical healing as well as other gifts, both spiritual and earthly.[39]

Although by the 1980s glossolalia had become widespread among denominations, it was Cho Yonggi, founder and former head pastor of the Yoido Full Gospel Church who, in the 1960s, initially "introduced glossolalia as the typical outward sign" that a person has received the Holy Spirit.[40] At that point, glossolalia was still part of an unorthodox theology that shocked many older Protestant groups established before the Korean War. The ubiquity of glossolalia in South Korean Protestant Christianity just a few decades later is a key feature of what is sometimes called the "pentecostalization" of Korean Christianity, an orientation to prosperity and spiritual gifts that has now penetrated the various denominations.[41] The Yoido Full Gospel Church is generally understood to be the emanating source of these practices and orientations. The Pentecostal orientations of Korean Christianity in the past half-century, even among non-Pentecostal denominations, in turn, are part of a broader evangelicalism that characterizes Korean Christianity more generally.[42]

For many Christians, even those who speak in tongues, the forms of Full Gospel worship are linked not only with the impoverished origins of the church and its congregation but also with the purportedly superstitious, even shamanistic tendencies of its theology. For them, the Yoido Full Gospel Church is an example of the dangerous religious syncretism that emerged in South Korea following the war as the rural flooded the urban, bringing along indigenous, unenlightened, shamanic "folk" practices and superstition.[43] Some pejoratively characterize these churches as shamanism in a Protestant guise, and of "absorb[ing] huge chunks of indigenous Korean shamanism and demon possession into its worship," where "the degree of importation is so extensive that some wonder out loud what has absorbed what."[44] Indeed, members of the Yoido Full Gospel Church historically belonged to groups stereotypically associated with shamanic practices. Notably, women constitute the majority of shamans in Korea, and many shamans and their clients became Christians when Cho organized "cells" in which responsibility often was delegated to women.[45]

In this way, my Christian interlocutors and other observers could see clear formal and functional continuities and syncretic mixtures between shamanic practices and Christian practices that focused on solving "this-worldly" problems.[46] They saw the charismatic role of the shaman herself (occasionally himself) as a conduit of otherworldly power, a spiritual portal that had been appropriated in the role of pastors, who were mostly male, as well as the vast numbers of female deaconesses and cell leaders who carried out the work of the church on a smaller, more personal scale.[47] Consider the following characterization by a Presbyterian scholar of Korean Pentecostalism, Yoo Boo-Woong, writing in the mid-1980s:

> [Cho's] healing ministry is based on the baptism of the Holy Spirit, speaking in tongues and driving away demons (evil spirits) from sick persons by the name of Jesus. His role in Sunday morning worship looks exactly like that of a shaman or *mudang*. The only difference is that a shaman performs his wonders in the name of spirits while Rev. Cho exorcises evil spirits and heals the sick in the name of Jesus.[48]

Others view positively the infusion of indigenous elements into the church, characterizing it as an important localization and contextualization strategy for gaining missiological traction in Korea. They understand that, as the Pentecostal scholar Kim Ig-Jin put it, "the phenomenal aspects of shamanism can best be compared to those of Pentecostalism because both are connected with spiritual dynamism among the masses in modern Korea."[49] Cho himself, however, offers his theology as the true alternative to shamanistic practices, and has elaborated it in a number of publications and sermons. In 1979, Cho published *The Fourth Dimension* (*4-Ch'awŏn*), in which he claims that the fourth dimension is a spiritual realm that exists beyond and controls the "geometrically" analyzable three dimensions of physical space. In the fourth dimension, either good or evil can be created.[50] It is a realm to which Christians are called to fight against deceptive, devil-induced fourth-dimensional phenomena, such as healing miracles attributed to other non-Christian spiritual practices.[51] Cho himself states that he is consciously seeking "to show the miraculous power of God to those who still believed in shamanism."[52]

Proponents view Cho as reproducing an "original Pentecostalism" based on biblical principles that have been lost.[53] Conceived as "nothing but pure biblical faith," Cho's theology is supposed to be a return to the Bible's original teachings: "salvation, baptism with the Holy Spirit, healing, and the second coming of Christ."[54] By focusing on healing the physical body with the help of the Holy Spirit, the Yoido Church "regards itself as the body of the living Christ [and] emphasizes healing as an important factor in fulfilling its mission"—as Jesus himself was supposed to have done.[55] Cho views his theology as "clarify[ing] the relationship between revelation and experience because the ultimate object of God's revelation is focused upon humans, not upon the Bible."[56] Glossolalia is crucial within Full Gospel theology to resolving the conflict between the denotational distance of scriptural proposition and the phatic phenomenology of "presence."[57]

Conclusion It is largely with the growth and urbanization of postwar Pentecostalism in the 1960s, and especially the increasing influence of the Yoido Full Gospel Church, that glossolalia emerges in the 1980s and '90s as a widespread component of Korean Christian worship across denominations. As much as the gifts of twentieth-century Christianity were said to be given by God, they were also clearly understood and talked about as the product of Koreans' labor, both individual and collective. Korean Christians like Samonim saw themselves as worthy of such gifts, because they suffered more, prayed more, tithed more, trained more missionaries, and displayed more commitment of faith. To her, God recognized their sacrifices and labors and had rewarded them with health, financial prosperity, individual positions of status, and political power. After all, her husband was a pastor at the single largest megachurch in the world.

My Full Gospel hosts tried to impress upon me the theological imperative to speak in tongues. Glossolalia was, they reminded me, one of many spiritual gifts (ŭnsa) given to humankind and was available for me too. They listed for me the numerous benefits of praying in tongues that the Bible had promised and that they had experienced. I had studied the sermons of Cho Yonggi, the founding pastor of their church, and could recognize in their arguments the list of benefits that Cho often enumerated—first and foremost, that praying in tongues convinces Christians of the fullness of the Holy Spirit.[58] Glossolalia also offers Christians a secret language to communicate with God (especially to confess and repent); it edifies or strengthens faith; it relieves weariness of the heart and allows for psychological release; it allows for the expression of the inexpressible through groans and sighs; it becomes prophecy if interpreted; and it helps Christians pray for long periods of time. In listing these various benefits, they emphasized the importance overall of encountering the Holy Spirit, of realizing that the Holy Spirit was indeed a person with whom a Christian could have spiritual contact, and of recognizing the presence of the Holy Spirit in others. They instructed me to look at their church for a place where one could have a powerful, direct, one-on-one encounter with the Holy Spirit and observe the spirit at work in thousands of others at the same time. I now turn to this ritual center.

2

The Limits of Language

On Wednesday mornings at the Yoido Full Gospel Church in Seoul, more than ten thousand congregants gather for a sermon and to pray for healing. After the sermon, the pastor opens the prayer by asking the congregation to stand, address the deity, and summon the deity with a full-throated, archaic hyperdeferential vocative: "Chu yŏ!" ("O Lord!"). They call out three times, and then the thousands of people in the main sanctuary break into loud group prayer. The excerpt below is taken from a Wednesday-morning service that took place July 17, 2013. The head pastor, Young-hoon Lee, had given a sermon titled "When the Holy Spirit of Truth Comes." After invoking the deity, Lee prayed with the congregation, beginning with a quick repetition of "hallelujah." He chanted this phrase on a B-flat, the tonic of the accompanying hymn, "Old Rugged Cross." As the prayerful were enveloped by the cacophony they themselves produced, their prayers transitioned into glossolalia—that is, speaking or praying in tongues (excerpt 2.1).

Excerpt 2.1

1. *Uri ka onŭl tarŭn kŏttŭl ŭl ta ttŏnago Chunim sŏngnyŏng ch'ungman haesŏ Yesunim hamkke hayŏ chuopsosŏ. Yesunim hamkke hayŏ chuopsosŏ.*
   Today we depart from everything, and as the Holy Spirit of the Lord
       fills [us], Jesus, [we ask that you] be with us. Jesus, be with us.
2. *"Chu yŏ" k'ŭge se pŏn ŭro kido hamnida!*
   [We] pray [by calling out] "Lord" three times loudly!
3. *Chu yŏ! Chu yŏ! Chu yŏ!*
   Lord! Lord! Lord!
4. Hallelujah, hallelujah, hallelujah!
       [glossolalia]

Christians in South Korea by and large learn to speak in tongues through vocalized group prayer (*t'ongsŏng kido*) like this. This is true even if they first produce glossolalia, or continue to practice it, alone. Forms of group prayer share a common feature: synchronous but unsynchronized vocalizations carried out in groups that create a cacophony of sound; this cacophony hinders the interpretability of any single voice but one's own. Simply put, since everyone is speaking at once but saying different things, no one can understand what anyone else is saying. Incorporating an ideology of sincerity and the Protestant holy priesthood of all believers into institutions founded on charismatic authority, *t'ongsŏng kido* can be found in nearly every corner of Korean Protestant Christianity, in South Korea and throughout the diaspora.[1]

A foundational and legendary, if exaggerated, moment for this sort of prayer practice was the Pyŏngyang Great Revival of 1907, when hundreds of recent converts broke out into cries of repentance, and revival activity spread throughout the peninsula. Echoing John in Revelation (14:2), William Blair wrote in his memoir, *The Korean Pentecost*:

> So many began praying that [the missionary Graham] Lee said, "If you want to pray like that, all pray," and the whole audience began to pray out loud, all together. The effect was indescribable. Not confusion, but a vast harmony of sound and spirit, a mingling together of souls moved by an irresistible impulse of prayer. The prayer sounded to me like the falling of many waters, an ocean of prayer beating against God's throne.[2]

As if anticipating Durkheim's *Elementary Forms of Religious Life*, Blair marveled at how "every man forgot every other. Each was face to face with God. I can hear yet that fearful sound of hundreds of men pleading with God for life, for mercy. The cry went out over the city till the heathen were in consternation."[3] Graham Lee recounted the "indescribable effect" of "hundreds of men praying together in audible prayer," where confession mixed with weeping, wailing, even falling to the floor and screaming, which the pastors managed to quiet only by singing hymns.[4]

However, unlike the 1906 Azusa Street revival in Los Angeles that sparked the Pentecostal movement in the United States, the written record of the 1907 revival in Pyŏngyang does not mention speaking in tongues.[5] It is largely with the growth and urbanization of postwar Pentecostalism in the 1960s—and especially the increasing influence of the Yoido Full Gospel Church in particular—that glossolalia emerged in the 1980s and '90s as a widespread component of Korean Christian worship across denominations. It was Cho Yonggi, founder and former head pastor of the church, who is credited with initially introducing in the 1960s "glossolalia as the typical outward sign" that a person has received the Holy Spirit.[6]

In this chapter, I look closely at the place of glossolalia in cacophonic group prayer. In these contexts, glossolalia is the concrete production of individuals making speech-like utterances, while cacophony is the result of many individuals doing this, all at the same time, in the same place. First, I consider the conceptual problems that emerge from trying to understand glossolalia as language. Then I turn to analyze the way glossolalia and cacophony are fruitful disruptions of "normal" speech, because each separately enhances practitioners' sense of their direct, personal communication and sensate connection with deity, and the combination of the two even more so.[7] I aim to show how the immersive, overwhelming semiotic effects of glossolalia and cacophony impose limits on speech that, together, undermine "normal" linguistic functions while intensifying the very act of communication itself. During cacophonous glossolalia, practitioners collaborate to place limits on four areas of "normal" speech: denotation, prosody, participant roles, and social indexicality. The ritual teleology of these imposed limits is, however, an experience of virtual language that exceeds the limits of "normal" speech. This allows practitioners to construe the limits (as imposed constraint) that glossolalic practice places on linguistic functionality as a generative, enhanced form of language that exceeds the limits (as extreme boundary) of linguistic functionality.

Ideological Core, Ideological Limits

The problem of glossolalia-as-language led William Samarin to conclude that glossolalia "always turns out to be the same thing: strings of syllables, made up of sounds taken from among those that the speaker knows, put together more or less haphazardly but which nevertheless emerge as word-like and sentence-like units because of realistic, language-like rhythm and melody."[8] He called it a "façade" of language, echoing earlier judgments that examples of this seemingly spiritually inspired, speech-like behavior was a kind of semiotic alchemy—producing some of the effects of language without being "real" language.[9] Samarin's conclusion that glossolalia is made of "common human stuff" draws an analytic line between two ways of segmenting this "stuff" into sounds: a grammar-driven segmentability of speech understood as linearly unfolding linguistic signs, and a more brute-reality segmentability of speech in terms of syllables. This line continues to shape anthropological approaches to glossolalia.

The grammar-driven approach to segmentation begins with phonemes, the "oppositive, relative, negative" categories of speech sounds that, as individual units, contribute to denotation by differentiating more complex linguistic units.[10] According to grammatical "rules," phonemes can combine to produce morphemes, the minimal units of what linguists and philosophers call "sense." These may be further combined to produce more complex syntactic units and, ultimately, denotational text. Denotation is most commonly associated with lexemes, those semantically saturated linguistic units often conflated with "words for things" in folk ideologies of language. Lexemes can be isolated through grammatical analysis by separating among syntactic units what appear to have a kind of stand-alone semantic "content" from those that do not. For example, *speaks* and *speaking* both are formed from a verb stem, the lexeme *speak*; *-s* and *-ing* have grammatical but not lexical "sense." Phonemes (as the purely "negative" units) and lexemes (as the semantically "full" units) are functionally linked through a grammar.[11] Within this structuralist linguistic paradigm, the phonological plane of speech is defined not merely by its rules of linear combination nor merely by the distinctive features through which it is organized, but also by the way it is integrated systematically into more complex planes of linguistic function. Glossolalia therefore cannot be said to have even phonology, let alone grammar or semantics.[12]

In the more phenomenological approach to segmentation, the brute reality of speech consists of a string of syllables assembled by phonetic articulations. One of the hallmarks of glossolalia is that it is perfectly syllabic. Because the syllables draw phonetically from phonological systems with which the speaker is familiar, and because they seem to follow some minimal rules of combination, the utterances would seem to be interpretable in phoneme-to-morpheme terms. In this view, the sounds should combine to produce denotationally coherent utterances. Glossolalic utterances are not, however, interpretable in these terms: the syllables can never actually be construed as morphemes, so the utterance never rises to the level of linguistic "sense." Instead, phonetic residue is reconstituted to masquerade as a phonological system. Only through mystical acts of "interpretation," bypassing grammatical equivalences across codes, can glossolalic utterances be said to contain or produce denotation.[13]

This analytic split between the phonological segmentability of speech and the syllabic segmentability of pseudo-speech has led anthropologists to chart different methodological routes into the problem of language in glossolalia. The ethnographic record of denotationally unintelligible speech has focused on contextualization to explain how it can produce, effectuate, "do" something that is taken to be real, rather than merely passively corresponding to something real outside of itself.[14] Anthropological treatments of religious speech genres have demonstrated how religious assertions find, as Webb Keane put it, "support in the concrete forms of speech practices as much by what they presuppose as by what they depict"—from the moral demands of semiotic overdeterminacy to the performative productivity of semiotic underdeterminacy.[15] Aware that charismatics are inclined to locate spiritual presence in semantic absence, anthropologists of glossolalia have often focused on the "problem of presence" itself.[16] They have treated glossolalia, for example, as a correlate of trance or dissociation, as the foregrounding of bodily activity, or as part of a learned repertoire of techniques for producing psychologically sensate experiences of the unseen.[17] These perspectives have emphasized the "intensity" of religious practice more generally, whether methodologically collective, methodologically individual, or anthropologically aware that, as Edward Sapir long ago observed, "societies tend to differ according to whether they find the last court of appeal in matters religious in the social act or in the private emotional experience."[18] And yet, one problem lingers. As William Samarin observed but did not explain, "Glossolalia is indeed like language in some ways, but this is only because the speaker (unconsciously) wants it to be like language."[19] There remains a fundamental, unanswered question: Why do they want it to be language?

Since the 1970s, anthropologists increasingly have conceptualized denotation, and the formal linguistic structures that make it possible, within a broader theorization of culture as semiosis (sign processes). This understanding views pragmatics, the domain of indexicality, as logically and empirically prior to (and encompassing) denotation, or the symbolic function of language.[20] Semantics and pragmatics do not form an opposition; rather, semantics is a narrow, residual domain of pragmatics. To make this observation methodologically viable, Michael Silverstein helpfully clarified a crucial scalar, semiotic distinction: culture may be understood as a "construct for the meaning system of *socialized* behavior," whereas language, more narrowly, is a "systematic construct to explain the meaningfulness of *speech* behavior."[21] Speech (whether vocalized, inscribed, or manually articulated) *is* socialized behavior, of course, but it is socialized behavior with the unique semiotic function of denotation. Although language is unique within culture for this true symbolic mode (denotation), the bulk of speech actually involves the indexical and iconic modes, making speech formally similar to and practically continuous with the more expansive domain of cultural semiosis.

Glossolalists insist that speaking in tongues is a specifically linguistic medium, albeit mystical and mysterious, despite the absence of a true symbolic mode, or even the structured linguistic processes that would make such a mode possible. A pressing question remains how and why glossolalia's ideological status as language is central to its appeal, even as it lacks in practice the very semiotic mode that would differentiate it from the rest of cultural semiosis.

The ideological conundrum of glossolalia for practitioners is the dynamic that should analytically and methodologically define glossolalia for anthropologists: glossolalia should be conceptualized for anthropological analysis as cultural semiosis that is said to contain, and can therefore be justified by, an ideological core of language, but that in fact is produced at the ideological limits of language. An ideological core refers to the absolute necessary element that orients a cultural category (in this case, language), is prototypical or emblematic of the category, and is the conceptual focal point in terms of which other elements are assimilated to the category. The ideological limit refers to the threshold for assimilation to the category (perceived as either an imposed constraint or an extreme boundary). For example, within the ideological limits of language, some sounds are treated as phonemes, syllables as morphemes, strings of syllables as words, and so on, because these elements can be functionally related to an ideological core (denotation). Beyond the ideological limits of language, these sounds seem to lose their linguistic value. For example, a person at a birthday party blows out candles on a cake, producing a sound that resembles the onset of the English word *who*.[22] Is it speech? Christians face the same problem when evaluating speaking in tongues in the context of prayer. They must decide if a string of syllables is really speech or merely speech-like.

For Korean Christian practitioners of glossolalia, two related propositions follow from the assertion that glossolalia is the spoken actualization of a specific, real language. First, unintelligible speech in an unknown language—however transcendent and ineffable—can be rendered intelligible through the gift of interpretation, revealing propositional truth formulated as denotational text. Although denotation is absent in practice, it is there in potential. The emphasis on denotation appropriates the more familiar model of biblical truth that is immutably given in scripture and set into circulation by sharing the Word across speech events.[23]

Second, the unintelligibility of glossolalic utterance is a complex sign of contact between the prayerful and their deity. Korean glossolalists, like Pentecostal theologians, disagree about whether to take this sign of the deity's presence in the evidential sense of hard proof of the baptism of the Holy Spirit or in a more sacramental sense of the dynamic and variable media of personal spiritual encounter.[24] The emphasis on contact highlights the communicative grounds of a "live and direct" or "fusional" encounter with the spirit that reappears consistently in Christians' accounts of glossolalic experience.[25] In a specifically spiritual perspective, the view of glossolalia-as-contact, in which the deity directly plants the Word in the mouths of the prayerful, is familiar to South Koreans from shamanic spirit possession.[26] This is why both Christian and non-Christian Koreans have sometimes viewed some Christian practices as contaminated by the residue of shamanic superstition as well as, for vocal practice specifically, repetitive Buddhist chanting. And it was often in reaction to the scent of syncretism (if not outright fraud and fakery) that Korean Christians contested and negotiated the ideological limits of language, as they decided whether speech-like behavior—their own or someone else's—was or was not "real" glossolalia.

This fundamentally phatic dimension of glossolalia also fits within a broader Korean understanding of speech as a pragmatic medium of social contact. Koreans reflect explicitly on how the interactional dimensions of Korean speech situate speakers in a complex matrix of social relations through its elaborate formal system of honorifics and speech styles. They do not make the error of treating speech as "mere words," of "naively suppose[ing] that speech is nothing but the piling up of lexations"—a tendency that Benjamin Whorf long ago observed among the native speakers, not to mention philosophers and scientists, of Standard Average European languages.[27] This awareness presents particular challenges for Christian assertions of universal, egalitarian access to God, as even the Korean gloss for the Word or speech of God is already marked by its honorific form, *malssŭm*, rather than the unmarked *mal*.[28]

The ideology of denotation depends, crudely put, on assumptions about how the "meaning" of "words" relates to "things." Technically put, this assumption begins from the semantico-referential function, or the functional process by which a denotational form corresponds both to a conceptual class and to range of denotata or referents that may be "picked out" by that form. The typified denotational form mediates between the semantic category and the range of referents in the world via the form's mobilization in referring and predicating expressions; i.e., in speech. The philosophical characterization of this functional relation is between *intension* (note the spelling) and *extension*, between conceptual classes and the range of "things" to which those concepts correspond. When glossolalia is interpreted, and the unintelligible is rendered into intelligible denotational text, an image of semantico-referential, or denotational, equivalence is produced between the unknown and the known.

However, the experience of glossolalia-as-language in South Korean Christianity also depends fundamentally on speech as a site of social contact, for it is through contact that the interpretation of glossolalia is possible; and it is these interpretations, formulated as propositions, commands, and prophecy, that encourage Christians, once again, to use glossolalia as a means of spiritual contact. In shifting from the denotational to the phatic, or contact-focused, dimension of glossolalia, the narrow problem of linguistic *intension* and *extension* expands, semiotically, to the broader problem of sociopsychological *intensity* and, its classical if now archaic counterpart, *extensity*. Samuel Taylor Coleridge captured this nineteenth-century duality crisply:

> Intensity and extensity combinable only by blessed spirits. Hence it is that lovers in their fresh state, incapable of fathoming the intensity of their feelings, help the thought out by extension—commute, as it were—and thus think the passion as wide in time and space as it is deep in essence—hence, *Auf ewig dein!*[29]

Concentration and distribution, focus and resonance, compounding and resounding—this double tension intersected repeatedly in descriptions of glossolalia, which returned again and again to the way the intensional-extensional dimensions of divine denotation were linked to the intensifying-extensifying dimensions of divine contact.[30] For it was through this combination that Christians could agree that, despite the radical unintelligibility of speech and the radical individuation of contact, each ineffable instance throughout a population was an effect of the same fundamental force: the Holy Spirit.

From "wordless groans" to opaque vocalizations interpretable through spiritual gifts, glossolalia's value as language—whether ancient, foreign, the "language of heaven," or the "tongues of angels"—rests on an ideological commitment to the promise of denotation, and to denotation as a product of social contact. The more undeniable the feelings of contact, the more convincingly the presumed potential for denotation can be converted into the pragmatics of virtual language.[31] Treating glossolalia narrowly as linguistic utterance focuses attention on this ideological core—namely, the promise of denotation and the special socio-spiritual contact that denotation is thought to anchor. Treating glossolalia as semiotic practice broadens the focus to consider a wide range and a vast scale of operations beyond syllables that allow culture generally to manifest in a specific experience of language. It is through this dynamic that cultural semiosis at the limits of language allows Korean Christians to posit glossolalia as language, and collaboratively to transform the intensity of unintelligibility into the clarity of propositional truth.

The Productivity of Limits

At the Yoido Full Gospel Church, events of prayerful cacophony and mass glossolalia follow a predictable pattern of both suppression and amplification. Repetitive utterances help the prayerful completely suppress denotation. The compounding effects of repetition also, but less obviously, suppress prosodic variation, narrowing the pitch contour toward fluid vocalizations that can be tuned in various ways—via pitch, rhythm, and tempo—to the ubiquitous musical accompaniment, whether it be a pulsating Korean gospel band (as above) or the austere, droning chords of a hymn played on the organ. The cacophony produced by groups of people praying together suppresses the audibility of individual speech sounds, opening up private communicative spaces for individuals to engage in focused, intimate, even secret communication with the deity. And their denotationally opaque vocalizations, buffered by noise, suppresses role distinctions between speaker and addressee, "I" and "you," the prayerful and the deity, creating a disorienting communicative space where it is unclear who is speaking. Combined, these semiotic processes place limits on linguistic functions while producing ideological commitments to language itself.

LIMITS TO DENOTATION: "IF WE OPEN OUR MOUTH WIDE BEFORE GOD, GOD FILLS IT UP EVEN TODAY"

It takes socialization and training to speak fluently while suppressing denotation. On Sunday, July 13, 2008, at the fourth service of the day, Pastor Cho stood before his congregation in the main sanctuary of the church and announced that God had sent him and the congregation a glossolalic message. He recited the glossolalic message and then interpreted (t'ongyŏk) it into Korean for the audience. The audience shouted "Amen!" rhythmically and enthusiastically as Cho recited the lines of his interpretation, and they applauded when he finished.

The example of glossolalia below follows standard Korean phonology, with the exception of some sound placements found only in loan words (e.g., onset [l]). This allowed me to easily render it into Han'gŭl as well as romanized Korean using the McCune–Reischauer system.[32] Han'gŭl is a phonemic alphabet written in syllabic blocks. This writing system gives the syllable considerable ideological loading, even though, as the linguist Samuel Martin observed, in Korean "the syllable can be defined and described wholly in terms the phoneme sequences which compose it."[33] While the phonetic material of Cho's glossolalic utterance is taken entirely from the sounds of Korean, it is, predictably, a drastically reduced swatch of the available phonetic repertoire (see tables 2.1, 2.2).[34] Yet, in interpreting his own glossolalic utterance, Cho generated denotational text that, syllable for syllable, far exceeds the glossolalic source from which it was drawn (excerpt 2.2):

Excerpt 2.2[35]

INTRODUCTION

Hananim kkesŏ uri ege pangŏn ŭi meseji rŭl chusigo kyesineyo.
God is giving us a message of glossolalia.

GLOSSOLALIA

T'ip'iya lasyak'ap'at'e lashiyada loyaroba k'annak'i lik'ik'ik'o nak'achi lashik'ap'at'ari nimik'iniya ap'at'ak'ak'aya shik'ik'ik'o p'aya.

INTERPRETATION

1. *Nae sarang hanŭn adŭlttal a, nŏ nŭn nae ka ŏdi ittago saenggak hanŭnya?*
   My beloved sons and daughters, where do you think I am?
2. *Nae ka kumalli changch'ŏn mŏlli hanŭl e ittago saenggak hanŭnya?*
   Do you think I am in the vast, distant heavens?
3. *Ttangkkŭt esŏ ittago saenggak hanŭnya?*
   Do you think [I am] at the end of the earth?
4. *Ttang ŭl p'aya, na rŭl ch'ajŭl su ittago saenggak hanŭnya?*
   Dig in the earth, do you think you can find me?
5. *Anira! Sipchaga rŭl t'onghayŏ nae ka nŏhŭi sok e tŭrŏwa itko.*
   No! Through the cross I come into you.
6. *Nŏhŭi sum kwa hamkke itko nŏhŭi saengmyŏng sok e hamkke ittoda.*[36]
   [I am] with your breath and also with you inside your life.
7. *Nae ka nŏ rŭl puttŭrŏ chugo nŏ rŭl towa chugi rŭl wŏnhana*
   I want to hold you and help you, but
8. *Nŏhŭi ka na rŭl morŭnŭndoda. Na rŭl alla. Na rŭl kkaedarŭra!*
   Oh, you don't know me! Know me! Realize me!
9. *Na rŭl ŭiji hara. Nae ka nŏhŭi ŭi kido rŭl tŭtko*
   Rely on me! I hear your prayers, and
10. *Nŏhŭi son ŭl putchaba chugo nŏhŭi rŭl ikkŭrŏ churira.*
    [I] will hold your hands and lead you.
11. *Kip'ilk'o nae ka sara kyesin nŭngnyŏk ŭl nŏ ege nat'anae churira.*[37]
    Surely I will disclose to you the living power.
12. *Yŏnggwang ŭl poyŏ churira. Ttŭt taero toege mandŭrŏ churira.*
    [I] will show you glory. I will make it happen according to [someone's] will.[38]
13. *Hananim ŭi yŏnggwang ŭi ttŭt i imhayŏsŏ nŏhŭi sok e nat'anage toege hal kŏt ida.*
    [I] will make the meaning of God's glory present, so that it will appear inside you.
14. *Turyŏwŏ malgo nollaji malmyŏ tamdae hago kanghara.*
    Do not be afraid, do not be alarmed, be bold and strong.

TABLE 2.1. Phonetic inventory of excerpt 2.2 (consonants)

	Bilabial	Alveolar	Postalveolar	Velar	Glottal
Nasal	m ㅁ	n ㄴ		ŋ ㅇ	
Plain stop	p-b ㅂ	t-d ㄷ	tɕ-dʑ ㅈ	k-g ㄱ	
Tense stop	p͈ ㅃ	t͈ ㄸ	t͈ɕ ㅉ	k͈ ㄲ	
Aspirated stop	pʰ ㅍ	tʰ ㅌ	tɕʰ ㅊ	kʰ ㅋ	
Plain fricative		s-ɕ ㅅ			h ㅎ
Tense fricative		s͈-ɕ͈ ㅆ			
Liquid		l-r ㄹ			

TABLE 2.2. Phonetic inventory of excerpt 2.2 (vowels)

	Yang/light			Yin/dark			Dark/neutral	
Simple	a ㅏ o ㅗ ɛ ㅐ wɛ ㅚ			ʌ ㅓ u ㅜ e ㅔ wi ㅟ			ɯ ㅡ i ㅣ	
Palatalized diphthongs	ya ㅑ yo ㅛ yɛ ㅒ			yʌ ㅕ yu ㅠ ye ㅖ				
Combined diphthongs	wa ㅘ wɛ ㅙ			wʌ ㅝ we ㅞ			ɰi ㅢ	

CONCLUSION

I wa kach'i Chunim kkesŏ malssŭm hasimnida. Hallelluya. Hananim kamsa hamnida.
The Lord speaks in this way. Hallelujah. Thank you, God.

In the next example, which Cho produced at the third Sunday service on September 26, 2004, the glossolalic utterance is parsed into individual text-utterances, for which Cho then provided a text-sentence interpretation, implying almost a one-to-one metasemantic equivalence across morphemes (excerpt 2.3; G indicates glossolalia; I indicates interpretation). Moreover, he repeated the phonetic sequence *yaraba* twenty times, as well as single instances of two variants, *yarabi* and *yŏrŏbŏ* (*ŏ* is the vowel harmonic opposite of *a*).[39] This gives the impression of regular pragmatic and even possibly denotational function, perhaps a name for the deity or the equivalent of a sentence ending in Korean (e.g., *-(sŭ)mnida*). Its repetition suggests that the listener could reasonably quote the form and ask: "Pastor Cho, what does *yaraba* mean?"

Excerpt 2.3[40]

INTRODUCTION

Pangŏn t'ongyŏk pangŏn yeŏn i imhayŏ issŭmnida. (Amen)
Glossolalia interpretation and glossolalia prophecy are present. (Amen)

GLOSSOLALIA (G) AND INTERPRETATION (I)

G: *Nae yaraba roshi lik'i yaraba na yaraba shik'u yaraba sat'a yaraba sannaribi.*

I: *Na ŭi adŭl ttaldŭl a nae mal e kwi rŭl kiurira: nae ka ŏje to nŏhŭi wa kach'i <u>kyesyŏtko</u> onŭl to hamkke itko naeil to hamkke innora.* (Amen)⁴¹

Listen to me, my sons and daughters: I was with you yesterday, today I am with you, and tomorrow I am with you. (Amen)

G: *Nik'io lashi yaraba k'a na i i k'a na yŏrŏbŏ shi yaraba k'annari.*

I: *Pora hŭgam i tagaogo kwangp'ung i purŏ onŭndoda musŏun il i irŏnal kŏt iroda.*

For behold, darkness is coming, and a mighty wind is blowing, and a terrible thing will happen.

G: *Ramok'o'ko ya lishiya nak'a k'a shi yaraba k'an yaraba syŏriyedŭri.*

I: *Kŭrŏna na rŭl ŭiji hanŭn cha nŭn pukkŭrŏum ŭl tangch'i aniharira.* (Amen) *Nae ka hŭgam esŏ kwangmyŏng i toego ŏdum esŏ pit ŭro nŏhŭi rŭl puttŭrŏ chul kŏt igo,* (Amen) *olmu esŏ kŏnjyŏ chul kŏt ira.* (Amen)

But he who trusts in me will not be ashamed. (Amen) I will be a light in darkness, in the darkness [I will] hold you by means of light, (Amen) [I will] save you from a snare. (Amen)

G: *Mu yaraba syania k'a yaraba k'a mia ori yaraba k'an yaraba lasyari yaraba k'anari.*

I: *Nŏhŭi ka Hananim irago purŭsinŭn Hananim ŭn ch'ŏnji rŭl chiŭsin Hananim iyo.*⁴² (Amen) *Hanŭl kwa hanŭldŭl ŭi hanŭl kwa ttang kwa kŭ kaunde modŭn kŏt ŭl chiŭsin Hananim ira.* (Amen)

The god you call God is the god who created heaven and earth. (Amen) [He is] the god who created heaven, the heaven of heavens, and everything between heaven and earth. (Amen)

G: *Ori yaraba k'a yaraba shi yaraba k'an yaraba k'a yarabi yaraba sannari yaraba k'annari.*

I: *Kŭ nŭn pyŏnyŏkchi anihasigo ŏje to onŭl to tongil hasimyŏ* (amen) *nŏ ŭi nunmul ŭl posigo nŏhŭi kido e kwi rŭl kiurisimyŏ* (amen) *orŭn son ŭro nŏ rŭl putchabasŏ mal hagi rŭl turyŏwŏ malla. Nae ka nŏ wa hamkke hanira.* (Amen) *Nollaji malla. Nae ka nŏ rŭl towajurirago mal hanŭn kŏt inira.* (Amen)

He does not change, and he is the same yesterday and today and (Amen) he sees your tears and listens to your prayers with his ears and (Amen) he says while holding you with the right hand, do not be frightened. I am with you. (Amen) Do not be alarmed. I am telling you that I will help you. (Amen)

CONCLUSION

I wa kach'i Hananim kkesŏ malssŭm hasimnida. Hallelluya. Uri Hananim kke paksu ro kamsahamnida. [applause]

The Lord speaks in this way. Hallelujah. We thank our God with applause. [*applause*]

TABLE 2.3. Phonetic inventory of excerpt 2.3 (consonants)

	Bilabial	Alveolar	Postalveolar	Velar	Glottal
Nasal	m ㅁ	n ㄴ		ŋ ㅇ	
Plain stop	p-b ㅂ	t-d ㄷ	tɕ-dʑ ㅈ	k-g ㄱ	
Tense stop	p̬ ㅃ	t̬ ㄸ	t̬ɕ ㅉ	k̬ ㄲ	
Aspirated stop	pʰ ㅍ	tʰ ㅌ	tɕʰ ㅊ	kʰ ㅋ	
Plain fricative		s-ɕ ㅅ			h ㅎ
Tense fricative		s̬-ɕ̬ ㅆ			
Liquid		l-ɾ ㄹ			

TABLE 2.4. Phonetic inventory of excerpt 2.3 (vowels)*

	Yang/light				Yin/dark				Dark/neutral	
Simple	a ㅏ	o ㅗ	ɛ ㅐ	wɛ ㅙ	ʌ ㅓ	u ㅜ	e ㅔ	wi ㅟ	ɯ ㅡ	i ㅣ
Palatalized diphthongs	ya ㅑ	yo ㅛ	yɛ ㅒ		yʌ ㅕ	yu ㅠ	ye ㅖ			
Combined diphthongs	wa ㅘ	wɛ ㅙ			wʌ ㅝ	we ㅞ			ɯi ㅢ	

*Although this example of Cho's glossolalia appears to include more vowels—specifically, from the "yin/dark" category—these count for only very few instances (e.g., three of the four instances of ŏ [ʌ] are in *yŏrŏbŏ*).

Cho himself claims that speaking in tongues like this allows him to pray at least three hours a day. He also instructs his congregants to pray for hours at a time as a form of spiritual endurance training. According to him, the spirit can come at any time, but after an hour or so of prayer a person runs out of things to say. This, he suggests, is the perfect time to speak in tongues. In these moments, as they tire of repeating themselves because they have run out of things to say, members of the church do not necessarily consider their unintelligible utterances to be the speech of the spirit. Rather, as some admitted (even acknowledging the heterodox implications of these admissions), they often treat these sounds as a practical orientation to the speech of spirit, engaging in glossolalic practice with the goal of producing inspired glossolalic utterances. It can take practice and experience to develop the skills of discernment to know whether the spirit is "really" speaking (see chapter 6). This repetitive narrowing of the degrees of phonetic freedom can be frustrating, or it can be an arousing, pleasurable, intermediate stage on the way to producing the mysterious speech of the spirit. As Cho tells his congregants, riffing on Psalm 81:10, "If we open our mouth wide before God, God fills it up even today."[43] One can use glossolalic forms to "open" the spiritual mouth, just as one might practice pronouncing new words—the syllables contain the potential for denotation.

LIMITS TO PROSODY: "THE HOLY SPIRIT WILL COME DIRECTLY TO LEAD YOUR LIPS AND VOCAL CORDS"

The ideal of holy speech passing fluently through the mouths of the faithful was clear when Christians described the "flow" (*hŭrŭm*) of prayer. Prayer that flowed like water was a sonorant stream of vocalization, with legato, open syllables connected by a single breath. Such prayer takes on a quasi-musical character, harnessing the capacity of prosody not only to focus and intensify denotation but also to redirect attention from denotation to intonation, to override denotation, and, ultimately, to become a crucial mode of orientation in the total absence of denotation.[44]

The sonorant flow of glossolalia came to the fore when practitioners described glossolalia in terms of singing and treated vocalization itself as a semiotically coherent intermediary point on the way to glossolalia. They told me of singing in tongues and chanting in tongues. Hyejin even dreamed of singing operatic arias in tongues (see chapter 1). Pastor Cho himself explained it this way on February 15, 2009, in a sermon on the benefits (*yuik*) of praying in tongues: even though we do not have all the lyrics memorized, we can join in singing the hymns without the hymnal. "If we sing hymns in tongues," he said, "the Holy Spirit will come directly to lead your lips and vocal cords [*mokchŏng*]."

This appeal to singing makes sense of the way limits to prosodic variation intensify the production of markedly holy speech. For example, a part-time organist and choir conductor in her late twenties, who is the daughter of a pastor of a Yoido Full Gospel satellite church, explained to me how she had learned to pray in tongues following Cho's direction. In a small coffee shop in Seoul, she explained that she had received the gift of tongues in her third year of high school. She received glossolalia suddenly while Cho was leading a Friday-night prayer session. More than ten thousand people were speaking in tongues together. They prayed all night. And then she explained a method for learning to speak in tongues. As captured in Pastor Lee's invocation of the deity quoted at the beginning of this chapter, a way to release the tongue is to say "hallelujah" continuously. She demonstrated this method for me by repeating "hallelujah" three times quickly, after which she said, "At some point glossolalia suddenly breaks out [*tŏjida*]." As a transition into glossolalia, this Christian's utterance of "hallelujah" not only formally limited denotation to repetitive syllables but also demarcated itself tonally from her other speech.

As she repeated "hallelujah," she raised and fixed her pitch and increased her tempo to produce a concentrated, fluid form of vocalization that departed dramatically from her "normal" speech, orienting instead toward glossolalia in a chanted, almost sung, quasi-musical way.

This kind of phased transition was common among Christians who described their experiences speaking in tongues, especially when they emphasized the repeated recitation of scripture as a technique of intensification. When congregants observed scripture "flowing" from Cho's mouth as he preached, they received a model for their prayers. Normally, Cho began his sermons by speaking emphatically but still in a relatively normal or unmarked sermonic style, framing his comments around relevant Bible verses. He emphasized a certain point that the selected scripture was supposed to clarify and affirm as a means of hermeneutical explanation. His prosody approximated "normal" if somewhat excited oratorical speech. He then transitioned into another style characterized by extended repetition—a familiar feature of ritual speech. At this point, his speech assumed a clear rhythmic structure and a fixed pitch or repeated intonation contour. The poetics of parallelism and redundancy function as an intensifier, emphasizing his hermeneutical explanation and also rhythmically indexing the coming of a more intense overall experience. Intensification served as a transition from hermeneutical explanation to the recitation of the Bible verse around which the sermon was organized. When he finally did recite the Bible verse, he changed the pitch (raising or lowering it), increased the speed of his speech, and produced syllables rapidly and rhythmically so that the verse was practically chanted. The transition to recitation is a transition from denotation that he himself authored to textual chunks (verses) that he was merely animating.[45]

The passages below are taken from just this sort of episode, a sermon given by Cho on October 29, 2006, called "The Outer Person and the Inner Person" (*Kŏtsaram kwa soksaram*). The passages exhibit the three phases of oration discussed above, interspersed with shouts of "Amen!" from the audience (excerpt 2.4). A pitch analysis of these passages (figure 2.1) visualizes the increasing concentration and stabilization of pitch and utterance segments toward a rapidly produced chant-like form, from (A) explanation to (B) intensification to (C) recitation.

Excerpt 2.4

    A. Explanation: *Soksaram i saerowŏ chigo him ŭl ŏtko nŭngnyŏk ŭl ŏdŏsŏ kŏtsaram ŭro salji malgo ije uri nŭn soksaram ŭro saraya toegessŭmnida. (Amen!) Soksaram i ŏttŏk'e saerowŏ chimnikka? Malssŭm ŭro saerowŏ chinŭn kŏt imnida. (Amen!) Malssŭm ŭl t'onghaesŏ yŏngchŏk in nae ka nugunji rŭl palgyŏn hage toenŭn kŏt imnida. Soksaram i ŏttŏhan saram inya?*

The inner person is renewed and receives strength and power. We should not live as the outer person, but now we should live as the inner person. (Amen!) How can the inner person be renewed? [The inner person] can be renewed through the Word. (Amen!) Through the Word, I can discover who I am spiritually. What kind of person is the inner person?

B. Intensification: *Ŭiroun saram, kŏrukhan saram, ch'iryo padŭn saram, ch'ukpok padŭn saram, yŏngsaeng pongnak ŭl ŏdŭn saram, yŏnghon i chaldoego pŏmsa e chaldoemyŏ kanggŏn hage toen saram i soksaram ida. Soksaram ŭn t'aekhasin choksok iyo, wang kat'ŭn chesajang iyo, kŏrukhan nara yo, kŭ ŭi soyu toen paeksŏng i toeŏtta.*

The inner person is a righteous person, a holy person, a healed person, a blessed person, a person who has received the blessing of eternal life, a person who prospers in all things and is healthy, just as his soul prospers. The inner person is [of God's] chosen people, a king-like priest, a holy nation; the inner person becomes one of God's own subjects.

A. Explanation: *Soksaram ŭn almyŏn alsurok kŏtsaram e taehaesŏ kanghage irŏnal su innŭn kŏt imnida. (Amen!)*

The more we know the inner person, the more we can rise strongly against the outer person. (Amen!)

B. Intensification: *Kŏtsaram ŭi konggyŏk ŭl mullich'igo kŏtsaram ŭl ttara kaji annŭn kŏt imnida. Yuhok e nŏmŏ kaji annŭn kŏt imnida.*

[The inner person] drives away the attacks of the outer person and does not follow the outer person. [The inner person] is not taken by temptation.

A. Explanation: *Kŭrŏmŭro soksaram ŭl malssŭm ŭro uri ka kanghage haeya toenŭn kŏt imnida.*

Therefore, we must make the inner person strong with the Word.

C. Recitation: *Roma 12:2 e, "Nŏhŭi nŭn i sedae rŭl ponbatchi malgo ojik maŭm ŭl saeropke ham ŭro pyŏnhwa rŭl pada Hananim ŭi sŏn hasigo kippŏ hasigo onjŏnhasin ttŭt i muŏt inji punbyŏl hadorok hara."*

Romans 12:2, "Do not emulate this era, but be transformed solely by renewing your heart-mind, that you may discern what is the good and pleasing and perfect will of God."

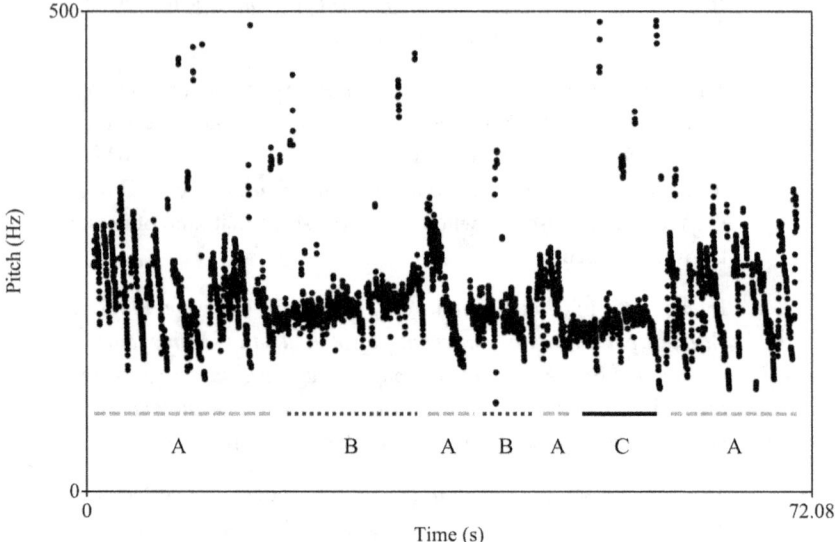

FIGURE 2.1. Pitch visualization of excerpt 2.4

> A. Explanation: *Malssŭm ŭro uri nŭn saerowŏ chimnida. Ttohan na ŭi ŭiin ŭn midŭm ŭro malmiama sallirago haessŭmŭro soksaram ŭn yuksin i chunŭn kamgakchŏk in chŏngbo ro salji ank'o malssŭm i chunŭn chŏngbo ro samnida.*
>
> Through the Word we are renewed. Also, as it is said, "My righteous ones shall live by faith"—the inner person does not live according to the sensory information given by the flesh, but lives according the information given by the Word.

As Cho moves closer to the recitation, the stylistic delivery marks the shift from self-animated, self-authored hermeneutics (as "direct speech") to self-animated, other-authored scripture (as "quoted speech"). But the effect of narrowing the pitch contour and increasing the speed to make this transition is to present himself as if he were simply "opening his mouth" and letting it be filled up by the Word of God. The flow of recitation is the climax and release from intensification. In this arrangement, the Bible verse serves as the authoritative Word, which, like a ventriloquist, speaks through Cho to the audience as if it were not merely memorized but actually embodied within, or passing through, him.[46] Like scripture flowing from Cho's mouth while preaching, glossolalia in prayer should emerge as a sonorant flow, allowing Christians to speak secrets "in" or "with" the spirit.

LIMITS TO PARTICIPANT ROLES: SPEAKING IN TONGUES "SO THE DEVIL CANNOT UNDERSTAND"

Korean Christians often described speaking in tongues as having a secret conversation with God. The conversation itself is not a secret. Its secret properties are based on the denotational unintelligibility of the conversation—the inability of (most) others to decode the denotational substance of speech, even while they might understand in a general sense what the genre of conversation is "about" (e.g., worship, confession, repentance). As Cho explained on September 26, 2004, glossolalia is a "secret language with God"; it is "speech that is just between us and God." He continued by claiming that if we use ordinary speech, "the devil comes to know and can interfere in advance. However, if we speak in tongues to tell God all of our private inner feelings so the devil cannot understand our soul or our heart," then "the devil is helpless and unable to obstruct us."[47]

If God is the super-addressee, Satan is the super-overhearer. For these Christians, glossolalia prevents Satan, the devil, evil spirits, as well as human others (*nam*) from hearing (and presumably acting on) the juicy or even banal details of one's life revealed through verbalized confession and repentance (see chapter 5). They sometimes compared praying in tongues to slang, where slang is characterized as a secret register used by young people to speak privately with one another.[48]

Some were adamant that Satan and others would use their secrets against them. Their caution about "others" is significant, since they emphasize group prayer as a centerpiece of the Korean Protestant experience. In settings of group prayer, the threat of eavesdropping can be counteracted by both glossolalia and the noise of the group itself, modeling the anonymity of the urban crowd. The noise facilitates privacy through a kind of civil inattention that is afforded by a cacophony in which no individual's utterances can be interpreted. While there are events of group glossolalic prayer organized around a specific prayer topic, where a sense of a unified, amplified megaspeaker emerges out of the collaborative din, in the regular rituals of *t'ongsŏng kido*, the participants are more often praying together *severally*, rather than in unity. Ratified interactional participant roles can be restricted solely to dyadic channels between individuals among the prayerful and their deity—a special, spiritual, one-on-one meeting within a multitude.

The pastor's daughter quoted above felt constantly under scrutiny, even surveillance, at church. She explained that when she had "uncomfortable things" to reveal in prayer, she preferred to say them in large groups or completely alone, for example, at home in her room or in an individual prayer cell at a mountain retreat. She explained that she was not very proficient at speaking in tongues and, aware of the potential for "learner error" in this acquired language, she feared that she might accidentally reveal a secret during prayers. She suspected that others would listen to her prayers because, she admitted, she herself would do the same. For her, a small prayer group was like a small town where everyone constantly overhears—eavesdrops on—everyone else.

The aggregate of sentiments expressed publicly but with the security of individual privacy—enveloped by cacophony and masked by glossolalia—seems to produce a perfect Christian secret society mediated by universal, simultaneous access to both public and private confession, made possible by sharing unintelligible secrets with God. The severe threat of rumors in churches, some claimed, was exactly why the gift of interpretation was given only to those who could keep a secret—to those who spread the gospel rather than gossip. Producing cacophony through glossolalic group prayer instantiates not only the excesses of spiritual contact but also the special personal relationship that individual Christians are supposed to have with the deity: a relationship of overwhelming intimacy, privacy, and secrecy, in which everything can be revealed through confession and repentance without saying anything at all.

LIMITS TO SOCIAL INDEXICALITY: BLENDING IN WHILE "BURSTING WITH GRACE"

Freed from denotation, focused by narrowed prosody, and made private by cacophony, the dyadic interactions between the deity and prayerful individuals are nonetheless subject to a limit of their own: the social indexicality that formally pervades the Korean language. This indexicality takes the form of honorifics and speech styles—a baroque, elaborate signaling of uneven participant roles according to intimacy, status, and generalized forms of social differentiation.[49] The obligatory and archaic deference and demeanor indexicals normally reserved for addressing the deity give way to a feeling of phaticity that, by dissolving the dyad, combines submission with empowerment, intimacy with awe. Practitioners often described this permeable state of spiritual sociality in bodily terms that are familiar, sensuous, vivid, and affectively charged. They moreover described the deity's presence both outside ("enveloped by grace," "bathing in grace") and inside (a heart "spilling over with grace," "bursting with grace") the individual person.

On these themes, an evangelist (*chŏndosa*) in his midthirties tried to teach me how to speak in tongues.[50] The evangelist was raised a Presbyterian but decided, against the wishes of his parents, to attend Hansei University, the theological seminary attached to the Yoido Full Gospel Church. Although he participated in daily events of group prayer and glossolalia, he said he also spoke in tongues for hours every night in the privacy of his room. In a noisy restaurant, after we had finished our cheeseburgers, he explained that glossolalia was common, easy, and available to all. His technique was to focus his heart-mind (*maŭm*) on the deity specifically and completely.[51] He insisted that one should never try; rather, a person should simply ask. And then he demonstrated for me. After addressing the deity and entreating the deity to lead his prayers, he transitioned into rapid-fire tongues (he mentioned that people who pray slowly have a harder time speaking in tongues). As he did so, he alternated among three different conversations with three distinct styles: a relatively unmarked polite mode addressed to me; a formulaic, overtly honorific mode addressed to his deity; and glossolalic utterances devoid of person deixis or honorifics. With each style, his pitch became increasingly fixed, from variable prosody to formulaic prosodic contours to a fixed and markedly lower pitch.

The evangelist insisted that the phonetic and prosodic sound patterns of glossolalia could be very simple at first. And while many people did begin speaking in tongues in a very simple way—with "starter tongues" (*ch'obangŏn*) sometimes described as infantile babble, baby talk, or "la la la" glossolalia—it was possible for glossolalia to undergo ornate semiotic enregisterment. There was occasionally conflict among Christians over which of them excelled at glossolalia. Some Christians described being cautious about their own glossolalia because it would make their friends envious and cause discord within their church groups. Many congregations strongly pressured members to participate, enthusiastically, in gatherings of group prayer; sometimes glossolalia was a prerequisite for such participation. And prayer style also regulated participation: there was much discussion among Christians about other Christians whose prayers—glossolalic and otherwise—were distracting. Others' prayers were considered disruptive if they were too loud or otherwise stood out from the sound of the group. Those who first learned to speak in tongues sometimes prayed too loudly and had to be corrected by their more experienced peers. Christians accused other Christians whose prayers were consistently disruptive of engaging in a kind of worldly boasting, of effectively bragging about their faith and their special relationship with God. Disruptive prayers even generated judgments of satanic, demonic, or ghostly influence, resembling a witchcraft accusation. "Not all prayer is clean," insisted one seasoned glossolalist, who emphasized the importance of spiritual discernment while speaking in tongues. Indeed, the Bible contains passages pointing to deceitful speech, metonymically anchord to tongues and lips. These kinds of statements suggest that boastful prayer violates the ritual limits to participant roles and social indexicality more broadly, because it is through these two kinds of semiosis that social differentiation—differentiation among the prayerful as a function of their individual relations with God—can be made explicit.

Although people insisted that they should not listen to one another during prayer, they admitted that they sometimes did. Sometimes people listened with curiosity to the glossolalic sounds of their neighbors. Often, however, listening was the unwanted effect of another's intrusive behavior. In these contexts of collaborative sound-making, a relationship emerges between glossolalic practices in worship contexts and honorific practices in the broader social context of being a Christian in Korean society. Although the cacophony produced from glossolalic practices bypassed ordinary verbal interaction laden with honorific usage, it still faced the problem of social indexicality in the form of group participation, an activity that required neither transcendence, nor dissociative trance, nor embodied ecstasy, but rather, as in everyday speech, careful encryption, self-monitoring, and deference to others.

The Communicative Production of Reality

As members of the Yoido Full Gospel Church contact the deity through glossolalia en masse, they enact a basic principle of their faith: "If we stand firmly on the Word of God, think the Word, believe the Word, speak the Word, go forth according to the Word, in the end we will be able to experience that which is true and real," as Pastor Cho puts it in a sermon called "Illusion and Reality" (*Hŏsang kwa silsang*), delivered March 28, 1999. "The Word" (*malssŭm*) in this passage is a spiritual entity, encompassing the denotational conception of language as a vehicle for propositional truth and a broader pragmatic conception of language as a medium of social interaction that makes denotation possible.[52]

As the sanctuary erupts with the sound of mass glossolalia, long-shot images of the congregation and close-up images of individual congregants are projected on large screens to the right and left of the towering backlit cross behind the pulpit. Within the cacophonous acoustic space, the promise of denotation is fulfilled and the reality of contact made manifest in the voices and hands of roaming intercessors. These intercessors move about the congregation, standing on pews above the prayerful, placing their hands on the person's head or back to pray over them. As the congregants' bodies begin to sway and shake from prayer, they rise and wave their outstretched arms. Some congregants strain toward the intercessors, leaning over adjacent pews, striving with their arms and torsos to make physical contact with these roaming conduits of the Holy Spirit.

THE LIMITS OF LANGUAGE   59

    The excerpt below (excerpt 2.5) captures the moment when a roaming intercessor approached me at a service on July 17, 2013. Amid the cacophony and frenetic bodily movement, some voices droned on the same B-flat tonic that began the prayer session on "hallelujah," sometimes harmonizing with the pitch, departing from it, and returning to it again. As the intercessor approached, his voice came through increasingly clearly, in part because of the direction of his speech (all the congregants were directed toward the cross, while the roaming intercessors were mostly face to face with the prayerful) and in part because of the denotationally transparent Korean that he was speaking against the cacophony of others' glossolalia. He stood on the pew in front of me, placed his hands on my head, and uttered the initial phrases of his formulaic intercessory prayers, also on a B-flat. He departed from this pitch only in the final cadences of each sentence, when he produced a prosodic thrust that was calibrated to match the quick shoves of his hands and the final verb and sentence endings that finished each phrase (Korean syntax is verb final). These sentence endings alternated between the hyperdeferential combination of the honorific infix *-si-* and the archaic honorific imperative *opsosŏ*, and the plain combination of the future verb suffix *-l* and the archaic imperative *chiŏda*. This alternation explicitly signaled a change in addressee, with contrasting forms of illocutionary force manifesting as the difference between supplication and command. Furthermore, the command pattern [verb]*-l chiŏda*, while usually directed at a second-person addressee (e.g., "Behold!" [*Pol chiŏda!*], "[You shall] praise God!" [*Hananim ŭl ch'anyang hal chiŏda!*]), was expanded to include a third-person referent. This fashion of speaking effectively proclaimed prophecy and performatively brought that prophecy to reality by "going forth according to the Word" (as in "It shall be done!").[53]

    Below, I have underlined the passages that were uttered on the fixed B-flat tonic of the hymn. Furthermore, I have differentiated the phrases that are addressed to the deity as a form of supplication in respectful, honorific speech (to the left), and the phrases that use the spiritual power afforded by this supplication to performatively command and influence or give prophecy about states of affairs on earth produced without such honorifics (to the right).[54]

Excerpt 2.5

                    [glossolalia]
                    Kido hamnida.
                    [We] pray.
<u>*Yesu sŏngnyŏng ŭl simŏ chusigo*</u>
Please plant the Holy Spirit of Jesus, and

  ŭnhye ŭi yŏng isigo
  [you] are the spirit of grace, and
  pok chusigo
  give the blessing, and
  kan'gu hayŏ chusiopsosŏ
  we earnestly desire, and you give.[55]
  Kŭrŏch'iman sarang hage towa chusigo
  But help us to love, and
  Abŏji yŏksa hayŏ chusiopsosŏ
  Father, please work in us.
          Choe saham i (?) mŏjianŭl chiŏda![56]
          The forgiveness of sins shall [?] before long!
          Chu ŭnhye ka imhal chiŏda!
          The grace of the Lord shall come!
          Kijŏk i irŏnal chiŏda!
          Miracles shall occur!

Nŭnghi towa chusigo
Ably help [us], and
Ŭnhye rŭl tŏhayŏ chusiopsosŏ!
add [your] grace [to us]!
Chu man para podorok towa chusigo
Help us look only at [you], Lord, and
Chu rŭl ŭiji hamkke kijŏk i irŏnal chul mitsŭmnida!
We believe that [we will make] miracles together if we rely on the Lord!
          Chu ŭi nŭngnyŏk i imhal chiŏda!
          The power of the Lord shall come!
      [glossolalia]

  When the intercessor finished and moved on to the next person, the recording captured others still regularly praying on this tonal center, harmonizing with it, departing from it, and then returning again. The role of pitch here, combined with fixed rhythm and increased tempo, seems to provide a semiotic mode of spiritual contact with the deity (through supplication), one that "carries over" to the mode of spiritual authorization (through blunt command) to speak "in the name of Jesus" in the world. That is, the alternating intercessory supplications and commands are riding on the collaborative cacophonous glossolalia and its tonal center as a complex, morally saturated phonosonic nexus, wherein the intercessors and the prayerful align and reinforce a specific kind of phonic engagement with a specific kind of sonic orientation.

  Glossolalic cacophony produces the reality described by Cho through carefully calibrated, layered, co-metricalized processes of poetic intensification, or the intensification of style qua textural densification.⁵⁷ Through these compounding processes, dynamic semiosis seems to congeal into something with a palpably real presence.⁵⁸ For the prayerful in settings of cacophonous glossolalia, this collaborative semiotic intensification produces the collective reality of the spirit. At the service on July 17, 2013, the ordered sequencing of supplication, a triplicate vocative (*Chu yŏ!*) and sustained repetition of "hallelujah" on the tonic of a hymn both suppressed some elements of "normal" speech while intensifying others as a way of transitioning into cacophonous glossolalia. Glossolalia proceeded like this for about ten minutes until, as in the final excerpt below (excerpt 2.6), Pastor Lee drew the congregants back into a "normal" communicative space by taking up the melody of the hymn and singing it, with the congregants following in kind. Glossolalic cacophony turned to melody, and then melody turned into relatively unmarked speech; that is, the congregants returned to where they began. In his final prayer, Lee denotationally gathered together the individual prayers of the congregants into a comprehensive intercessory prayer for healing, and in so doing, like the individual intercessors during the prayer session, he began on a fixed pitch as his tonal anchor, and his prayers moved, in parallel and in a compounding fashion, rapidly toward a powerful prosodic cadence that departed from this tone with a calibrated thrust. In response to each thrust, the congregation shouted "Amen!" As above, honorific supplication is to the left, blunt command is to the right, and utterances on a fixed pitch are underlined.

Excerpt 2.6

[glossolalia]
[singing]
[spoken to the congregation:]
Kak kasŭm e son ŭl ŏnjŭsipsio.
Please place your hand on your heart.
Midŭm ŭro, munje ka palsaeng haettamyŏn kasŭm e son ŏnko kido hasipsio.
With faith, place your hand on your troubled heart and pray.
[spoken to God:]
Sarang kwa ŭnhye wa chabi ka yŏngwŏn hasin Hananim abŏji
God the Father, whose love, grace, and mercy are eternal,
Yesunim ŭi irŭm ŭro Chu ŭi sŏngnyŏng kkesŏ
in the name of Jesus, the Holy Spirit of the Lord,
i sigan uri rŭl manjyŏ chusigil wŏnhamnida. (Amen)
at this hour we want you to touch us. (Amen)
Sangch'ŏ ibŭn uri maŭm ŭl manjyŏ chusigo (Amen)
Touch our wounded hearts and (Amen)

naksim hanŭn simnyŏng enŭn wiro hayŏ chusigo (Amen)
lift up our depressed spirits and (Amen)
kot'ong kwa koeroum e innŭn kŭ maŭm e p'yŏngan ham ŭl chugil wŏnhamnida. (Amen)
into the hearts in pain and suffering, we want you to put peace. (Amen)
[spoken in the name of Jesus:]
Nasaret Yesu Kŭrisŭdo ŭi irŭm ŭro myŏng hanoni
In the name of Jesus Christ of Nazareth, I command
<u>*Modŭn chilbyŏng ŭn mŏrikkŭt put'ŏ palkkŭt kkaji modu ttŏna kal*</u> *chiŏda! (Amen!)*
every disease from the tip of the head to the tip of the feet shall go away! (Amen!)
<u>*Simhan tut'ong, pulmyŏnchŭng, uulchŭng (?) chŏngsin chirhwan, ch'imae hyŏnsang mullŏ kara! (Amen!)*</u>
Severe headache, insomnia, depression (?), psychological disease, phenomena of dementia be gone! (Amen!)
<u>*Simjangpyŏng i mullŏ kal*</u> *chiŏda! (Amen!)*
Heart disease shall be gone! (Amen!)
<u>*[?] mullŏ kal*</u> *chiŏda! (Amen!)*
[?] shall be gone! (Amen!)
<u>*Kwanjŏllyŏm i mullŏ kal*</u> *chiŏda! (Amen!)*
Arthritis shall be gone! (Amen!)
<u>*Aksŏng [?]) to ttŏna kal*</u> *chiŏda! (Amen!)*
Malignant [?] also shall be gone! (Amen!)
<u>*Kohyŏrap kwa tangnyo nŭn mullŏ kara! (Amen!)*</u>
Hypertension and diabetes be gone! (Amen!)
<u>*Mok kwa p'ye t'ongchŭng to*</u> *mullŏ kal chiŏda! (Amen!)*
Pains of the neck and lungs also shall be gone! (Amen!)

In these mass events of speaking in tongues at the Yoido Full Gospel Church, glossolalists intensified some features of cultural semiosis while suppressing others as they moved from everyday forms of speech to a narrowed communicative space. In this narrowed space, musical pitch, rhythm, and tempo emerge as semiotic points of orientation to which other sounds may be indexically anchored within a cacophonous environment. Although such vocalizations are, practically speaking, produced at the ideological limits of language, their status as language is reinforced as church members integrate these sounds into commands and prophecies—denotational text uttered in Korean.

Conclusion The positive valence of collective effervescence is pronounced in the data I have analyzed. In these combined events of glossolalia and cacophony, the prayerful suppress and limit the normal functions of language and communication more broadly to pass through a narrowed, intensified channel of spiritual semiotics. As the prayerful move away from intelligible denotation, variable prosody, inclusive interaction, and differentiated social indexicality, they find a new semiotic orientation in pitch, rhythm, and tempo. This kind of pitched intensification in prayer takes place in huge gatherings like the one described above, as well as within small, intimate groups (as small as two). This collaborative intensity is the goal as the prayerful enter the prayer space. And as features of the synchronous prayers also become increasingly synchronized, this intensity is materialized by a cacophony that is anchored to a tonal, rhythmic center, becoming the very source from which to draw power in denotational prayer once they depart from it. Via glossolalia, they collaboratively produce cacophony with a perceptible but evasive semiotic point of orientation, a sensory environment that is at once disorienting and orienting, overwhelming and stabilizing.

Although prayer is defined locally as communication with God and glossolalia is defined in this context as secret communication with God, there is plenty of evidence that interaction qua broadly cultural semiosis is taking place with others, even though it is not denotational and is not usually acknowledged as interaction. On the one hand, glossolalia serves as a privileged medium for sharing secrets with God. On the other hand, it also might allow the prayerful to tune in intersubjectively with others quasi-musically, through pitch, rhythm, and tempo, below the level of awareness. Cacophonous glossolalia allows the prayerful to disconnect from others denotationally while connecting with others through a broader, covert set of pragmatic processes ritually organized into poetic form.

The powerfully felt effects of glossolalia—the sensation of secrecy as intimacy and concealment as contact—lie not only in overt, unintelligible speech alone, nor even in the extremely personal, private space of spiritual connection, but also in the more covert modes of sociality in which the prayerful place themselves: hiding secrets from others while telling secrets in the presence of others, and orienting to the deity linguistically while orienting to other humans musically. When these Christians are making private, secret, intimate contact with the deity, they also are making plenty of contact with one another. Although glossolalia and cacophony jointly suppress denotation to generate spiritual contact, they also jointly draw on social contact to fulfill the promise of enhanced denotation. When the prayerful return to forms of communication that they take to be more directly intelligible to one another, they say that their hearts are refreshed and that their speech seems purer and more potent. Some have even made a bold new proposal that expands this ritual process into an ambitious religious program: now that so many Korean Christians can speak in tongues, now that glossolalia is so habitual, now that unintelligibility is so familiar, it is time to move on to prophecy. For they have taken speech to the ideological limits of language and converted a collaborative cultural experience that is intense beyond words into the social force of propositional truth.

3

Feeling the Same Thing

Circulation and the Spirit of Sameness

In the previous chapter, I showed how the compounded unintelligibility of glossolalia and cacophony could be ritually transformed into an experience of contact with the divine. The process of producing this contact is so thickly mediated by social action that the mediation itself could seem to disappear, generating an impression of unmediated, absolute spiritual presence. I also showed how the production of unintelligibility as cultural semiosis at the limits of language has a refreshing, reinforcing, undergirding effect on certain propositional forms taken to be emblematic of Christian speech. Similarly, the process of reinforcing denotation is so thickly mediated that it could seem to appear unmediated, to present itself as completely transparent, eternal propositional truth. There is a parallel between ideologies of denotation and pneumatologies of the Holy Spirit: just as an ideology of transparent denotation draws attention away from—even stands in for—the vast pragmatic labor of social mediation involved in speech (especially propositions claimed to be eternally true), a concept of the Holy Spirit as divine mediator draws attention away from—even stands in for—the vast pragmatic labor of social mediation that produces encounters with the divine (however immediate and undeniable they may feel).

It is common for Christians to conceptualize the Holy Spirit as the materializing agent that facilitates phatic intimacy with the deity, just as they conceptualize it as the agent that inspires biblical scripture to come alive, to be experienced as the "living" Word.[1] When the spirit, scripture, and glossolalia are considered together, it is as if scripture and glossolalia form two branches of a spiritual hyperbola, with glossolalia straining asymptotically from propositional truth toward spiritual contact, and scripture straining asymptotically from spiritual contact toward propositional truth. The link between glossolalia and scripture emerges when Christians characterize the Bible both as the dynamic medium that links individual humans with the deity and as the absolute stabilization of propositional content. In such characterizations, the Word is conceptualized both as an ongoing speech event and as a fixed representational framework, one that is both adaptable and the same across time, space, and language. Practitioners often related glossolalia to scripture, partly because scriptural repetition could lead to glossolalia, but also because glossolalia was sometimes experienced as if the speaker had been given a Bible or hymnal in an unknown language from which to read or sing. Such descriptions helped make sense of the complicated issue of personal agency in glossolalia, when practitioners were certain that their speech had a source outside of themselves but they still maintained some consciousness of and even control over their utterances. Like glossolalia, scripture involves an ambivalent, competitive, and yet potentially complementary relation between spiritual presence and static denotational proposition.[2]

Christians rely on the semiotics of sameness to manage this ambivalence. That is, they find ways to treat the Word as denotationally stable across every utterance, within and across semiotic communities. Likewise, they find ways to assert that the kinds of experiences of divine contact produced through glossolalia are in fact the same across every encounter. Just as they must agree that the Word always "says" the same thing, they must agree that, in their heightened experiences of contact with the Holy Spirit produced through the Word, they always "feel" the same thing. This is not to say that their proprioceptive "feelings" are the same; in fact, these might be quite different. Rather, it is to say that they feel, sense, or perceive the effects of the same divine object or causal agent. It is a practical theological solution to the more general evidentiary challenge, posed by Franz Boas, that "though like causes have like effects, like effects have not like causes."[3] Despite sociohistorical differences of speech and radically individuated spiritual encounters, the Word and the spirit should be, in principle, the same. A semiotics of sameness across instances of perceptual difference is vital to the entire enterprise.

This chapter looks more closely at the problem of social mediation between spiritual contact and literal denotation, focusing specifically on the conceptualization of the Word (*malssŭm*). My aim is to situate glossolalia among other Christian speech practices that are oriented to the Word as an emblem of ideal Christian speech and a medium of spiritual contact. Consider, for example, the Kingdom Awakening Portal, a "web based communication network connecting and encouraging the Body in kingdom awakening."[4] The following quote is an excerpt from a posting in one of the portal's forums called "From around God's Network," where users report on Christian evangelism and revival activity outside the United States. In the quote, the American revivalist Jan Jansen of Global Fire Ministries describes a four-thousand-person revival meeting in Seoul, South Korea, led by her husband, Jeff Jansen. It took place at a church at the theological fringes, which formerly was known as the Great Faith Church (K'ŭn midŭm kyohoe) until scandal and claims of heresy forced the church to change its name and denomination.[5] During the revival event, a technological medium of communication became a channel for transporting the Holy Spirit:

> Jeff released cell phone miracles one night. As he felt the faith of the centurion soldier rise up, he released healing into the atmosphere and released a healing wave that would not be limited by space or distance. Notably, one woman who was not intendance [sic], but in her living room at home, had been in a car accident and had a rib grossly out of place and a twisted spine. She was in great pain and required surgery. Someone in attendance called her on the cell phone when the healing wave was released, and she testified that she felt the heat and the power of God come upon her and that her rib just popped right back into place right before her eyes.[6]

Reports of such cell phone miracles and anointments are not uncommon among charismatics. They were reported in South Korea as well, where some informants recounted the way they prayed via technological mediation with others—often through their churches' live-streaming online prayer portals—and felt the spirit pass through their computer or tablet or phone. Even at their churches, they often listened to sermons and received blessings from a video screen; sometimes they had to worship via live video feed in one of the megachurch's overflow chapels, and sometimes they had to worship via previously recorded material when a pastor was out of town.[7]

These examples are a straightforward illustration of a central argument of this chapter—namely, that language ideology provides groups with a model for characterizing and explaining their notion that they share deeply felt experiences of the same unseen things in the world. Rather than language being opposed or complementary to embodied, experiential encounters with the divine, it is precisely an ideology of language that provides the conditions of possibility for and means of conceptualizing such experiences. In the case of the cell phone miracles, online prayer communities, or video sermons: as the Word travels, so does the spirit.

In this chapter, I further explore the concept of spiritual and semiotic "movement" as a means to asserting sameness across spiritual events. I do so by placing Yoido Full Gospel's theological treatment of the Word and the Holy Spirit in contrast with a more familiar, Protestant mainline understanding of a Seoul megachurch, Sarang ŭi Kyohoe (Church of Love). Although many Sarang Church members do speak in tongues, glossolalia is not emphasized as central to the church's worship or theological paradigm. Together, Sarang Church and Yoido Full Gospel Church exemplify at an institutional level the two different orientations to the asymptotic hyperbola of proposition and presence: at one end, an emphasis on denotation and its social effects, and on the other, an emphasis on spiritual contact and its supernatural effects. In both churches, however, the movement of the Word is apperceived to trace a pathway between speakers and between social groups, and between spiritual and earthly realms. The logic of this dynamic relationship is projected onto the speech-like behavior of glossolalia to justify it as language spoken by and with the spirit.

My approach is to focus on the sermons of these two pastors that characterize and draw the Word and the Holy Spirit together in terms of movement. Reverend Oh Jung-hyun (O Chŏnghyŏn) of the Presbyterian Sarang Community Church and Reverend Cho Yonggi of the Pentecostal Yoido Full Gospel Church both direct their congregants to engage in specific styles of communicative interaction and language use organized around the Word. These directives provide a model for conceptualizing other nonlinguistic but semiotically rich and religiously powerful experiences (e.g., the "fire" of the Holy Spirit) by linking the perceived behavior of the unseen agents of such experiences to the perceived behavior of linguistic tokens. Reverend Oh encourages his congregants to circulate and share the Word in order to create a community of shared beliefs based on shared meanings that are immutably given in scripture. Adhering to these words in the company of others, the congregants set the conditions of possibility for the Holy Spirit to inhabit the social body of like-minded/like-worded Christians. By contrast, Reverend Cho treats the Word as a gateway into the spiritual realm, emphasizing the way the sovereign God directly plants the Word in each yielding person. These different language ideological models of the Word shape how the different institutions treat the movement of the spirit among their congregants and throughout the world.

Pastors Oh and Cho link the behavior of the Word with the behavior of the Holy Spirit through a series of conceptual moves that connect a linguistic and broader semiotic ideology at one end, to the logic of the church institution at the other.[8] They attempt to align institutional biblical hermeneutics, congregants' behaviors, and congregants' individual and collective religious experiences of the deity. Each pastor makes theological claims to truth and reality that provide the basis of a semiotic ideology which characterizes the experienceable form of a spiritual entity or event as a certain type of readable sign or multimodal ensemble of signs. They do so through their linguistic ideological treatments of the Word, which oscillate between accounts of interdiscursivity and intertextuality.[9]

Interdiscursivity describes a relationship between events of semiotic production that highlight a directionality between a source and a target. I use the term in my analysis to account for descriptions of semiotic tokens that appear to "move" from point A to point B in some culturally conceptualized deictic plane (in time, through space, between minds, etc., from "here" to "there"). Pastors Oh and Cho mobilize local Christian theories of interdiscursivity by focusing on the means, mediums, and pathways by which the Word is understood to move. Within an evangelical Christian framework, the Word has momentum. It is incumbent upon the recipient of the Word to support its holy trajectory through the world via further evangelism—to make one's own event of semiotic production a past event from the point of view of some other future event of utterance to which it bears an interdiscursive relation.

Intertextuality, by contrast, is logically achronic and directionally neutral. It describes a relationship in which "two or more texts-in-context (individuable objects) become tokens of a type, thus 'the same' in some respect or respects."[10] Rather than focusing on the movement or directionality of signs from a source to a target, potentially emphasizing the differences between originary and subsequent entextualizations, intertextual relations focus our attention on the elements of textual sameness (iconicity) across events.[11] Insofar as intertextuality concerns two or more tokens of a type, it also draws attention to the contextual sameness or difference across events—in a sense, outward into the social rather than forward or backward between events.[12] The pastors shift from a perspective of interdiscursivity to one of intertextuality when they emphasize the eternal sameness of the Word, and especially when they emphasize the way the Word "incorporat[es] aspects of context, such that the resultant text carries elements of its history of use within it."[13] From interdiscursivity to intertextuality, the Word not only moves through the world, but also changes the world as it moves.

Fire is the operative metaphor—and phenomenal reality—that is literalized when the semiotics of sameness produces the image of an unchanging Word moving through time and space, transforming populations, and setting individual hearts ablaze.[14] It is through vast complexes of interdiscursivity and intertextuality that the Word can be said to be the same across different semiotic events, and likewise that mystical encounters with the divine can be said to be the same across different events. It is the globalized, transhistorical analogy of chapter 2, verse 3 of the Acts of the Apostles, depicting the branching of a single flame, cloven into fiery tips like tongues, resting on and working through individuals across time and space. A Christian phenomenology of the Word and its power depends, fundamentally and unavoidably, on these semiotic processes. Semiotic ideology, in this case, is anchored to and only analyzable through a specifically linguistic ideology.

Let me emphasize that I am not simply arguing that the sameness of their representations produces the sameness of their experiences. Rather, I am pointing out the analogical logic by which they project a model of circulation based on an ideology of sameness of utterances onto an assertion of sameness of spiritual experience. Their respective language ideologies, biblical hermeneutics, models of nonlinguistic spiritual experience, and ecclesiastical structures come into alignment. In both cases, I look at the way the logic of sameness across different events contributes to the communal viability of these institutions by providing the ideological grounds for explaining the sense of a shared experience of entities not available for systematic, public demonstration or manipulation. In both cases, social mediation itself is a problem to be solved—emphasized as Christian fellowship in some respects, suppressed as worldly corruption in others. But on the whole, the likeness of conceptualization between the Word and the Holy Spirit—i.e., their analogical relation—makes it possible for glossolalia to be experienced as language.

The Word as Denotational Entity

Sarang Church (Sarang ŭi kyohoe), or the Church of Love, is a Presbyterian megachurch located in a wealthy area of Seoul, south of the Han River. It claims to have eighty thousand members. The church was established in 1978 by the Reverend Oak Han-Heum (Ok Hanhŭm), who died in 2010. After Oak's retirement in 2003, leadership of the church was transferred to Pastor Oh Jung-hyun. Pastor Oh received special notoriety when it was exposed that he had plagiarized major portions of his doctoral thesis, and when he presided over the three-hundred-billion-wŏn ($270 million) construction of a mammoth new church building in an affluent and expensive district of southern Seoul.[15]

Sarang Church is known in Korea for its "discipleship training" (*cheja hullyŏn*) program, a seminar designed to develop leadership among the laity. The program has been used to train hundreds of pastors and has been replicated in numerous churches throughout Korea, as well as in ethnic-Korean churches throughout the world.[16] Discipleship training at Sarang is based on the Nevius method, named for the nineteenth-century Christian missionary John Nevius, who emphasized "the Bible as the basis of all Christian work and

[an] elaborate system of Bible classes by which that book could be studied and applied to the believer's heart."[17] This missiological method is often characterized as emphasizing self-propagandizing, self-governing, and self-supporting missions, rather than straightforward evangelizing by foreign missionaries.[18] A version of the program is still carried out in the church's current operations, with a commitment to self-study and a belief in biblical inerrancy guiding the church's evangelical and exegetical style.

Along these lines, in 2006 Pastor Oh gave a sermon titled "How Do We Tame the Tongue?" (*Hyŏ rŭl ŏttŏk'e kildŭrilkka?*). The sermon was not about glossolalia. The stated aim of the sermon, based on James 3:1–4, was to convince the congregation that "our small tongue controls our whole body, our mouth rules our whole body, our words rule all our actions." The reason: members of the congregation had been spreading rumors, threatening the potential discipleship of other members.[19] Here, both the content and the pathways of circulation were targeted for regulation and control.

In this sermon, Pastor Oh claims that the health of the church as a whole is threatened by the misuse of *mal*—here, glossable as "words," "speech," or "language"—among individuals who spread rumors. Congregants are instructed to open their mouths and display the health of their words before God:

Excerpt 3.1

> "A" hamyŏnsŏ hyŏ rŭl naemi nŭn kŭ kŏt i ai ŭi kŏn'gang kŏmjin ŭl hanŭn kŏt imnida. Onŭl i sigan, i yebae rŭl tŭrŭmyŏnsŏ, i malssŭm ŭl tŭrŭmyŏnsŏ, chŏ wa yŏrŏbun tŭl i Chunim ap esŏ "A" hasigi paramnida. Yŏrŏbun hyŏ rŭl naemirŏsŏ uri ŭi yŏnghon ŭi kŏn'gang kŏmjin, uri ŭi yŏnghon ŭi ch'eon, uri yŏnghon ŭi sujun ŭl ch'ŭkchŏng hal su ittorok ŭnhye rŭl chusigi rŭl paramnida.

> We can measure children's health by having them say "Ah" and stick out their tongues. Today, at this time, as you listen to this worship, as you listen to this Word, I hope that we all say "Ah" before God. As you all stick out your tongues, I hope that we are given the grace to have our spiritual health examined, our spiritual temperature taken, our spiritual level measured.

The sermon culminates in Oh's instruction to church members to replace their un-Christian words with the Word in order to heal the church. Similarly, in a 2005 sermon titled "Longing for a Revival of the Word" (*Malssŭm ŭi puhŭng ŭl kalmangham*), Pastor Oh offers an example of how the good Word of the Bible stands in contrast to the bad words of rumor—again, the gospel versus gossip. He also suggests that words more generally move like material objects in the world. He connects the spreading of the fire of the Holy Spirit with the spreading of the right kinds of words at the Pyŏngyang Great Revival of 1907. Then, to make the point that the fire of the Holy Spirit follows the pathway of the Word, Pastor Oh sketches the historical movement of the Word among Christians. He explains how the fire passed through time and space from person to person: from Martin Luther to John Knox, to John Wesley, and finally to the Christians of Pyŏngyang:

Excerpt 3.2

> *Saram tŭl ŭi maŭm sok e Hananim ŭi malssŭm i imhanŭn kot mada pul i t'agi sijak haessŭmnida. Pulgil i imhaessŭmnida. Kŭraesŏ uri ka ch'anyang hago kido hanŭn kaunde esŏ irŏn ch'alna e i pul i put'ŏssŭmyŏn chok'ettago t'ansik ŭl hasidŏn Chu isiyŏ. Onŭl uri kyohoe ppun man anira yŏrŏbun kaein kakcha i Han'guk sahoe e i malssŭm e pul ŭl tŏnjisisa, tasi hanbŏn yŏnggwang i ch'ungjŏkhage hayŏ chuopsosŏ.*

> Wherever the Word of God reached people's heart-minds, the fire was set ablaze. The fire came. So, "O Lord," you sighed, wanting the fire to catch at the moment when we sang hymns and prayed. Today, throw the fire of the Word not only on our church but also on everyone, each individual, [and] Korean society, so that once again the glory of God will be fulfilled.

When Oh directs the congregants to spread the Word throughout the world, he downplays the possibility that these words might be recontextualized differently in different situations. That is, he commits to an absolute, inerrable semiotic form that would not undergo transformation in its "movement" from one context to another. Oh emphasizes this assertion in his sermon by distinguishing the Word from text:

Excerpt 3.3

> *Onŭl uri minjok ŭi munje ka muŏt imnikka? Malssŭm ap esŏ chasin ŭl pitch'uŏboji mot hanŭn kŏt imnida. Chigŭm uri Han'guk kyohoe naejŏk ŭro to munje ka issŭmnida. Kŭ kŏt i mwŏnyamyŏn sowi Sŏnggyŏng pip'yŏng irago haesŏ, "textual criticism" irago, i kŏt i mani yŏnghyang ŭl mich'ŏsŏ. Sŏnggyŏng pip'yŏng ŭi t'ŭkching i mwŏnyamyŏn chagi ka wŏnhanŭn kŏt man "pick up" hanŭn kŏeyo. Sŏnggyŏng nae e chagi ka choahanŭn kŏt man "pick up" hanŭn kŏeyo. Chagi ka maŭm e an tŭnŭn kot tŭlŭn kŭnyang tŏnjyŏbŏryŏ. Ye rŭl tŭrŏsŏ, tongsŏngae. Sŏnggyŏng esŏ nŭn andoendago kŭraettjanayo.*

> What is our nation's problem today? The problem is we cannot reflect upon ourselves according to the Word of God. These days our Korean

churches also have some inner problems. The thing is that so-called biblical criticism, that is, "textual criticism" [Eng.], is having a lot of influence. The distinguishing feature of biblical criticism is that one "pick(s) up" [Eng.] only the things one oneself wants. It is to "pick up" [Eng.] only the things one oneself likes in the Bible. [They] throw away the things they don't like. For example, homosexuality. In the Bible, isn't it prohibited?[20]

"The Word" in this formulation is made up of decontextualizable denotational nuggets that can be exchanged and circulated among individuals, creating Christian behaviors and institutions wherever they are received. "The Word" conceptualized as denotation is central to this assertion of literalness. For Oh, text is a secular theoretical concept that ignores the eternal truth of the Word by treating words as situational, conditional, underdetermined, and open to interpretation.

According to Oh, those who have the right words available to them have the potential to experience material change, but they must first put the Word to use in their social interactions. Many sermons dealing with this kind of change were dedicated to a Christian concept of healing. However, in line with Calvinist theology, Oh continually reinforces the claim that individuals themselves cannot call on God to make material changes on earth. He explains that miracles [*kijŏk*] recede among people as the complete [*wanjŏnhan*] Christian gospel becomes available. This explanation is meant to account for the presence of miracles in the Bible and the relative absence of them among present-day Koreans. Along these lines, Oh's 2007 sermon "God Who Heals" (*Ch'iyu hasinŭn Hananim*) argues that the availability of the gospel in a society—that is, the presence of the Word—is inversely related to God's direct material involvement in individuals' material lives:

Excerpt 3.4

> *Agusŭt'in ŭn che ka chom chosa rŭl haennŭndeyo. AD sa segi, o segi, kŭ ijŏn kkajiman hadŏrado ch'ŏttchae kyohoe put'ŏ han sam paengnyŏn tongan man hadŏrado ch'iyu wa kijŏk ŭi hyŏnjang i koengjanghi mani kirok toeŏ issŏyo. Shilche jŏk ŭro aju kijŏkchŏk in yukch'e ch'iyu ka mani irŏnassŏyo. Kŭnde sa segi ihu put'ŏ kijŏkchŏk in ch'iyu ka mak kŭrŏk'e hŭnhan kŏn anieyo. Kŭ iyu ka mwŏnya. Kŭ iyu nŭn Hananim ŭi malssŭm i wanjŏnhi, AD sa segi kyŏng e kuyak kwa shinyak ŭi, i chŏnggyŏng, 66 kwŏn ŭi sŏnggyŏng i wanjŏnhi toego nan taŭm put'ŏ nŭn Hananim ŭi malssŭm i uri sam e p'iryoch'ungbunjogŏn ida, irŏk'e saenggak ŭl haesŏ kŭ i jŏn mank'ŭm kŭrŏk'e yukch'e kijŏkchŏk in ch'iyu ka mani nat'anaji anassŏyo. Hajiman chigŭm to Sŏnggyŏng i wanjŏnhage pŏnyŏk toeji anŭn kot iradŭnji Sŏnggyŏng i wanjŏnhi ŏmnŭn kot tŭl kat'ŭnde, yerŭl tŭrŏsŏ hajamyŏn Papua New Guinea na,*

> *Amazon ŭi chŏnggŭl ina, kwagŏ Chungguk kyohoe kat'ŭn tenŭnyo, yukch'e ŭi kijŏkchŏk in ch'iyu tŭl i irŏnatsŭmnida.*
>
> I did a little research on Augustine. Up until the fourth century, the fifth century, for about three hundred years after the first church, there are very many records of acts of healing and miracles. In fact, many very miraculous physical healings occurred. But after the fourth century, miraculous healings just ceased to be that common. What is the reason? The reason is that around the fourth century, the Word of God was complete with the canon of Old Testament and New Testament, complete with the sixty-six books of the Bible. And from this time the Word of God became a necessary and sufficient condition for our lives. In this vein, there were not as many miraculous physical healings as in the former times. However, in places where the Bible has not yet been completely translated, where the Bible is not complete—for example, in places like Papua New Guinea, the jungle of the Amazon, or churches in China in the past—miraculous physical healings have taken place.

The language ideology that construes the Word as efficacious in the world depends on a shared social sense of the efficacy and consequentiality of discursive practice. Words command social action as they "move" from places like Europe to places like Papua New Guinea, altering people's relationships with the material world and with one another.

Along these same lines, healing, as a religious concept in this model, is treated not as a physical transformation, but as a sociopsychological one led by the Word. This is apparent when Oh declares in the same sermon, "We cannot be limited to physical healing only. The healing spoken of by God is healing of a person's character [*in'gyŏk*]." Oh argues this by setting his own theory apart from what he treats as three extreme perspectives:

Excerpt 3.5

> *Onŭl nal e do Hananim kkesŏ nŭn ch'iyu hasinŭn'ga? Yŏrŏbun ŭn ŏttŏk'e saenggak hasimnikka? Yŏgi e taehaesŏ se kaji t'aedo ka issŏyo. Chŏttchae t'aedonŭn akka Sigmund Freud ch'ŏrŏm onŭl nal kŭrŏn ch'iyu ŏpta. [. . .] Tubŏntchae ro nŭn aju kŭktanjŏk in sedaejuŭi ipchang e innŭn pun tŭl inde Yesu ŭi sidae ttae nŭn kanŭng haennŭnde kŭ ihu e nŭn ŏpta, pulganŭnghada. [. . .] Iwa nŭn talli, kŭrŏssŭmnida, Hananim kkesŏ nŭn onŭl to ch'iyu hasindago hwaksin hago punmyŏng han ch'iyu e taehaesŏ ipchang innŭn pun tŭl i itsŭmnida. [. . .] Kŭrŏna han'gaji chosim hal kŏt ŭn ch'iyu rŭl pap mŏktŭt i namyong hanŭn ipchang e sŏgo sipchi anayo. Waenyamyŏn kŭktanjŏk in sinbijuŭija radŭnji kŏjit yaksok ŭl nambal hanŭn pun tŭl i issŏyo. Mujogŏn ch'iyu pannŭnda kŭrŏgo. Kŭraesŏ yosae*

> *Han'guk kyohoe nae e to yŏngjŏk in tolp'ari tŭl i manayo. Sunjin han sŏngdo tŭl ŭl kkoeŏgajigo idŭk ŭl ch'wihanŭn kyŏngu ka itsŭmnida.*
>
> Does God still heal these days? What do you think? There are three attitudes here. The first attitude, like that of Sigmund Freud, these days [is that] there is no such healing. [. . .] Second, there are people who have a very extreme dispensationalist perspective and say that when Jesus lived it was possible, but now there is none, it is impossible. [. . .] And then, unlike this, yes, there are people who are convinced that God is still healing today. Their view is that God is clearly healing. [. . .] But one thing to be careful about—[we] don't want to take a stance that misuses healing as if it were like having a meal. This is because there are extreme mystics or those who carelessly issue many false promises. They say you can be healed unconditionally. Nowadays many spiritual quacks have even entered the Korean church. There are cases where they lure in naive Christians and use them to make a profit.

Oh offers an example from his days as a theological student in the United States, where a professor would anoint his ill students' foreheads with olive oil and pray for them. The professor cited James 5:14 as his authority: "Is any one of you sick? He should call the elders of the church to pray over him and anoint him with oil in the name of the Lord." Oh admits to his congregation that he doesn't know how many of the students had actually been healed by the professor, and advises them to be careful (*chosimhada*) of such things.

Oh emphasizes the point that Christians should focus on healing themselves socially and psychologically by controlling their tongues. They should heal the "whole person" (*onsaram*) by establishing social relations through discursive practice according to God's will as revealed by the Word. This way, according to Oh, contemporary Christians presume neither to command nor to rule out the participation of God in their material lives. According to Oh, the speech that organizes the social world either paves or blocks the way for God's works. In the same sermon on healing mentioned above, Oh describes the way in which the "faith of friends" was necessary, even in the Bible, for a miracle to take place:

Excerpt 3.6

> *Yŏrŏbun chal asinŭndaero Yesunim kkesŏ nŭn Maga pogŭm e nollaun ch'iyu rŭl hasil ttae, Maga pogŭm i chang o chŏl e pomyŏnyo, Chunimkkesŏ mwŏrago hanyamyŏn, chungp'ung pyŏngja ka innŭnde kŭ chungp'ung pyŏngja rŭl terigo, ch'in'gu tŭl i chibung ŭl ttŭdŏgajigo Yesunimkke teryŏgassŏyo. Yesunim i ch'iyuhaejushinŭndeyo. Maga pogŭm i chang o chŏl che ka ch'am choahanŭn Sŏnggyŏnggujŏl chung e hanaeyo. Han pŏn pogetsŭmnida. Kach'i ilketsŭmnida. Yesu kkesŏ kŭ tŭl ŭi midŭm ŭl posigo chungp'ungbyŏngja ege*

> *irŭsidoe 'chagŭn chaya, ne choe ŭi saham ŭl padannŭnira' hasini." Halleluya. Chal pwayo. Yŏgi ponikka, Yesu kkesŏ "kŭ tŭl ŭi midŭm ŭl posigo," kŭ tŭl i nugu nyamyŏn ch'in'gu tŭl ieyo. I chungp'ungbyŏngja ka pyŏng i nannŭn'ge, chungp'ungbyŏngja kaein ŭi midŭm to midŭm ijiman ch'in'gu tŭl ŭi midŭm ŭl posigo chungp'ungbyŏngja ege irŭsidoe "ne choe saham patko nŏ pyŏngi nannŭnda." Halleluya. [. . .] Yŏrŏbun honjasŏ ap'ŭm ŭi chim ŭl chigo nagaji masipsio. Kongdong ŭro taechŏ hasipsio.*

> As you all know well, there is an amazing story of a healing by Jesus if you look in the Gospel of Mark, chapter two, verse five. What does it say the Lord said? There was a paralytic. Friends removed part of the roof and brought the paralytic to Jesus. Jesus healed him. Mark, chapter two, verse five is one of my favorite passages from the Bible. Let's look at it and read it together. "When Jesus saw their faith, he said to the paralytic, 'Son, your sins are forgiven.'" Hallelujah. Look closely. If you look here, when Jesus "saw their faith," the "their" means the friends. The paralytic recovered from his illness, because Jesus saw the friends' faith, not just the paralytic's faith, and he said, "Son, your sins are forgiven and you are healed of your illness." Hallelujah. [. . .] Don't bear your pain and go forth alone. Deal [with your problems] together [with other people].

The interdiscursivity of the Word, put into circulation through speech and spread through broader networks of social interaction, establishes the grounds for healing to take place. In this system, the physical miracle is the work of God, but this work will be done only if God recognizes the social work achieved through shared discourse among individuals. Social healing is treated as a precondition for a healing visit by the Holy Spirit, not a cause.

In the 2007 sermon "Overcoming the Limits of the Flesh" (*Yuksin ŭi han'gye ttwiŏnŏmgi*), Oh argues that Christians are eligible for material benefits from God only if the person has done the requisite sociolinguistic work. By accepting the social efficacy of the Word, one can overcome physical limitations. This involves shifting one's attention from selfish "worldly pleasures" (*hyŏnse ŭi chŭlgŏum*) to a communal "holy concern" (*sinsŏnghan kŭnsim*), which paves the way for the will of God to be manifested materially:

Excerpt 3.7

> *Chŭlgŏum ŭl kŭnsim ŭro pakkugo sŭlp'ŏhago aet'ong hamyŏ, yŏgi e innŭn kŏt chŏrŏm, kŭ yamal ro unŭn saram iya mal ro ch'am kyŏmson han saram i toel su issŭmnida. Kŭrigo i kyŏmson ŭl t'onghayŏ yuksin ŭi han'gye rŭl ttwiŏ nŏmgo, irŏk'e toel ttae, sip chŏl e: "Chu ap esŏ natch'wŏra, kŭrihamyŏn Chu kkesŏ nŏhŭi rŭl nop'isirira."*

Those who change pleasure into concern, who grieve and mourn, and as written here indeed, who cry, can become truly humble in the end. And through this humbleness we overcome the limits of the flesh. Only then, as in [James, chapter four,] verse ten: "Lower yourselves before the Lord, and he will lift you up."

Here, the interdiscursivity of appropriate words between events—good words, kind words, holy words—and the intertextual sameness of the Word across events combine to become the basis for healing, social, psychological, and physical.[21] It is this same process that produces the "fire" of revival: the Word passed from one person to the next until whole communities are set "ablaze." To "receive" the word is to "catch" the fire.

Korean Christians often point out that Korea's first dealings with Christianity were in the form of self-evangelism. In 1784, a Korean Confucian scholar received a Catholic baptism in Beijing and returned to Korea to evangelize, sparking enough Catholic conversions that the Confucian leaders of Korea began to suppress the religion with violence.[22] However, Protestant Christianity generally is understood to have come to Korea approximately eighty years later. Pastor Oh's account of the travels of the Word drew on the story of Robert Jermain Thomas, a Welsh missionary to China who died in Korea. Oh's account resembled the story that was told to me in slightly different versions by Christians in Seoul. In 1866, Robert Thomas caught a ride on the *General Sherman*, an American boat sent from China to Korea to establish trade relations through gunboat diplomacy. When the boat ran aground in the Taedong River headed for Pyŏngyang, villagers and soldiers were instructed by the local government to attack the boat. For two weeks, the foreign sailors and the Koreans battled one another. Finally, the Koreans set fire to the *Sherman*. Thomas leaped from the burning boat and cried out, "Jesus! Jesus!" while offering Bibles to his attackers. By some accounts, Thomas was decapitated. By others, he was beaten to death. However he may have died, one of his killers was supposed to have been so taken by the expression on Thomas's face that he became convinced he had killed a good man and decided to keep one of the Bibles. Making good use of this rare object, he used its pages to insulate his walls. The part of the story that Oh emphasized is this: by seeing the Word every day (which at that time would have been in Chinese), the killer of a Christian missionary was himself converted to Christianity. Like Saul's transformation into Paul, the killer himself became an evangelist: many people were said to have come the killer's house to read the Word on his walls and were converted.[23]

By the late 1880s, the Scottish Presbyterian missionary John Ross, assisted by Korean and missionary co-translators, had finished translating the New Testament into Korean, and other foreign missionaries had established sites that would become some of the most important medical and educational institutions in modern Korea.[24] Starting with "In the beginning was the Word" (John 1:1) and moving on to Jesus's teachings and the events of the New Testament, then to the birth of Protestantism when Luther translated the Word into German, and finally to the introduction of the Word into the Korean language, the "fire"—as coordinated movement of the Word and the spirit—was "led by God" (*Hananim i indo hasyŏssŭmnida*).

Whereas Pastor Oh gave an entire sermon on "longing" for a revival of the Word of this kind, I now turn to Pastor Cho Yonggi, whose influential theology and church are based, fundamentally, on the continued revival of the Word through glossolalia, the sensuous experience of fire through healing, and the power of the Holy Spirit to intervene directly in the lives of his congregants as continuous blessings in the present day.

The Word as Spiritual Entity

At the Yoido Full Gospel Church, Cho Yonggi has long claimed in his sermons that the Word is the pathway to contact with the deity. However, for Cho, the efficacy of the Word is not based primarily on the social consequences of its circulation; rather, it is realized through its power to make fourth-dimensional phenomena accessible to Christians (see chapter 1). In Pastor Cho's 2006 sermon "Believe in God" (*Hananim ŭl midŭra*), he outlines the way in which forms of speech and modes of thought affect one's faith and ultimately one's salvation. Cho argues against praying in the present tense (*hyŏnjaehyŏng*) or in the future tense (*miraehyŏng*), because such prayers are "always accompanied by doubts." Cho instructs his congregants to pray in the past tense (*kwagŏhyŏng*), telling them that God had already kept his promise in "Christ on the Cross." If we pray for what has already been fulfilled, Cho says, "the devil [*magwi*] shuts his mouth" and cannot spread further doubt. If Christians pray properly, Cho says, quoting Psalm 81:10, God will fill their mouths with the Word:

Excerpt 3.8

> *Hŭgam ŭn kwangmyŏng ŭro, mujilsŏ nŭn chilsŏ ro, chugŭm ŭn saengmyŏng ŭro, ch'u nŭn mi ro, kanan ŭn puyo ro, chilbyŏng ŭn kŏn'gang ŭro, p'aebae nŭn sŭngni ro mandŭlgi rŭl wŏnhasinŭn kŏt imnida. Hananim ŭn uri*

kaunde osyŏsŏ saeroun yŏnggwangsŭrŏpko arŭmdaun ch'angjo rŭl irusigi rŭl wŏnhasinŭn kŏt imnida. Uri ka Hananim ap e ip ŭl nŏlke yŏlmyŏn Hananim i onŭl nal to ch'aewŏ chusinŭn kŏt imnida.

[God] wants to change total darkness into light, disorder into order, death into life, ugliness into beauty, poverty into wealth, disease into health, defeat into victory. God comes among us and wants to accomplish a new, glorious, and beautiful creation. If we open our mouth wide before God, God fills it up even today.

By situating the event of narration in relation to a narrated event that is marked as already accomplished, Cho emphasizes biblical narrative as historical fact, thereby positioning the gifts of the Holy Spirit as already granted, the work of Jesus as already accomplished, and truth as already revealed.

In this formula, faith becomes the ability to call on and register the ongoing existence and participation of the Holy Spirit, manifested phenomenally in the fourth dimension. In the same sermon, Cho claims that "ninety percent of the promises of the Word have already been fulfilled." He asserts that the rationality [*isŏng*] of science is a doubting rationality and is detrimental to faith. This becomes clear in Cho's recitation of the story of how Abraham and his wife, Sarah, were able to bear a child, even though he was one hundred years old and she was ninety.

Excerpt 3.9

Kwahakchŏk ŭro isŏngjŏk ŭro saenggak hal ttae ŭisim i tŭrŏogo kamgak ŭl t'onghaesŏ kyŏnghŏm ŭl t'onghaesŏ ŭisim i tŭrŏol manhamnida. Kŭ nŭn ŭisimhaji ank'i ro kyŏlsimhago chakku Hananim kkesŏ yaksok hasin kŏt ŭl irul chul mitko kamsawa ch'anyang ŭl tŭrin kŏt imnida.

If [Abraham] had thought scientifically and rationally, doubts could have entered him; through his senses, through his experiences, doubts alone would have entered him. He was determined not to doubt, and he believed continually that God had fulfilled what he had promised, so he gave thanks and praise.

And similarly:

Excerpt 3.10

Pedŭro ka t'aeŏnal ttae putŏ anjŭnbaeng i toen saram ŭl yak ŭl chuŏsŏ koch'in kŏt animnida. Ch'im ŭl noasŏ koch'yŏjun kŏt animnida. Susul ŭl haesŏ koch'in kŏt animnida. Malssŭm ŭro koch'in kŏt imnida. [...] Malssŭm sŏnŏn ŭl ttara t'aesan i pada ro omgyŏganŭn kijŏg i irŏnago man kŏt imnida.

Peter did not use medicine to heal the person crippled from birth. He did not heal him with acupuncture. He did not heal him with surgery. He healed him with the Word. [. . .] According to the proclamation of the Word, the miracle of moving a big mountain to the sea had taken place.

Cho reiterates in the sermon that the events reported in the Bible, such as childbirth at ninety or moving mountains, are "nonscientific, nonrational, nonexperiential, and nonsensory" (*pigwahakchŏk igo piisŏngjŏk igo pich'ehŏmjŏk igo pigamgakchŏk in kŏt imnida*). Gifts such as these are already given and require fourth-dimensional consciousness for their manifestation in the lives of believers. Knowledge of and access to these gifts are not made through commonly circulating words among members of a group, but instead through direct individual intimacy—albeit en masse—with God. Similar to his comparison of glossolalia to the intimacy of slang, in a 2006 sermon, "The Blessing of the Descent of the Holy Spirit" (*Sŏngnyŏng kangnim ŭi ch'ukpok*), Cho argues the following:

Excerpt 3.11

> *Yŏrŏbun uri ka pimil ŭl mal hanŭn sai ka toemyŏn koengjanghi ch'inhan sai jiyo. Ch'inhaji anŭn saram ege pimil mal haji anssŭmnida. Na hago koengjanghi ch'inhaesŏ unmyŏng kongdongch'e ka toeŏya pimil ŭl mal hamnida. Uri ka pot'ong ta Hananim kke mal hamyŏn yŏp e saram tŭl i ta tŭtchiyo. Kŭrŏna pangŏn ŭro mal hamyŏn yŏp e saram i tŭrŏ to morŭmnida. Waenyahamyŏn kŭ ka yŏng ŭro Hananim kwa pimil ŭl mal hamnida. Pangŏn ŭro mal hamyŏn kŭ mank'ŭm Hananim kwa uri rŭl ch'inmil hage mandŭrŏ chunŭn kŏt imnida.*

> If we share secrets with another person, then the person is very close to us. We do not tell secrets to those who are not close to us. We tell secrets only when we become very close and become a community with a shared destiny. Ordinarily, if we tell everything to God, the person next to us hears everything. But if we speak in tongues, then the person next to us does not understand even though they hear us. It is because we are telling our secrets to God through the spirit. If we speak in tongues, it makes us very intimate with God.

The function of this transformation of the public words of prayer into the private "secrets of the spirit" is the alignment of the individual with God. That is, with the consciousness of the fourth dimension—the realm of spiritual perception in which pneumatological phenomena are known—the language ideology is transformed from one of individuals relating to one another via speech and interaction before God, into a structure of individuals united in their direct, individual relationships with the Holy Spirit.

Excerpt 3.12

> Kŭraesŏ pul i imhayŏttanŭn kŏt ŭn uri ŭi saenghwal sok e naenggi rŭl ŏpsaejugo Hananim ŭi ttattŭt'an sarang ŭro ch'aewŏ chumŭro kippŭm ŭl hoebok haejugo na anin uri tŭl i son chapko ap esŏ kkŭrŏjumyŏ twiesŏ milmyŏ hyŏmnyŏkhaesŏ saragal su innŭn kajŏng kwa sahoe wa kukka wa segye rŭl mandŭrŏ chunŭn kŏt imnida.

> Thus, the coming of the fire means that it removes the frigidness in our life and restores the joy by filling our life up with the warm love of God. It also makes a family, a society, a nation, and a world in which "we," not "I," hold hands—pulling from the front and pushing from the back—and live in cooperation.

Where Pastor Oh's model depicts the circulation of the Word as setting the pathway for social cohesion through discursive interaction among members of a community, Cho's model depicts the Word placed directly by God in each individual's open mouth (or heart). In *The Fourth Dimension*, Cho explains this process by differentiating between two senses of the Word: logos and rhema. He writes, "Logos is the general Word of God, stretching from Genesis to Revelation," but "rhema is a specific word to a specific person in a specific situation."[25] And he explains further how the Holy Spirit places the Word qua rhema directly in a believer:

> Rhema is produced out of logos. Logos is like the pool of Bethesda. You may listen to the Word of God and you may study the Bible, but only when the Holy Spirit comes and quickens a scripture or scriptures to your heart, burning them in your soul and letting you know that they apply directly to your specific situation, does logos become rhema. Logos is given to everybody. Logos is common to Koreans, Europeans, Africans, and Americans. It is given to all so that they may gain knowledge about God; but rhema is not given to everyone. Rhema is given to that specific person who is waiting upon the Lord until the Holy Spirit quickens logos into rhema.[26]

In Cho's model, Christian fellowship is a result of, rather than a prerequisite for, individual contact with God via the Holy Spirit. This fellowship emerges out of the chronotopic lamination of one kind of relationship to the Word onto another kind. One relationship pertains to the historical space-time of the Word, emphasizing the interdiscursivity among past events in which the Word appeared (much like Oh's narrative of the way the Word eventually made it to Korea). The second relationship pertains to the narrative of the Holy Spirit delivering the Word directly into the mouth of the believer, when "scripture no longer belongs to the 'said word' of God [logos] but is instantly the 'saying word' of God [rhema]" for many individuals at once (inverting the directive from praying in the past tense to receiving the presence of God through scripture in the present tense).[27] The union of a historical human chronotope of the Word and a particular interactional chronotope of the Holy Spirit's movement as it carries the Word from the spiritual to the earthly realm creates for believers an experience of the "nonrational" suprachronotopy of what Cho calls the fourth dimension (i.e., a dimension not bound by the temporal and spatial frames of earthly human experience).

Instead of focusing on the primacy of speech as a sociolinguistic medium with potential spiritual efficacy, Cho treats speech as a spiritual medium with potential sociomaterial efficacy. Like Oh, Cho uses the metaphor of fire to conceptualize a theory of interdiscursivity and the experience of the Holy Spirit among the congregants. However, it is different from Oh's construal of fire as the sensation of the Holy Spirit accompanying the circulation of the Word via social interaction. Cho conceptualizes it instead as the unidirectional transmission of fire that takes place when the Holy Spirit itself "enters" the body from the fourth dimension. This process seems to take place in one of two ways. When alignment with and connection to God through the presence of the Holy Spirit is achieved through glossolalia, prayer is the medium. When alignment with and connection to God through the presence of the Holy Spirit is achieved through physical healing, touch is the medium (recalling the "spiritual quacks" described by Oh above). This is made clear in Cho's 2003 sermon "The Grace of Jesus's Cure" (*Yesunim ŭi ch'iryo ŭi ŭnhye*):

Excerpt 3.13

> *Kwisin ŭn malssŭm ŭro tchoch'anaejiman ŭn pyŏng ŭl koch'ilttae nŭn kirŭm ŭl parŭgo haessŭmnida. Chŏ to suyoil nal ansu halttae nŭn kirŭm ŭl pallasŏ ansu hago kido hamnida.*

> [The disciples] expelled demons with the Word but healed the sick by anointing them with oil. When I lay my hands on the sick during the Wednesday service, I also anoint the sick with oil and lay my hands on them and pray for them.

When individuals come into contact with the fire of the Holy Spirit, it manifests as glossolalia and healing, and both are considered cleansing processes—the former of the spiritual relationship with God, and the latter of the material being in the world:

> Sŏngnyŏng ŭi pul ŭn tŏrŏum ŭl t'aeunŭn sodokhanŭn pul imnida. I sesang e kajang choŭn sodok pangbŏp ŭn pullossŏ t'aeunŭn kŏt i cheil choŭn sodok pangbŏp imnida. Sŏngnyŏng i pullossŏ nat'anan kŏt ŭn uri rŭl sodokhae chugettanŭn kŏt imnida.

> The fire of the Holy Spirit is the sanitizing [sodokhanŭn] fire that burns filthiness. The best method in the world for sanitizing is burning with fire. The Holy Spirit coming as fire means that [God] wants to sanitize us.[28]

In keeping with the directive to pray in the past tense, Full Gospel semiotic ideology claims that "sorrows and diseases are also false and vain images" because "the truth is, when we come under the cross, Jesus has put an end to sorrows and diseases and has brought us joy and healing."[29] Communication with God becomes a process of manifesting materially the reality already posited in the denotational text; i.e., the Word. Above, I discussed the way Reverend Oh interprets the "faith of friends" story from Mark 2:5 as an account of Jesus's recognition of, and reward for, the socialization of faith through the Word. Cho offers a different interpretation. He writes, "Jesus saw their faith and responded by saying, 'It will be done as you believed,'" and explains that it was the power of the friends' faith—their faith that he would be healed—acting directly in that situation, which healed the paralytic.[30]

The Word, then, is not merely the inerrable, inspired speech of God, but also a fourth-dimensional entity:

Excerpt 3.14

> Kŭrŏmŭro uri ka Hananim ŭi malssŭm wi e kutsege sŏsŏ malssŭm ŭl saenggak hago malssŭm ŭl mitko malssŭm ŭl mal hago malssŭm ŭl ttara naagamyŏn chongguk e kasŏ i kŏt i ch'am toego shilchilchŏk in kŏt iranŭn kŏt ŭl ch'ehŏm hal su itke toenŭn kŏt imnida.

> Therefore, if we stand firmly on the Word of God, think the Word, believe the Word, speak the Word, go forth according to the Word, in the end we will be able to experience that this is true and real.[31]

Cho reinforces this point in the chapter "The Creative Power of the Spoken Word" from his book *The Fourth Dimension*. Cho writes, "[Jesus Christ is] not high up in the sky, or below the ground. Jesus is in His Word," and argues that in the very expression of faith through spoken prayer, one comes closer to experiencing Jesus.[32] When one's speech transitions from an orientation toward the Word as given (logos) to the Word as placed directly in one's mouth by the Holy Spirit (rhema), one experiences the "ultimate true reality." Glossolalia is the path to this reality.

Similar to Pastor Oh's sermon on taming the tongue, Pastor Cho writes that "ultimately your word molds your life."[33] But then he diverges from Oh's Presbyterian sociopsychological model of words by advancing a neurological theory which posits that "the speech center in the brain has total dominion over all the other nerves."[34] Here, Cho goes so far as to claim that humans are biologically wired to be under the control of the fourth dimension: if the fourth-dimensional Holy Spirit places the Word in a person, then the person's speech controls the third-dimensional physical body. The Holy Spirit, which inhabits this fourth dimension, is viewed not as a substance or pure experience, but as a person, as a commanding being who carries the Word to individuals. As Cho writes in his book designed to help ordinary businesspeople become great:

> In 1964, I found out the Holy Spirit was a person. It was an epoch-making event that dramatically changed my life. Before that time I thought of the Holy Spirit as an experience, not as a person. From the time when I found the Holy Spirit as a person, when I went to bed I said, "Dear Holy Spirit, I sleep now. Tomorrow morning I will see you again."[35]

Cho's early publication, *Pneumatology* (*Sŏngnyŏngnon*, literally "theory of the Holy Spirit"), which he penned in 1971, lays out in detail the concrete personification of the Holy Spirit and its gifts (*ŭnsa*).[36] He incorporated this foundational pneumatology into the two-volume *Truth of Full Gospel*, published in 1979, wherein he dedicates a whole chapter to answer the question "What kind of person is the Holy Spirit?" (*Sŏngnyŏng ŭn ŏttŏn pun in'ga?*).[37] In *The Fourth Dimension*, he explains that Koreans want to know where, exactly, to find God, and thus he wrote an entire chapter titled "God's Address" (the answer is that he dwells inside of us—"his address is your address").[38] And elsewhere Cho develops a prayer method that he calls "positional affirmation prayer" (*wich'i hwagin kido*), through which a person focuses explicitly on the nature of their different relationships with the deity. Readers are instructed to affirm one's position relative to God by speaking to God in different ways on different topics that are indexically related to specific socio-spiritual relational types. Cho names the distinct relations in the following order. First, God is creator (*ch'angjoju*) and redeemer, and a person is his creation (*p'ijomul*) and the redeemed. Second, God is shepherd (*mokcha*), and a person is the sheep or lamb (*yang*). Third, God is potter (*t'ogijangi*), and a person is his clay (*chinhŭk*). Fourth, God is vine (*p'odonamu*), and a person is a branch (*kaji*).

Finally, fifth, God is bridegroom (*sillang*), and a person is his bride (*sinbu*). Each of these relations outlines a positional relation between the deity and the human according to a calculus of status and intimacy, each with a specific combination of authority and control on the one hand, and tenderness and closeness on the other.[39] These frameworks of spatial and social deixis are intended to help materialize Full Gospel theology in everyday life.

Some followers have asserted that Cho himself has healing powers. However, Cho argues that he is merely a channel for the Holy Spirit, and that the Holy Spirit does all the healing. He writes, "The Holy Spirit sees a need, and then follows the operation with a gift to flow through someone to meet that need."[40] In Cho's explanation, the social aspects of interdiscursivity—the recursion of semiotic form across social events involving biographical individuals—are maintained but reconceptualized in terms of the properties of this fourth dimension. In church services and other sacred spaces, the Holy Spirit "travels" via both prayer and physical contact from one person to another (hence, interdiscursively), and its works manifest as glossolalia and healing, both of which are interpreted as evidence of a more general structural relationship with God (hence, intertextually).

In the organizational structure of the Yoido Full Gospel Church, Cho, before his retirement, acted as senior pastor but insisted that Jesus Christ remained the "head" of the church.[41] Unlike Sarang Church's treatment of the Word within a public sphere–like model of circulation, the thoroughly charismatic character of the Yoido Full Gospel Church develops a unidirectional broadcast model of communication, where the Holy Spirit enters Cho from Jesus Christ and Cho passes the fire onto the congregants, either directly or via deacons and cell groups, by prayer and by touch, as performative emblems of denotation and contact. The phatic dimension of speech, as semiotically continuous with touch, is emphasized. The organizational structure of the church itself and communicative interaction among its congregants are organized around Cho's theory of the pathway of the Holy Spirit. In his 2006 sermon "Acting by Faith, Not by Sight" (*Midŭm ŭro haenghago ponŭn kŏt ŭro haji anŭm*), Cho explains the mediating function of the Holy Spirit:

Excerpt 3.15

> Uri yuksin ŭi nun ŭro pogo yuksin ŭi kwi ro tŭtko yuksin ŭi maŭm ŭro kkaedatchiman hanŭl nara nŭn sŏngnyŏng ŭl t'onghaesŏ pogo sŏngnyŏng ŭl t'onghaesŏ tŭtko sŏngnyŏng ŭl t'onghaesŏ kkaedatsŭmnida. Sŏngnyŏng i yŏrŏbun ŭi nun iyo, Sŏngnyŏngi yŏrŏbun ŭi kwi yo, Sŏngnyŏng i yŏrŏbun ŭi kkaedannŭn maŭm in kŏt imnida. Sŏngnyŏng ŏpsinŭn amu kŏ tto al su ŏpsŭmnida.

We see with the eyes of the flesh, hear with the ears of the flesh, and understand with the heart of the flesh. But the Kingdom of Heaven is seen through the Holy Spirit, heard through the Holy Spirit, and understood through the Holy Spirit. The Holy Spirit is your eyes; the Holy Spirit is your ears; the Holy Spirit is your heart of understanding. You can know nothing apart from the Holy Spirit.

Being able to "act by faith, not by sight" means one must "serve and obey God" [*Hananimŭl sŏmgigo sunjonghaeya hamnida*], which involves "proclaiming boldly" [*tamdaehage sŏnŏnhada*] the Word. These bold proclamations are intended to "overcome the test of seeing" [*ponŭn kŏt ŭi sihŏmŭl igyŏnaeda*] through fourth-dimensional realizations of God's ongoing work. This position, according to Cho, is the "full gospel" part of his theology: to return to the "full account," which includes the repeated and generous works of the Holy Spirit in the lives of Christians. This return has its foundation in Cho's own personal healing as a young man, which brings the full account of the gospel, Cho's first meeting with the Holy Spirit, and the continuous manifestation of the charisms of the Holy Spirit through healing and glossolalia for believers into intertextual alignment one with another.

Within this linguistically anchored semiotic ideology that views speech and physical contact as opening fourth-dimensional channels for the Holy Spirit to travel, glossolalia and physical healing become manifestations of intertextual events built on a theory of the interdiscursivity of signs of fourth-dimensional phenomena made entextualizable through the speech of Christian faith. Cho tells his congregants:

Excerpt 3.16

> *Hananim ŭl ŭijihago Hananim ŭl mitkosŏ kijŏk ŭl kidaehago kkum ŭl kajigo midŭm ŭl kajigo ipsul ŭi kobaek ŭl hamyŏ uri maŭm sok e ŭisimhaji ank'o ch'anyang hago nagamyŏn Hananim ŭi kijŏk i pandŭsi irŏnanŭn kŏt imnida. Uri ŭi sam chung e kijŏk ŭi ch'ehŏm i issŏya toenŭn kŏt imnida. Kidokkyo sinang i tarŭn chonggyo wa mwŏga tarŭmnikka? Tarŭn chonggyo nŭn iron kwa nolli rossŏ karŭch'ijiman uri nŭn sara kyesin Hananim kwa hamkke sanŭn Hananim ŭi kajok i toenŭn kŏt imnida.*

> If we depend on God, believe in God, expect miracles, have dreams, have faith, confess with our lips, and do not doubt in our heart, going forth with praise, then miracles of God will certainly take place. We must experience miracles in the midst of our lives. What is the difference between the Christian faith and other religions? Other religions teach based on theory and logic, but we become the family of God who live with the living God.[42]

Indeed, for Cho, visions and dreams are the "language" of the fourth dimension.[43] The miracles are proof of the theology and are manifestations of what the congregants should already believe to be true. The gap between faith and experience becomes a question of perceiving what one proclaims "boldly" (*tamdaeham ŭro*) to be reality. When proclamation and perception coincide, the Christian experiences healing and glossolalia—which means God has used the Holy Spirit to place the full Word in the person. In effect, one cannot truly speak the Word without also experiencing the Word. When this happens, individuals become aligned to semiotic form in structurally iconic ways, such as when an ensemble of sensations is "felt"—through the intensionalizing effect of multimodal entextualization—as holy fire and construed as contact with the Holy Spirit via the fourth dimension. And these events of glossolalia and healing become the building blocks, the intertextual units, of an institution that has its foundational moment in Cho's own glossolalia and healing experiences. As with the Presbyterian Sarang Community Church, these structures of personal relationship with the Holy Spirit become indexical icons of the larger institutional organization.

Conclusion I began this chapter by considering how a technology of speech transmission becomes a technology of pneumatological transmission for a particular group of Christians. For them, many of the properties of their particular phenomenology of language are projected onto a Christian phenomenology of the Holy Spirit, relating the qualities and behaviors of one to the other. This projection from the language ideology of the Word to the semiotic ideology of the spirit produces a whole set of analogies for describing a realm of personal individual experience not directly available to others. Reverend Oh puts forth a Lockean model of Christian self-confirmation (of Christian baptism, really), resting on the notion that the circulation and sharing of the Word creates a community of shared beliefs through shared meanings. And Reverend Cho puts forth a Hobbesian model of Christian self-confirmation, in which only the sovereign God is able to plant the Word directly in a person. Pastor Oh commands his congregants to open their mouths "before God" to display the circulation of the Word to both God and to their neighbors; Pastor Cho commands his congregants to open their mouths wide so that God can "fill [them] up" with the Word, which is carried by the Holy Spirit as it moves through the fourth dimension. Pastor Oh characterizes this movement as a kind of exchange among members of a community. Pastor Cho characterizes the movement as a kind of delivery from a supernatural realm that is carried out by a supernatural being. And as Pastor Oh points out, the notion of a "text" as segmentable, analyzable, and recontextualizable is not compatible with a theology that posits the Word to be spiritually eternal, transcendent, and true. From this ideological assertion about the fundamental sameness of the Word comes the authority to explain believers' experiences of the fire of the Holy Spirit that accompanied the Word in the Pyŏngyang Great Revival of 1907 as experiences of the same thing.

As long as the Word, like the spirit, is conceptualized in terms of movement, then missionaries are authorized to direct that movement by "spreading the Good News" and "carrying the Word to the ends of the earth." Likewise, average Christians in Pastor Oh's church can contribute to the trajectory of the Word by receiving it and sharing it with fellow Christians, thereby inviting the Holy Spirit into their lives and their communities. In Cho's church, average Christians invoke the fourth-dimensional movement of the Holy Spirit as it carries the Word between sacred spaces by modeling this movement within the sacred space itself: individual Christian bodies become conduits for the Holy Spirit to move throughout the congregation, and glossolalic speech becomes the expression of the Word as it is placed directly in the mouths of these sacred vessels. And it is this concept of movement that links their individual discursive practices to the church institutions of which they are a part. By linking a model of the moving Word with a model of the moving spirit, they gain assurance that they are not just saying the same thing but are in fact experiencing—feeling—the same thing.

4

Fusion and Force

Billy Graham and Billy Kim

In the spring of 1973, construction for the new sanctuary of the Full Gospel Central Church was nearly completed. The church had grown to a membership of eighteen thousand, which its building in the Sŏdaemun district of Seoul could no longer accommodate. The mammoth domal structure would host the 10th Pentecostal World Conference in September of that year, and its pastor, Cho Yonggi, would preside over the conference as the general superintendent of the Assemblies of God in Korea. That same spring, just steps from the construction site, the American evangelist Billy Graham held one of his famous crusades. The evangelical campaign took place on Yoido, an island along the Han River. Although this island would emerge over the next decades as a dense urban center of government, finance, and broadcasting, in 1973 it still was largely an empty plot of sandy earth.[1] General Park Chung-hee, the autocratic ruler of South Korea from 1961 until his assassination in 1979, gave permission for organizers to hold their crusade on an asphalt expanse on Yoido that was used for official state events and military demonstrations. The area had been used as an airstrip by the US military and by South Koreans as a limited international airport until the construction of Gimpo Airport in 1958. Prior to that, it had been used by the Japanese colonial government. On May 30, the first day of the crusade, more than three hundred thousand people attended. Each day, the crusade grew in attendance. On June 3, the fifth and final day, Graham preached to a crowd estimated to exceed one million (figure 4.1).[2] It was the largest crowd ever amassed for a Billy Graham event.[3]

Next to Billy Graham at the pulpit, and backed by a choir of six thousand singers, was Billy Jang Hwan Kim, the South Korean minister of Suwŏn Baptist Church, who reproduced Graham's sermon verbally and peri-verbally—utterance by utterance, tone by tone, gesture by gesture—for the Korean-speaking

FIGURE 4.1. Billy Graham (*left, at pulpit*), Billy Kim (*right, at pulpit*), and participants at the 1973 crusade in Seoul

FIGURE 4.2. The 1973 crusade in Seoul and the construction of the Yoido Full Gospel Church

audience.⁴ Christian leaders in South Korea praised Kim's performance. Pastor Kim Kyong Nae, secretary general of the crusade, described Kim's interpretation as capturing Graham's "spiritual flow" (*yŏngchŏk in hŭrŭm*) and characterized the interaction of the two preachers as one of "harmony."⁵ Pastor Pang Chiil, a member of the organizing committee for the crusade, claimed that Kim had not translated (*pŏnyŏk*) Graham's sermon at all. Rather, according to Pastor Pang, Kim seemed to have given his own sermon, which, Pang claimed, is why it had made such a deep impression (*kammyŏng*) on the audience.⁶ There was similar praise from US Christians who witnessed Kim's performance. According to Billy Graham's official biographer, "Billy Kim actually enhanced Billy Graham. In gesture, tone, force of expression, the two men became as one in a way almost uncanny. A missionary fluent in Korean who knew Graham personally thought that Kim's voice even sounded like Graham's. Some TV viewers, tuning in unawares, supposed Kim the preacher and Billy Graham the interpreter for the American forces."⁷ Henry Holley, Billy Graham's crusade director for Asia, put it simply: "The two of them functioned as one."⁸ At a press conference during his trip to Seoul, Graham himself thanked the thousands in Korea who had been "working and praying and preparing" for the success of the crusade and then added: "And I would be absolutely nothing were it not for my good voice, Billy Kim."⁹

Kim explained in his autobiography that he watched film footage of Billy Graham's preaching so that he could "practice the accents, gestures, and intonations of Billy Graham" in order to "become a Korean-speaking Billy Graham" for those five days.¹⁰ In documentary footage of the event, Kim explained that while his own style at the pulpit was different from Graham's—and while it was a great challenge to keep up with Graham's speed—for those five days he did not want to "divert," "change," or make Graham's message "any different" from what or how Graham preached.¹¹ Kim described the interactional effect of interpreting for Billy Graham as two voices becoming one voice.¹² He explained this accomplishment in supernatural terms: "Well, once I got in with him, I didn't even know what I was doing. And I think I was completely influenced by the force that, uh, you know, we call the Holy Spirit."¹³

Although this account is not, strictly speaking, an example of speaking in tongues, it does approximate the logic of tongues within a broader Korean Christian language ideology of the Word. It involves an explicit deferral of agency to the Holy Spirit that is linked directly to the purpose of evangelism, transforming the unintelligible into the intelligible—like tongues to prophecy. The sermon produces both a fusion of voices, similar to the kind of permeability of speech that takes place in glossolalia, as well as the ultimate separation of voices, in which one speaker interprets for the other. And the formal characteristics of this vocal fusion and separation adhere to similar intensifying, compounding poetics that are appropriated in the ritual production of glossolalia. Ultimately, the performance of Billy Graham and Billy Kim—neither of whom admits to or advocates for speaking in tongues—highlights the kind of cultural semiosis that puts pressure on speech, taking it to the ideological limits of language in order to produce an ideological core. The result is the spirit of sameness that reveals propositional truth spoken by the deity directly to individuals.

Interpretation and the Transitive "Principal" of Evangelism

In order to show how this event illuminates the logic of glossolalia in South Korea, I first want to reveal in detail the semiotic processes of synchronization and calibration by which Billy Kim's sequential interpretation of Billy Graham's sermon into Korean for a Korean-speaking audience had the semiotic effect of "fusing" two voices into one through a kind of "flow." These processes complicate the question of "who" was speaking at any given moment, and they suggest that we must investigate the cultural-conceptual frameworks that make these processes semiotically legitimate for participants. Second, I attempt to demonstrate how this semiotic fusion of voices drew on and intensified the very ideological principles of evangelism that brought these two men to the pulpit and justified their speech in Seoul in 1973. As I explain in detail in what follows, the broader pragmatic dimensions transforming the unintelligible into the intelligible expand the lens of analysis from the narrow translation of denotational text to a broader semiotic "transduction" of indexicality through which denotational texts emerge through interaction. The film recording captures the dynamic pragmatics of increasingly dense layering of temporal and spatial deixis across codes, the compounding of vocalizations and figurative voicings across speakers, and the way these semiotic dimensions of preaching link theological principles of radical universality to personal experiences of radical individuation.[14]

The event illuminates the historical context for South Korea's marked emphasis on fervent, large-scale participation by focusing on the geopolitical and historical pressure placed on postcolonial, Cold War South Koreans to convert, confess, and evangelize in the postwar period. Approximating the logic of glossolalia, this spectacular event illustrates the semiotic process by which Kim "transduced" the pragmatic dimensions of Graham's sermon beyond the narrow translation of his denotational text, with one Christian's voice seeming to be filled with the holy speech of another, and the miraculous union of the two men's voices being attributed to the work of the Holy Spirit.

The first step is to shift focus from the denotational (semantico-referential) translation of "words for things" across codes to the pragmatic (indexical) "transduction" of the broader set of semiotic phenomena through which textuality—the "thinginess" of communicative media—emerges and congeals.[15] This expansion from the relatively narrow function of denotation to the broader polyfunctionality of pragmatics makes available for analysis the various self-authorizing ideological dimensions of language that are invoked in speech, contribute to performative efficacy in interaction, and must be managed—that is, transduced—in events of translation.[16]

In the genre of the evangelical sermon, the complex, often unclear relationship between the preacher and the authorship of the utterances preached can be mobilized for strategic ends: a marked liveliness of preaching can be construed as inspired and therefore authorized; stranger sociability among members of an audience who are unknown to one another can be accommodated and shaped into Christian fellowship; conversions can be claimed when the speech of the audience manifests in utterances that resemble those of the preacher.[17] At a press conference in Seoul during his 1973 visit, Graham drew explicitly on these aspects of the evangelical tradition when he announced that he had "come as a representative of the kingdom of God" and explained that his evangelical approach was based on his belief that "the Bible is the inspired word of God."[18] Nearly two decades earlier, Roland Barthes described Graham's crusade in Paris in 1955 in similar, if sarcastic, terms: "Here, from the first minute, Billy Graham is presented as a veritable prophet, into whom we beg the Spirit of God to consent to descend, on this very evening in particular: it is an Inspired Being who will speak, the public is invited to the spectacle of a possession: we are asked in advance to take Billy Graham's speeches quite literally for divine words."[19] On the topic of Graham's first "back-to-the-Bible campaign" in a predominantly Catholic country, when he preached to average crowds of eight thousand people, the evangelist himself reported that "it was the most amazing response I have ever seen. A new spirit seemed to form on the congregation after the initial difficulties of interpretation and acoustics. I feel that God did it."[20] According to the language ideology of this early instance of a Billy Graham revival performed in two linguistic codes, the Word was treated as if it had been delegated to Graham by the deity. Graham in turn delegated the Word to the Baptist Reverend Jacques Blocher, who stood beside Graham in Paris in 1955 and "repeated Graham's sermon in French into microphones and duplicated virtually every one of Graham's clenched fist and jabbing finger gestures."[21] This model would reach its apex of both virtuosity of performance and scale of attendance in Seoul in 1973.

In order to preach across different linguistic-cultural contexts, evangelists rely on an ideology of the literal denotation of biblical assertion as justification for attempting to preserve a fundamental likeness of speech across all possible conditions of semiotic difference.[22] This fundamental likeness—grounded in a specifically religious ideology of the Word as both eternal and flawless on the one hand, and living and adaptable to different sociohistorical conditions on the other—supports a metaphor of movement that is appropriated in the description of evangelism itself: Christians should "spread" the gospel, "carry" the Word, "bring" the truth, and so on (see chapter 3). This mode of conceptualizing semiosis as movement is made possible by a kind of cultural apperception, where a perceived serial ordering of these events over time, interdiscursively linking one with respect to another, and a perceived intertextual likeness across events of semiotic production combine to produce an effect similar to the lights that seem to "move" on a marquee.[23] The likeness of the Word across time and space, recorded in Bibles, carried by evangelists, and placed directly into the mouths of preachers and the prayerful, becomes the very material in terms of which the force of evangelical oratory can be conceptualized. This ideology of language as words in motion across both earthly and spiritual channels can be mobilized to resolve the logical tension between conceptualizations of the Word as both eternal and flawless as well as living and adaptive.

An ideology of the inerrancy of the Word also plays a role in the elicitation of confession and the induction of conversion. When one prays, preaches, or simply asserts biblical truths, one is supposed to align one's specific inner belief with collective outer forms of expression within a Christian model of "sincere," "earnest" speech.[24] The ideology of sincerity here depends on a notion of the individuated, distinct, radically personal relationship with the deity and such a relationship's mediation by various forms of spiritual semiosis. And yet the very media through which one prays, preaches, or asserts biblical truth are largely unoriginal and unindividuated. While a fundamental Christian assertion is that all people are biographically specific and radically individuated before God (for example, the very hairs of their heads being numbered, and so on), Christian speech should be thoroughly generic and radically universal insofar as it approximates eternal, flawless biblical assertions.[25] This basic contradiction is brought to the fore in the genre of the sermon. In her study of Jerry Falwell, an evangelical minister who rose to fame in the United States in the late 1970s and '80s, Susan Friend Harding notes:

> Preachers are not bound by intellectual property rights, and among them piracy is not a vice, it is a virtue. They may borrow aggressively from one

another, appropriating exegeses, illustrations, stories, quotations, logics, style, tone, gestures, and even entire sermons without citation. Their skills of imitation and impersonation, and whom they choose to imitate and impersonate, in part determines their audience and their reach.[26]

In precisely this way, the coordinated performance of Billy Graham and Billy Kim at the 1973 crusade serves as an extreme amplification of the way Christians, as Webb Keane writes, "must confirm their true faith in a public performance, one of an endless series of socially grounded affirmations. And such confirmations are themselves a discursive pedagogy, as they work to transform individuals . . . from listeners into sincere speakers of the language of faith."[27] In the live interpretation of sermons across codes, interpreters themselves are generally already known and self-identified as Christians, so the act of interpretation itself becomes at least a partial act of religious self-fashioning.

The 1973 crusade was preceded by revivals around South Korea that were designed to prepare South Koreans for Billy Graham's visit. These events were part of a larger trend following the Korean War, when numerous revivals and evangelistic campaigns in South Korea contributed to the dramatic growth of Protestant Christianity in the country from a mere 3 or 4 percent around 1960 to between 20 and 25 percent by the 1990s.[28] These orchestrated events of Korean Christian self-evangelism helped produce the ubiquitous evangelical ethos that is said to pervade contemporary South Korean Protestant Christianity. According to this ethos, the religious obligation is not merely to be a sincere speaker of the language of faith, but also to address that language persuasively to others: to evangelize, proselytize, missionize. In many ways, to be a Korean Christian is to be an evangelist.[29]

Christian evangelizing, proselytizing, and missionizing of the sort just described operates by speaking "in the name of Jesus" (*Yesunim ŭi irŭm ŭro*)—that is, by appropriating the authority and interest of Jesus, if not necessarily Jesus's precise utterances. According to Erving Goffman's classic "production format" model of participant roles in verbal interaction, the "author" composes an utterance, the "animator" materializes it, and the "principal" is responsible for or has an interest (in the legalistic sense) in it.[30] The ideal Christian speech that I discuss in this chapter operates—to make a Goffmanian pun—according to a transitive "principal" of evangelism. And the interpreter of evangelical speech—in 1973, Billy Kim interpreting for Billy Graham—becomes a kind of conduit, translating denotational text and transducing the cultural semiotics of sincerity, conviction, emotionality, and so forth. This process of semiotic transduction brings the eternal, flawless, living Word in its fullest, most potent sense, to a new audience in a new code.

In the analysis that follows, I focus on three semiotic dimensions that are particularly salient to the processes of sermonic transduction and the transitive "principal" of evangelism. These dimensions help us to understand how the sermon develops intersecting narratives that chart relations among different, often competing authors, animators, principals, and characterological figures. The first dimension is the way a particular combination of these narratives in the real-time unfolding of the sermon formulates a deictic scaffolding of time, space, and person—a narrative "chronotope"—of sacrifice and evangelism in terms of which to situate the 1973 crusade and its participants.[31] The second is the way the two pastors populate this emergent chronotope by manipulating their individual acts of vocalization in relation to an emergent moral voicing structure of characterological figures that serve as personified points of orientation for the judgment of speech, thought, and other actions. Finally, the third is the introduction of biblical scripture qua "authoritative word"—that is, a denotational model of ideal speech and, more broadly, a pragmatic model of social interaction that mediates between the allocentric orientation to universal truth and the egocentric orientation to individual conversion.[32] These three processes combine and compound to produce a poetic series of indexical constraints on the interactional space into which the attendees are invited to participate, effectively narrowing and fixing the degrees of pragmatic freedom to yield a remarkable oratorical force.[33] The intensifying interactions of the two pastors on stage reveal the complex semiotic processes that can transform a sermonic copy into an evangelical conduit for the movement—the "flow"—of the Word from speaker to speaker, from code to code, from country to country, from heaven to earth.

Chronotopic Formulations

"Twenty-two years ago, I was here in Korea. It was at Christmastime. And it was very cold. I'd never been so cold in all my life. And I toured along what is now the DMZ." Thus begins Billy Graham's final sermon of his Seoul crusade, which took place two decades after the armistice agreement that ended fighting in the Korean War in 1953. The first words of Graham's sermon formulate a moral chronotope of sacrifice that links the then-present event of utterance to the slaughter and tragedy of the Korean War two decades prior, and then two millennia further back to the crucifixion. Graham recounts the actions in 1951 of an American soldier on "Heartbreak Ridge" who threw himself onto a grenade to protect his fellow soldiers. The soldier died, but his friends were saved. This story operates as a familiar allegory of Christian self-sacrifice, which Graham later links to Jesus on the cross. As this moral space-time of sacrifice emerges from Graham's narrative, Graham introduces biblical scripture that, along with sacrifice, links the space-time dimensions of the narrative to its moral import. Graham and Kim, referring each to his own copy of the Bible, in English and Korean respectively, recite the passage (which Graham claims be one of the greatest "in all of literature") that the clergyman read at the funeral of the sacrificed soldier (excerpt 4.1, figs. 4.3–8).

Excerpt 4.1

[25:25–25:53]

1. G: And when they held the memorial service for that soldier,
2. K: *Kŭ kunin ŭl wihaesŏ yebae rŭl tŭryŏssŭl ttae e*
3. G: the clergyman took the *text* that I want to take today.
4. K: *Moksanim ŭi ponmun malssŭm i onŭl che ka yŏrŏbundŭl ege tŭrinŭn paro kŭ malssŭm imnida.*
5. G: It is found in John's Gospel in the Bible [John 15:13–14].
6. K: *Yohan pogŭm e innŭn malssŭm imnida.*

[25:54–26:11 omitted]
[26:12–26:28]

7. G: "Greater love hath no man than this, that he lay down his life for his friends."
8. K: "*Saram i chagi ch'in'gu rŭl wihayŏ moksum ŭl pŏrimyŏn i e tŏ k'ŭn sarang i ŏptago malssŭm haessŭmnida.*"
9. G: Now, Jesus said this just before he was going to go to the cross.
10. K: *Yesunim i i malssŭm ŭl hasin kŏt ŭn sipchaga kasigi chikchŏn e hasin malssŭm imnida.*

[26:29–26:41 omitted]
[26:42–27:42]

11. G: And he said, I have one commandment to leave with you.
12. K: *Nae ka nŏhŭidŭl ege kkok han kaji myŏngnyŏng ŭl chul t'eda.*
13. G: I want to say something I hope you'll never forget, he said.
14. K: *Ije chejadŭl ege nae ka hanŭn mal ŭl yŏngwŏnhi irŏbŏriji marara.*[34]
15. G: Love one another!
16. K: *Sŏro sarang hara!*

17. G: Love one another!
18. K: *Sŏro sarang hara!*

19. G: Love one another!
20. K: *Sŏro sarang hara!*

21. G: He said, I have only one commandment to leave.
22. K: *Nae ka kyemyŏng ŭl chul kŏt i hana pakke ŏmnŭnira.*

23. G: Love one another!
24. K: *Sŏro sarang hara!*

FIGURE 4.3

25. G: He was getting ready to die.
26. K: *Kŭ nŭn chukki chikchŏn imnida.*

27. G: He was getting ready to leave.
28. K: *Ije sesang ŭl ttŏnasil chikchŏn imnida.*

FIGURE 4.4

29. G: And the last words he said to the people was love each other.
30. K: *Saramdŭl ege majimak chusinŭn malssŭm i sŏro sarang hara.*[35]

FUSION AND FORCE 99

FIGURE 4.5

31. G: I say to you as Christians today:
32. K: *Onŭl sŏngdo yŏrŏbundŭl ege che ka malssŭm tŭrigo sip'ŭn kŏt ŭn:*

FIGURE 4.6

33. G: Love one another!
34. K: *Sŏro sarang hasyŏya toemnida!*

FIGURE 4.7

FIGURE 4.8

    35. G: And that is the message I want to leave as I go back to America: love one another in Korea!
    36. K: *Che ka ije Han'guk ŭl ttŏnasŏ Miguk e toraganŭnde majimak malssŭm i yŏrŏbundŭl ege sŏro sarang haranŭn malssŭm imnida!*

In this opening passage, the funeral of the soldier, as a spatiotemporal medial point (there/then) in the moral chronotope of sacrifice provides a deictic bridge between the distal point (way-over-there/way-back-then) of Jesus's Last Supper and the proximal point (here/now) of the sermon, in which the voice of Jesus, the recitation of Bible verse, and Graham's and Kim's coordinated commands to the audience become linked (table 4.1).

As Graham and Kim proceed with their coordinated oration, the tight alignment of their communicative actions is fixed by deixis across linguistic codes and amplified by nearly identical gestures.[36] This is made clearer by the shifting participant framework emergent from Kim's use of a relatively blunt command form in Korean to translate Graham's citation of the key phrase in the Bible passage being discussed: "Love one another!" (*Sŏro sarang hara!*).[37] This command would have been spoken from a position of authority—that is, by Jesus or "in the name of Jesus." The command is first translated as having been spoken by Jesus to his disciples (*cheja tŭl*) and then to "the people" (*saram tŭl*). When the command is directed explicitly at the audience in Seoul, Kim strategically adds honorific deference indexicals to contextualize the utterance as being uttered

TABLE 4.1. Moral chronotope of sacrifice and evangelism in excerpt 4.1

Distal	Medial	Proximal
Way over there / way back then	There / then	Here / now
Crucifixion	1951 funeral for US soldier	1973 crusade in Seoul
Jesus "getting ready to die" / "getting ready to leave"	Clergyman preparing for burial	"as I go back to America"
To the disciples and people	To family and friends of the departed	"to you as Christians today"
"Love one another!"	"Love one another!"	"Love one another!"
Sŏro sarang hara!	Sŏro sarang hara!	Sŏro sarang hasyŏya toemnida! (honorific)

"here" and "now" to "you" (*yŏrŏbun sŏro sarang hasyŏya toemnida!*).[38] Shifts in spatiotemporal deixis lay the track for interactional sameness across time and space: Jesus said these words before he was going to "leave" and "die," the clergyman said them at the American soldier's funeral, and Billy Graham said them before leaving for America. Across these different utterances and their utterers, the strident vocalizations and dramatic visual gestures remain constant.

The moral chronotope of sacrifice and evangelism that emerges from Graham's opening narrative establishes a framework of orientation that metapragmatically situates and fixes the pragmatics of the crusade in historic time and space. Furthermore, by signaling both the arrival of the message and the departure of the messenger, the crusade takes on the character of rupture that is part and parcel of "world-breaking" and "world-making" Christian conversion experiences.[39] The message itself, distributed among different speakers, and furthermore distributed among different Goffmanian participant roles—animator, author, principal—establishes relations of speech within a hierarchy of speech participants, which is then anchored to a key phrase that remains "the same" across all utterances in both languages; that is, denotationally "translatable" within the broader pragmatics of evangelical "transduction."

Voice and Voicing

In a country still raw from the Korean War, the sermonic event was situated within a moral Christian chronotope of transhistorical and transregional sacrifice. As the sermon proceeded, personifications of this moral space-time began to materialize in the sensuous qualities of the verbal medium itself—the "qualia" of the men's voices.[40] Their strident vocalizations, for example, when calling out "Love one another!" / "*Sorŏ sarang hara!*" became the qualitative stamp of an event suffused with the values of conviction and urgency. However, different social voices—such as those of Eve and Satan—enter the sermon as direct ethical and aesthetic contrasts to the strident voices of God, Jesus, and the two evangelists speaking "as themselves." Graham and Kim link these voices to actions—of Eve, Satan, and God in the Garden of Eden—that form a composite human first cause for which their deity-in-the-flesh later would be sacrificed and in terms of which their evangelism in 1973 could be justified (excerpt 4.2, figs. 4.9–14). According to the transitive "principal" of evangelism, their own ongoing phonic engagements with each other and with the audience produced a sonic framework of differentiation and value to which they could orient as they proceeded with their oratory.

Excerpt 4.2

[35:51–36:18]

1. G: There's one tree in the garden you're not to touch.
2. K: *Eden tongsan e innŭn yŏlmae* [fruit] *hana nŭn ttamŏkchi* [pick and eat] *rŭl marara.*

FIGURE 4.9

3. G: If you touch it, you'll die.
4. K: *Ne ka kŭ kŏt ŭl ttamŏgŭmyŏn* [pick and eat] *chungnŭnda.*

FIGURE 4.10

5. G: And Eve looked at it.
6. K: *Haewa ka kŭ yŏlmae rŭl poassŭmnida.*[41]

7. G: She was very curious.
8. K: *Koengjanghi hogisim ŭl kajigo pomnida.*

FIGURE 4.11

9. G: How would it taste?
10. K: *Ŏttŏk'e masissŭlkka?*

FIGURE 4.12

11. G: It looked good.
12. K: *Koengjanghi pogi enŭn t'amsŭrŏunde.*

13. G: And then the devil came and whispered in her ear.
14. K: *Kŭ taŭm e magwi ka kwi eda taego soksagimnida.*

FIGURE 4.13

15. G: He said, oh, take some of it.
16. K: *Chom mŏgŏ posyŏ.*

FIGURE 4.14

In Graham's and Kim's coordinated utterances, the moral figures are encountered not only through what they say but also through the way they say it. The complex bundling of nuances of vocal timbre, accent, and prosody contribute to distinctive register effects across metricalized segments of the sermon. That is, the effect of the specific combination and differentiation the vocalized features of the utterances is that these utterances could be interpreted first as biblical voicings of good and evil, purity and temptation, and then allegorically generalized according to a social range of characterological figures who are recognizable as "'speaking just like that'—or 'just like what one might expect from those people.'"[42] The vocal actions of the two preachers narrating the event and the characterological stereotypes of moral figures that emerged within the their narration exert moralizing pressure on certain forms of speech. This pressure produces voicing relations that both demarcate and blend the speech of characterological figures and the narrators. The

FUSION AND FORCE   105

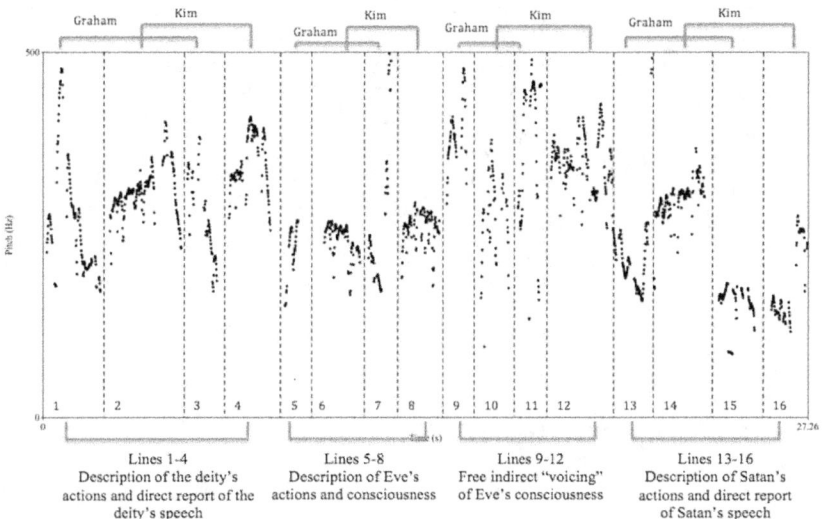

FIGURE 4.15. Pitch visualization of excerpt 4.2

identifiable characteristics of some of these voices leak into the evangelists' narrative framing of their actions (apart from their actual quoted utterances). With the help of pitch visualization, we can follow the way certain characterological voices leak—deictically and sensuously—into the narrating voices.

Figure 4.15 is a visualization of the variation of pitch over time in excerpt 4.2, which I have segmented and labeled according to line number (1, 2, 3, and so on), preacher (Graham or Kim), and relation between narrating and narrated voices (direct report, free indirect "voicing," and so forth). We can first notice the marked shift in intonation and timbre from lines 1–4, which contain direct reports of the deity's speech to Eve, to lines 5–8, which contain a description of Eve's actions and thoughts. In addition to shifting intonation and timbre, the two preachers also change their carriage and gestures (crossing their arms and leaning forward), bodily inhabiting as a first-person perspective what they describe in the third-person perspective: Eve looking at the fruit. Although lines 5–8 are objective descriptions of Eve's actions and thoughts, the signs of her subjective feelings of temptation come through in the description and begin to fuse the event of narration with elements of the narrated event. This process of fusion culminates when Eve's perspective breaks through and takes over verbally in lines 9–12. Here, the two preachers continue to gesture from Eve's perspective, now with the effect of speaking in free indirect style to convey Eve's curiosity and the seductive power of temptation: they embed the temporal, spatial, and person deixis of a

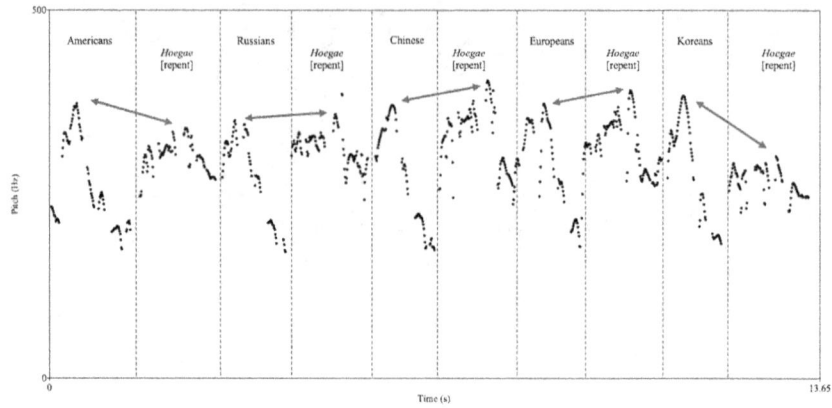

FIGURE 4.16. Pitch visualization of excerpt 4.3

subordinate clause within an indirect report without the matrix clause to frame it. Even though Eve's speech is never quoted directly in this particular excerpt of the sermon, we have a sense of her voice—we can "hear" it— because of its sequential position and, as shown in the pitch visualization, by the more erratic intonation that is linked to her temptation and agitation. In lines 9–12, Eve's perspective breaks through into the preachers' coordinated narration of her actions. Finally, as the preachers report on the nefarious actions and tempting speech of Satan (the devil) in lines 13–16, they return to an intonation pattern that most closely resembles Eve's initial curiosity in lines 5–8.

Let me offer another, contrasting example here of a moment in which the vocalizations of the two preachers again produce a characterological figure that they momentarily inhabit. What is interesting about this later moment is that Graham's and Kim's intonation patterns are different one from another, but they are still rhythmically calibrated across their sequential utterances. This excerpt takes place later in the sermon (excerpt 4.3, figure 4.16), as the two preachers fixate on foundational messages in the Bible, intensifying their vocalizations as concrete material manifestations of these intensified messages. Again quoting the deity's command, the preachers align themselves with the voice of God as they list with conviction and unwavering focus the peoples of the world who must repent. While there is clearly coordinated rhythmic emphasis across the English and the Korean utterances, the prosodic target of the emphasis emerges as different. Whereas Graham's prosodic emphasis lands on the various people—Americans, Russians, Chinese, Europeans, Koreans— who must repent, Kim's emphasis lands on the term *repent* (*hoegae*) itself. This

FUSION AND FORCE

potentially has to do with a prosodic difference between English's (subject-verb-object) highly productive form of phonological stress for semantic emphasis and Korean's (verb-final) use of particles and word order for emphasis and topic marking. The effect is a difference of sermonic focus: Graham's prosodic emphasis lands on the universality of the Christian message; Kim's lands on the act that Koreans, like others, must carry out. Combined, however, the two preachers rhythmically achieve a united command—a kind of *boom-chack, boom-chack, boom-chack* effect—that poetically links their voices into a single message, even while they remain prosodically different. It is as if Graham calls out, "Everyone!" to which Kim adds, "Repent!"

Excerpt 4.3

[46:18–46:26]

1. G: The Scripture says, God now commandeth all men everywhere to repent.
2. K: *Sŏnggyŏng ŭn mal hagi rŭl modŭn saram i hoegae hal kŏt ŭl myŏng hanora.*

[46:27–46:38 omitted]
[46:39–46:51]

3. G: **Americans** have to repent!
4. K: *Miguk saram to **hoegae** haeya toemnida!*
5. G: The **Russians** have to repent!
6. K: *Soryŏn saram to **hoegae** haeya toemnida!*
7. G: The **Chinese** have to repent!
8. K: *Chungguk saram to **hoegae** haeya toemnida!*
9. G: The **Europeans** have to repent!
10. K: *Kurap'a saram to **hoegae** haeya toemnida!*
11. G: The **Koreans** have to repent!
12. K: *Han'guk saram to **hoegae** haeya toemnida!*

In both cases, characterological figures become linked with vocal styles that are differentiable across segments of the emergent text. The compounding, repetitive, monologic pattern of command in excerpt 4.3—like Graham's earlier command to "love one another"—sharply contrasts with the more complex, nuanced polyphony in excerpt 4.2. This contrast is made possible through the textual poetics by which Graham and Kim phonically produce the sensuous vocal landmarks to which they sonically orient as they introduce the various figures of personhood into the sermon. The qualia that link their phonosonic voices to their characterological voicings produce a dense, sensuous narrative environment of competing moral perspectives. This density becomes the semiotic condition that allows Eve's voice—affected by the devil's temptation—to break through into the narrators' voices as an identifiable figure of alterity.[43] This space also produces the semiotic conditions that allow the deity's voice to break through into the narrators' voices both as a qualitative contrast to Eve's (and the devil's) voice within the narrative and as a generalized command to all in attendance and all peoples of the world ("Everyone repent!"). In this way, the formulation of a moral chronotope of evangelism and sacrifice introduced early in the sermon becomes filled with characterological attributes qua moral voicings in competition with one another. The coordinated utterances of the two preachers become increasingly fused as they navigate, side by side, utterance by utterance, the emergent polyphonic vocal space of their sermon.

Universalizing Individuation

By formulating a chronotope of sacrifice and evangelism and by populating the chronotope with sensuously differentiated, morally saturated characterological voices, the pastors are able to appropriate allegorical orientations and the transitive "principal" of evangelism to speak directly to members of the audience. They do this by generating the effect of addressing members of the audience individually (like a politician on stage pointing and smiling at individuals in a vast audience, as if there really were a single person out there corresponding to each point and smile). They simulate these targeted acts of address in order to ratify members of the audience as individuated participants in a massive interactional frame that is justified according to the universality of their message. Throughout the sermon, Graham addresses the audience with the second-person referential index *you*. To this he adds prosodic and gestural cues that specify that each *you* is aimed at a biographical individual (albeit unspecified), not at the entire audience. In transcript 4.4, which takes place early on in the sermon, Graham points in one direction to the audience and asks, "Do you believe in God?" (line 1). He then asks the same question, but points in another direction and shifts his prosody to differentiate the target of his address: "Do you believe in God?" (line 3). Kim responds to these shifts in footing by starting with a plural *you* (*yŏrŏbun*) (line 2), and then switches in the second utterance to singular *you* (*tangsin*) (line 4), which, in the general case of the second-person singular indexical, is normally

FUSION AND FORCE 109

avoided in Korean.[44] When Graham claims that God is a spirit and then points to an individual in the audience and announces, "Now, God doesn't have a body like yours" (line 11), Kim again uses the second-person plural indexical *yŏrŏbun* combined with the individuating gesture of pointing, but then he repairs the indexical contradiction (between a plural address and an individuating gesture) by pointing to himself, producing through gesture the indexical effects of a kind of last-minute *us*. Kim's rapid repair seamlessly links the scope of reference to the "everyone" that initiates Graham's earlier utterance in lines 5 and 7.

Excerpt 4.4

[30:19–30:42]

1. G: Do **you** believe in God?
2. K: **Yŏrŏbun** Hananim ŭl mitsŭmnikka?
3. G: Do **you** believe in God?
4. K: **Tangsin** to Hananim ŭl mitsŭmnikka?
5. G: **Everyone** believes in a supernatural being.
6. K: **Nugu tŭnji** ch'ojayŏnjŏk in Hananim ŭl mitsŭmnida.

FIGURE 4.17

7. G: **Everybody** believes there's a god somewhere.
8. K: **Nugu tŭnji** ŏdi tŭn, ŏdi tŭn, Hananim i kyesidago hanŭn kŏt ŭl kŭngjŏng hal kŏmnida.
9. G: Now, the Bible tells **us** what kind of a god he is.
10. K: Sŏnggyŏng ŭn ŏttŏhan Hananim irago hanŭn kŏt ŭl **uri** ege karik'yŏ chugo issŭmnida.[45]

FIGURE 4.18

[30:43–31:04 omitted]
[31:05–31:09]

11. G: Now, God doesn't have a body like **yours**.
12. K: *Hananim ŭn **yŏrŏbun** kwa kat'ŭn yukch'e rŭl kajigo kyesiji ansŭmnida.*

FIGURE 4.19

This pointing to the self, then, seems to be a key gesture in the transduction of Graham's complex web of temporal, spatial, and person deixis. The pastors point to the sky, indicating a supernatural being in heaven above as a cardinal, allocentric, and unchanging point orientation for all. They wave their Bibles—"held at arm's length like the universal can opener"—as a hybrid point of orientation with the unchanging, eternal Word as circulating text instantiated as multiple materialized copies, that is, two books (text-artifacts) that two persons can hold separately.[46] And they point to their individual bodies as thoroughly egocentric and inalienable, a site of radically personal Christian experience.

Historically situated, biographic individuals confront timeless universals through the processes of evangelical transduction across linguistic-cultural contexts. This moral web of indexicality becomes denser and more structured as the sermon proceeds, placing metapragmatic pressure on the pragmatics

FUSION AND FORCE   111

FIGURE 4.20 ALLOCENTRIC: a supernatural being in heaven above as a cardinal, allocentric, unchanging point of orientation for all.

FIGURE 4.21 HYBRID: the Bible as a hybrid point of orientation with the unchanging, eternal Word as circulating text instantiated as multiple materialized copies—here, two books (that is, text artifacts) that two persons can hold separately.

FIGURE 4.22 EGOCENTRIC: the body as thoroughly egocentric and personalized; time and space as radically individualized.

of its unfolding. That is, the underdeterminacy of the various indexical signs mobilized by the preachers becomes increasingly constrained and determined by the progressively clear, self-anchoring poetic dimensions of the sermon. In excerpt 4.5, deictic focus ultimately lands on the here-and-now of the crusade, when Graham and Kim tell the crowd, "We may never see a sight like this in Korea again" (line 7), "What a moment to receive Christ" (line 9), "He'll come to live in your heart" (line 15), and both men point to their own, individual hearts (see, again, figure 4.22). With this move, the pastors deictically enclose the space-time of entire sermon within the gathering itself, drawing purportedly universal, timeless truths revealed by historically situated events into the immediate here-and-now of the event and its participants.

Excerpt 4.5

[49:09–49:39]

1. G: There are tens of thousands of people here today that do not know Christ.
2. K: *Onŭl yogi suman-myŏng ŭi kunjung tŭl i Yesu rŭl morŭsinŭn pundŭl i kyesimnida.*
3. G: And this is the last hour of this crusade.
4. K: *I chŏndo chiphoe ŭi majimak sigan imnida.*
5. G: It will soon be over.
6. K: *Ije taŭm chu ihu enŭn* [after next week] *ta kkŭnmachi'imnida.*
7. G: We may never see a sight like this in Korea again.
8. K: *Uri nŭn Han'guk esŏ irŏhan kwanggyŏng ŭl tasi nŭn poji mothallŏnji morŭgessŭmnida.*
9. G: What a moment to receive Christ.
10. K: *Yesu rŭl minnŭn ŏlmana choŭn sun'gan imnikka?*
11. G: Let him come and change your life.
12. K: *Yesu ka yŏrŏbun maŭm tŭrŏwasŏ pyŏnhwa sik'yŏya toegessŭmnida.*

[49:40–49:54 omitted]
[49:55–0:01]

13. G: If you'll do that,
14. K: *Yŏrŏbun i kŭrŏk'e hasimyŏnŭn,*
15. G: He'll come to live in your heart.
16. K: *Yŏrŏbun maŭm e Yesunim kkesŏ sasil kŏmnida.*

"You Stand Up Right Now"

In his crusades, Graham often asked members of the audience to stand and approach the pulpit to receive Christ. With more than one million people in attendance at the Seoul event, this clearly was impossible. The final sermon there ended with Graham's request for people to stand and remain in place as a first step on the road not just to belief but also to evangelism. He asked them to "give up all other gods" and "take a public stand for Christ" within a moral chronotope of sacrifice and a voicing structure that blends individual, sincere utterances with universal, unoriginal content. The preachers told the audience that a "counselor" (*sangdamja*) would come to them with some literature. Like the two preachers with their Bibles and their utterances, these counselors would literalize the metaphor of the Word that travels to those who wish to receive it and actualize the deity that speaks to those who wish to hear it. Drawing together the semiotic resources of the sermon to produce a ritual culmination of spiritual presence in the here-and-now of conversion, Graham told the audience: "Stand up. And say, 'Today I want to receive Christ.' " The compounding of utterances, gestures, and now full-body action drew the attendees into a specifically South Korean Christian temporality of "now" and spatiality of "here" that was manifest as the presence of a living God speaking to and through a standing, uttering body.[47]

As Graham proceeded to command the audience to stand and speak, Kim transduced the force of the command into a form appropriate and effective for an audience that was still learning about the transitive "principal" of evangelism. Rather than directly reproducing Graham's blunt command in Korean, Kim made use of the three central indexical constraints I have discussed—the chronotopic formulation, the voicing structure, and the universalized individuation of the Word—to approximate the evangelical pressure of Graham's English utterance within a specifically Korean interactional frame. He achieved this specifically Korean cotextuality of denotation and interaction through a kind of deictic displacement. Rather than simply translating Graham's singular second-person address, Kim used the explicitly plural form (that is, *yŏrŏbun* rather than *tangsin*) but specified, repeatedly, that this address was limited to those who intended to or had made the personal, individual decision to believe. This adjustment foregrounded the invitation to the audience to inhabit the personal, individual role of "I/*Na*" in the phrase "I want to receive Christ. / *Na nŭn Yesu rŭl yŏngjŏp hagessŭmnida*." Furthermore, Kim took up Graham's directive to stand "right where you are / *kŭ chari esŏ*" and repeated it in multiple places where Graham did not, at once preventing a stampede and also reinforcing the individuated space-time of a person's conversion experience. Finally, similar to the early command to "love one another" (excerpt 4.1), Kim transformed the blunt command into a respectful request, this time adding the sentence-final verb *parada*: to hope, wish, ask, or request. The phrase "respectfully ask" in transcript 4.6 is an awkward and inadequate English approximation of the pragmatic force Kim's request to the audience in Korean. In this transcript (and earlier), I have noted in brackets these and other salient moments when Billy Kim departed from Billy Graham's phrasing to effectively transduce the force of Graham's evangelism specifically for the crowd in Seoul while preserving and adhering to universality of the Word. Each of Kim's modifications and strategic departures amplified Graham's message while shaping and transforming it for maximal interactional effect (figs. 4.23–26).

Excerpt 4.6

[50:19–52:18]

1. G: I'm going to ask you today to receive Christ.
2. K: *Na nŭn onŭl yŏrŏbun Yesu rŭl yŏngjŏp hagi rŭl wŏn hamnida.*
3. G: I'm going to ask you to do it **publicly**.
4. K: *Yŏrŏbun* **i kwanjungdŭl moim kaunde esŏ** *Yesu rŭl mitki—*
   [in the middle of this gathering of spectators]
5. G: I'm going to ask **you** to stand up right where you are.
6. K: **Yŏrŏbun** *i anja kyesin kŭ chari esŏ* **Yesu mitkiro chakchŏng hanŭn pundŭl ŭl** *irŏsŏ rago hagessŭmnida.*
   [the people who decide to believe in Jesus]
7. G: Stand up.
8. K: **Kŭ chari esŏ** *irŏsŏ* **chusigi paramnida**.
   [In that place]   [respectfully ask]
9. G: And say, today I want to receive Christ.
10. K: *Irŏsŏmyŏnsŏ na nŭn Yesu rŭl yŏngjŏp hagessŭmnida.*[48]
11. G: You may be a member of the church.
12. K: *Yŏrŏbun i kyohoe nagasinŭn pun inji morŭgessŭmnida.*
13. G: But you're not sure that Christ lives in your **heart**.
14. K: *Kŭrŏna yŏrŏbun* **maŭm e** *Kŭrisŭdo ka sanŭnji ajik morŭnŭn pun.*
    [heart-mind]

15. G: But you want to be sure.
16. K: *Kŭrŏna onŭl hwaksirhi algi rŭl wŏn hanŭn pun.*

17. G: But for thousands of you, it will be the **first time**.
18. K: *Ama suchŏn-myŏng ŭn **ch'ŏŭm ŭro Yesu rŭl mitke** toesil kŏmnida.*
    [first time to believe in Jesus]

19. G: I want **you** to stand up and say, today, I'm willing to turn from my sins. **I want Jesus in my heart**.
20. K: *Ije **ch'ŏŭm mitkiro chakchŏng hasinŭn pundŭl ŭn kŭ chari esŏ** irŏnasŏ*
    [the people who intend to believe for the first time, in that place]
    nae ka Yesu rŭl yŏngjŏp hago sae saram i toegessŭmnida.
    [I would receive Jesus and become a new person]

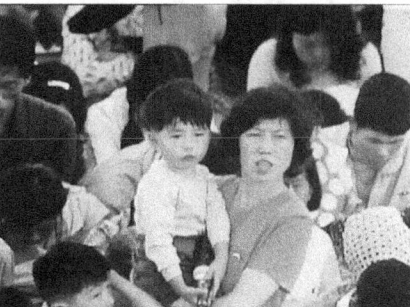

FIGURE 4.23

21. G: **Stand right where you are**.
22. K: ***Yŏrŏbundŭl kŭ anjŭn chari esŏ kŭdaero Yesunim minnŭn pundŭl ŭn, Yesu mitkiro chakchŏng hanŭn pundŭl ŭn irŏsŏ chusigi paramnida***.
    [All of you, the people who believe in Jesus, the people who decide to believe in Jesus, (we) respectfully ask you to stand in that place where you are sitting, just as you are.]

23. G: And keep standing.
24. K: *Kyesok sŏ **kyesigi paramnida**.*
    [respectfully ask]

25. G: And then in a few minutes, we're going to bring **you** some literature.
26. K: ***T'ŭkpyŏrhi sŏsin pundŭl ege nŭn*** *ch'aekcha rŭl tŭrigessŭmnida.*
    [Especially to the people who have stood]

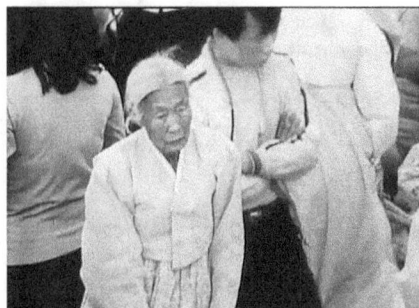
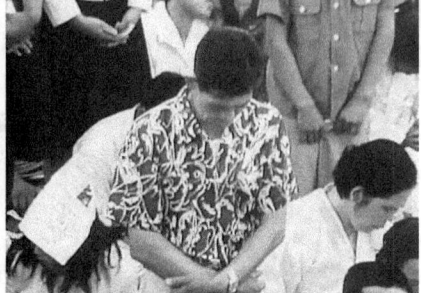

FIGURE 4.24

27. G: And we're going to have a prayer with **you**.
28. K: **_Kŭ sun'gan sŏn pundŭl ŭl wihaesŏ_** kido rŭl haedŭrigessŭmnida.
    [At that moment, for those people who have stood]

29. G: You don't need to move from where you are.
30. K: *Yŏrŏbun i sŏ innŭn chari esŏ umjigisil p'iryo ka ŏpsŭmnida.*

31. G: Just stand up and keep standing.
32. K: **_Kŭ chari esŏ_** *irŏna sŏ* **_chusigirŭl paramnida_**.
    [At that place]   [respectfully ask]

FIGURE 4.25

33. G: And say, on this day, this historic day, <u>**I receive Jesus Christ openly and publicly**</u>.
34. K: *Onŭl i yŏksajŏk in nal* <u>**na nŭn saramdŭl ap'esŏ Yesu rŭl mitkiro kyŏlsim hagessŭmnida**</u>.
    [I shall decide to believe in Jesus in front of people]

35. G: And a counselor will come to you where you are.
36. K: *Yŏrŏbun i sŏ kyesimyŏn ŭn sangdamja ka yŏrŏbun ŭl ch'ajagasil kŏmnida.*

37. G: You may be an American soldier.
38. K: *Yŏrŏbun i Miguk kunin idŭnji.*

39. G: You may be a Korean soldier.
40. K: *Han'guk kunin idŭnji.*

41. G: You may be an ordinary citizen.
42. K: *Ttohan kŭnyang **p'yŏngmin** idŭnji.*
    [commoner]

43. G: But God as spoken to you today.
44. K: *Hananim i yŏrŏbun ege malssŭm ŭl hasyŏttamyŏn.*

45. G: You stand up **right now**.
46. K: *Yŏrŏbun **i sigan e Yesu mitkiro chakchŏng hamyŏn** irŏsŏ **chusigi paramnida**.*
    [at this time, if you decide to believe in Jesus]   [respectfully ask]

47. G: **And say yes to Christ**.
48. K: ***Kŭrisŭdo rŭl yŏngjŏp hasigi paramnida***.
    [(We) respectfully ask you to receive Christ.]

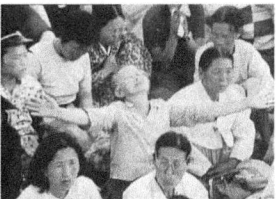

FIGURE 4.26

From lines 47 to 48, Billy Graham's blunt command in English becomes Billy Kim's respectful request in Korean. Graham told his audience that "God has spoken to you today" and instructed them to "say yes to Christ." Although many at the crusade were already Christians (the churches actively mobilized attendance), many others had not yet been instructed on how to respond to this deity. There are a number of possible glosses for *yes* in Korean, all of which are saturated with overt pragmatic value based on explicit norms of interaction. The most common is the generally "polite" form, *ne*. There is also *ye*, a markedly deferential form. *Ŭng* and *ŏ* are the least deferential and most informal (for example, normally used reciprocally among friends or asymmetrically to relative juniors). Eventually, Korean Christians would learn to use the most elaborate honorific forms, the highest levels of respect, the most archaic sentence endings, to address this deity. But Billy Kim, in June of 1973—after having insisted, beyond Graham's directives, that the audience stand *in their place*, and, crucially, that only *those who intend to believe* should stand—rather than bluntly commanding the audience to "say yes to Christ," respectfully asked them to receive Christ.

In the examples in this chapter, I showed how Graham's and Kim's individual utterances became increasingly calibrated as the two pastors aligned themselves to the chronotopic formulation of sacrifice and evangelism through which the crusade could be conceptualized and justified; to the temporal, spatial, and person deixis through which participants in the event could be drawn into and situated within this chronotope; and to the voicing structures in terms of which these participants could align with or distance themselves from different moral perspectives. In this final example, however, as the two pastors entered the crucial final phase of the sermon, they diverged more than at any other point. As Graham prepared to "go back to America," Kim spoke most directly to those who, like him, would remain in South Korea. It is as if, in the spatiotemporal model of the movement of the Word developed over the course of the sermon, the Word had nearly passed from Graham to Kim. There, within the internal poetic structure of the sermon, the Word was most fully Koreanized, was directed most specifically to the vast crowd gathered before them and adhered most tightly to the pragmatic expectations of Korean interaction. It is from this point—as those in attendance were asked to stand and speak, the crucial point of local "uptake" by more than one million individuals en masse—that the Word would emerge and circulate within a specifically South Korean domain of cultural semiosis, and thence out into the world in the form of Korean evangelical missions abroad.

With each coordinated multimodal event of semiotic production, the act of interpretation from English to Korean became an indexical icon of the long line of evangelists who had spoken across code and culture "in the name of Jesus." And to speak "in the name of Jesus," as the transitive "principal" of evangelism, continues to justify for Korean Protestants their missionary efforts throughout the world. Such a metapragmatic frame gives these evangelists the pragmatic authority not simply to speak as Christians, but to speak as Christian evangelists to others—to persuade and even command them; that is, to appropriate and channel the authority of the Word in all their interactions. This authorized use of illocutionary force was affirmed when Billy Graham said to his audience in Seoul in 1973, "You have the power to change all of Asia."

Conclusion   With Billy Graham and Billy Kim aligned at the pulpit, tightly calibrated across multiple semiotic modalities, with apparent parity and direct access to a deity still new to many Koreans, a structural position for South Korea was staged as a future source of world evangelism. In such an event, a Christian promise for postwar South Korea's place in the Cold War world was established, performed, and dispersed. Billy Kim's virtuosic transduction of Billy Graham in 1973 was a dramatic departure from what might at first seem like the studied voicelessness of interpreters that we are used to, for example, in institutional reports or broadcast news. Rather than serving as a transparent medium for the reproduction of information across codes, and rather than simply producing a sermonic copy of a famous preacher, Kim himself became a charismatic model of Korean evangelism and a charismatic source of evangelical momentum. In their 1973 crusade, Billy Kim and Billy Graham created a conduit for the movement of the Word.

In this conduit, it is Billy Kim who most clearly manifests the work of the Holy Spirit, for it is Kim who, like all priestly oracles, can transform the unintelligible into the intelligible. Just as witnesses of the two preachers at the 1973 crusade commented on the astonishing way in which Billy Kim captured the "flow" of Billy Graham, Christians who spoke to me about their glossolalia consistently emphasized the "flow" as one of the most valuable properties of prayer because it manifested the presence and abundance of the spirit. Just as Billy Kim expressed the challenge of keeping up with the speed of Graham's preaching, practitioners of glossolalia emphasized the importance of speed in prayer as a means of transitioning to tongues and generating enthusiasm for revival. Just as Kim's transduction of Graham's speech appeared not as mimicry or copying but as an inspired fusion of voices, united as they spoke in the name of Jesus, enthusiastic glossolalists celebrated the temporary deferral of agency they experienced when, unawares, they began to "blend" their voices with one another and sensed the Holy Spirit taking over their speech, transforming them and their neighbors into vehicles for directing the power of the spirit. Just as Kim's virtuosic transduction of Graham's preaching mobilized the dynamic pragmatics of oratory to produce the effect of universal denotational truth, glossolalia's promise of denotation through interpretation situates the pragmatics of transduction within a metapragmatics of translation. And just as Graham and Kim expressed their overwhelming feelings about the momentous, world-historical significance of their coordinated oratory for a gathering of more than one million in Seoul who had "the power to change all of Asia," charismatic Christians in South Korea often characterized their specifically glossolalic, highly individuated participation in events of group prayer as a formal necessity for Korea's emergence as the spiritual center of world evangelism. From coordinated sermonizing across languages to collaborative glossolalia in groups, the transitive "principal" of evangelism remained the ideological justification for the immense social pressures placed on Christians' speech behavior, and the personal responsibility that Christians were made to feel to participate in highly formalized ways. At the 1973 crusade in Seoul, Billy Graham and Billy Kim said to each member of the audience, "God has spoken to you today." It is to this radical individuation in glossolalia that I now turn.

5

Revelations

Gospel and Gossip

Korean Christianity in its most obvious manifestations seems to operate through spectacles of magnitude. Giant churches and massive evangelical campaigns are striking both for the excesses of human aggregation they display and for the immense crowd potential they seem to contain. Just as they easily bear witness, for believers, to the fire of the Holy Spirit working en masse in Korean society, they easily lend themselves to secular explanations built on vitalist metaphors of energy transfer and physical intensity. The characterization of glossolalia as total submission and possession fits comfortably with this image, depicting either a supreme force that places utterances directly into the mouths of speakers, or at least a crowd effect sufficient to generate enough social contagion to produce abundant experiences of the divine. It is the mass materialization of an evangelical project that aims to produce people to and through whom their God can be perceived to speak.

Korean Christianity is also unrelenting in the production of scandals of magnitude. Just as average Christians are confronted and often governed by the pressures of overwhelming semiotic circulation, so too are church leaders. Their transgressions begin as the topic of hearsay and rumor, eventually coming to light as profound distortions of the religious truths they proclaim and claim to uphold. Their stories are amplified at a scale commensurate with the size of their institutions. The head pastors of the well-known Samil Church and Manmin Church were eventually exposed for sexual extortion and even rape, of Sarang Church for financial misconduct and plagiarism, of Myung Sung Church and Somang Church for attempts to install the founding pastors' sons in dynastic succession, and of the Yoido Full Gospel Church for versions of all of the above. The massive condensation of Christian activity in the form of the megachurch is the product of dense, expansive, compounding social mediation with as much potential to spread the hopeful Word as to reveal uncomfortable facts.

Church leaders are always positioned between two regimes of revelation, organized by competing routes of circulation. Officially, they are mouthpieces for the gospel, the authoritative Word and its universal addressivity; they feed its voracious expansion. Like the promissory economics of capitalism or the politics of liberal democracy, the gospel is the idealized communicative dimension of the ever-expanding, always available, increasingly distributed access to a universal truth. But the gospel has a negative twin: gossip. From the perspective of pastors who caution the flock against gossip, gossip competes directly with the gospel, undermines the gospel, and often seems to have just as much momentum, power, and persuasion as the gospel. This inversion takes place across both denotation and interaction. Whereas the gospel is the vehicle for eternal truth, gossip is the vehicle for rumors. Whereas the gospel links humans to the deity, gossip links humans to one another. Whereas the gospel is massifying, homogenizing, and unifying, gossip is fracturing, heterogeneous, and divisive. Gospel is authoritative; gossip is subversive.

The competing revelatory capacities of gospel and gossip are organized by different architectures of transmission. Gospel follows the logic of a normative public—a self-reflexive, generalized addressivity that depends on different but interrelated processes and mediating technologies.[1] These processes are usually conceptualized according to three imperfect metaphors: broadcast, circulation, and exchange. Evangelical broadcast begins with the Word, continues from the moment the deity first breathed into Adam's nostrils and commanded him, and lives on through the inspiration and instruction of oratory and other semiotic technologies of textual atomization and dispersion.[2] Circulation describes the repeated re-entextualizations of the story of Jesus by the church's first evangelists as well as the eventual reproductions of inscribed, print, or digital vehicles for biblical textuality.[3] And exchange is shorthand for the communicative version of the balanced reciprocity that is presumed to exist in ideal contexts and genres of public interaction. In exchange, those with presumably equal access to circulation and broadcast move from stranger sociability to a not-quite-so strange communicative "marketplace of ideas," where they can discuss and debate what is circulated and broadcast—for example, in a public square, a coffee shop, or, in explicitly Christian settings, group Bible study and other activities of deliberative "fellowship."[4]

Gossip, born of intimate exchange, inverts this sequence. Exchange primarily dictates the routes and rapidity of circulation. And through circulation, a public secret, a virtual broadcast, is formed within a "hearsay public" until, if it is significantly scandalous, it penetrates the authorized public address of broadcast media and other similar platforms.[5] Like gossip, the substance of scandal is usually cultured in intimate, private, even secret communicative spaces—the small spaces of sociality, not the big ones—that promise, often naively, to form a secure communicative seal around themselves. The seal often breaks.

The aim of this chapter is to demonstrate how glossolalia belongs to an ensemble of genres, spaces, and tactics that form a pragmatic boundary between these two competing regimes of revelation. Just as the priesthood in Protestantism has been promised to all believers, in South Korea the esoteric, priestly genre of glossolalia has been, in effect, offered to all Protestants. It is not only church leaders who are at risk of exposure. Each member of a church or prayer group is both potentially a mouthpiece for the deity as well as a node within a circulatory route of speculation about others. All church members, from church leaders to newly minted Christians, sit at some intersection of gospel and gossip. It takes skill to belong, and seasoned members know how to balance these two pressures of speech—and especially how to avoid becoming the object of negative attention by knowing what to say and what not to say, or at least how not to say it. Glossolalia's exceptional capacity to produce enclosure, ambiguity, underdeterminacy, and even secrecy is a limit case among the various practices that form a semiotic buffer between gospel and gossip.

Sermons, guidebooks, and everyday practitioners in Korea commonly say that glossolalia allows Christians to say the unsayable. Two of the most commonly mentioned ways emphasize either overcoming the limits of denotation or overcoming the limits of phaticity. In the former, glossolalia is a means for communicating at the extreme boundaries of speech. This manifests as the scriptural reference to "groans" or "sighs too deep for words" (Romans 8:26). These groans and sighs (both translated as *t'ansik* in Korean), as well as shouts, chants, and murmurs, are characterized as a vocalized but often unintelligible means of expression that exceeds denotation. These forms lie at the ideological limits of language, pregnant with a spiritual fullness of signification. Indeed, there are whole traditions of speech that draw attention to these limits, genres of apophasis, or "mystical languages of unsaying," that confront through speech the very limits of speech to convey the divine.[6] In the latter, glossolalia makes possible persistent, long-term, focused prayer even after one "runs out of things to say." That is, it becomes a means for spiritual endurance that allows the prayerful to maintain spoken, phatic contact with the deity, to continually produce the presence of the Holy Spirit, without having to come up with denotationally coherent utterances. It is a way of staying in communicative touch without dwelling on communication.

Glossolalia becomes a medium for saying the unsayable in yet another important way. This is connected with excesses of spiritual meaning and maintaining spiritual contact, but it focuses attention in a different direction. Glossolalia yields social exclusion. Glossolalia becomes a medium of intimacy, privacy, and even secrecy that forecloses communication with others while being carried out in the presence of others. In its most spectacular manifestations, in the largest of Seoul's megachurches and other prayer gatherings, tens of thousands of people gather together in one spot to ignore one another.

At one angle, then, group glossolalia looks like the perfect antipublic: no exchange, no broadcast, no circulation. At another other, however, it is a kind of extreme version of the public promised by the Word: the deity broadcasting directly to the people, the Holy Spirit and the message circulating among them, and the ultimate stranger sociability in the form of their collective self-awareness as fellows, brothers and sisters, the body of Christ. In the Acts of the Apostles, speaking in tongues is both audible and, ideally, interpretable to others, transcending the limits of language, revealing the Word to all ears, and inviting outsiders (gentiles) into the body of Christ.[7] However, as in Paul's First Epistle to the Corinthians, glossolalia is also a medium of private devotion that separates individuals from one another through unintelligibility. As we saw earlier, Cho Yonggi expanded this latter characterization to describe glossolalia as a language of secrets. He compared it to the unintelligibility of slang, which severely excludes unwanted others from the communicative content. Esoteric speech, secret registers, insider slang, and other argots of exclusion, require a delicate calculus of information, form, and interaction to set the boundaries of inclusion and ratified participation.[8] The closer the interactants, the more privileged the information they can share. And the more privileged the information they share, the closer they become. This fits with an understanding of secrecy as a kind of exchange relation, with participants each telling secrets in units of equitable size and severity. Eventually, they come to "share" the secrets.[9] Speaking in tongues, in this sense, promises not so much to spread the gospel as to avoid gossip by taking talk out of circulation and encrypting it in special spiritual medium.

To explain how glossolalia contributes to the pragmatic boundary between competing regimes of revelation, I begin by reducing the scale from spectacles of magnitude to spaces of intimate exchange. I first turn to the historical, practical, theological center of glossolalia in South Korea: the Yoido Full Gospel Church. Instead of discussing Cho Yonggi, however, I focus on his mother-in-law and church cofounder, Choi Jashil. Her autobiographical account reveals a persistent connection between covert, furtive spiritual behavior and the successful work of evangelism and church growth. It also reveals the origins of secrecy in the theological orientation to tongues as one of the church's central modes of worship. I then turn to the place of glossolalia among other Christian communicative practices that people adopted to manage the risks of personal exposure through various forms of exclusion and concealment. Continuous and analogous with these other communicative practices, glossolalia can serve as a limit practice that promises safe participation in groups by countering the dangerous uncertainty of social relations with the severe underdeterminacy of form. Finally, I focus on small-group worship, which is promised as a space of security and comfort, where participants are made to feel safe to say the unsayable. Much of their participation in small groups took place through vocalization. In these small groups, one had to be careful to balance social participation with self-protection. I use the example a Christian retreat center outside Seoul to show how spatialization of social relations is fused to communicative contexts of prayer, where the promises and the risks of intimate speech are developed in relation to the problem of social belonging exclusion. Social pressures of participation manifest as the social organization and built environment of Christian communities.

The Prosperity of Secrecy

In 1958, Choi Jashil and Cho Yonggi cofounded the church that eventually would move to Yoido and become the largest Protestant congregation in the world. Cho (b. 1936) was twenty-one years younger than Choi (b. 1915), and eventually would marry her oldest daughter, becoming her son-in-law. They met as students at the Full Gospel Seminary in Seoul, and it was Choi who opened up her own house, purchased the military tent, and invited Cho to preach for the first service. Choi's autobiography, *I Was the Hallelujah Lady* (*Na nŭn halleluya ajumma yŏtta*), reads like a combination of personal testimony, a microhistory of twentieth-century Korea from the perspective of a woman entrepreneur, the annals of a rescue-and-healing mission, and a serialized account of demon-chasing, Satan-battling, ghost-confronting, serpent-destroying, exorcising, swashbuckling Christian adventure. At the heart of her testimony is the transitive "principal" of evangelism through which a Christian can appropriate spiritual authority and channel holy power (see chapter 4). As Choi herself puts it, speech and especially prayer have a terrifying power (*musŏun wiryŏk*). She became known for her witnessing on the streets of Seoul. Even without glossolalia, strictly speaking, her evangelism displayed some features that point toward the limits of language: ringing a bell made from an empty oxygen tank, singing hymns, and calling out "hallelujah!" to all who would listen. Her power of speech was strengthened by the self-deprivation of fasting (*kŭmsik*), the endurance of all-night (*chŏlya*) prayer, and the spiritual intimacy of glossolalia. As Choi reminds her readers, her approach to cultivating the Holy Spirit in her life, like those to whom she witnessed, was not a cerebral theology, but rather the faith from experience that each person personally possessed (*ch'ehŏm innŭn sinang ŭl soyuhada*).[10]

Choi's autobiography also reveals that she tended to do many things in secret. This was explicitly the case when it came to God. Repeatedly throughout her autobiography, she refers to her "private" time with God and her "secretive" or "covert" prayer and other activities. In fact, it was through explicit secrecy that she first made glossolalia a central component of her worship practice. Choi converted to Christianity early, at the age of twelve, while living in the northern part of Korea, which then was under Japanese colonial rule. Raised by an impoverished widowed seamstress, she grew up in conditions of starvation and began to contemplate suicide at an early age. Her mother experienced a chronic painful headache, which she likened to a chopstick stuck in her head. The affliction was healed by a preacher named Yi Sŏngbong during one of his tent revivals. After the healing, her mother began speaking in tongues regularly.[11] Choi explained that she did not understand her mother's experience until she herself experienced it years later. Before taking on the role of the *Hallelujah ajumma*, Choi had a career as a nurse in Chosan county on the northern frontier of the Japanese empire, then as a successful businessperson in Seoul running factories for matches and soap after liberation; she was a refugee in the Cheonggye Mountain south of the Han River during the Korean War, and after the war served as the chairperson of a business producing spindles for weaving in Jinhae at the far southern coast of the Korean Peninsula.

After experiencing a series of tragedies—her mother died, her eldest daughter died, her husband left her, and her business collapsed—she traveled to Seoul (leaving three children behind), visited numerous pharmacies for toxic pills, and took a taxi up to Mount Samgak (also known as Pukhansan) to commit suicide. She stopped at a brook to take a drink, and just as she was about to swallow the pills, a gust of wind blew them from her hand into the water. Taking this as a sign that God did not want her to commit suicide (the apostles experienced a "mighty" or "violent" wind before they broke into glossolalia), she decided to starve herself instead. She walked further into the mountains, looking for a place where no one would discover her body. She eventually found a cave hidden in a dense thicket and lay down to die. She planned to stay seven days but became unbearably hungry after only three days and descended the mountain for food. She repeated the attempt a few times until she encountered a friend who took her to a revival, where she again met Yi Sŏngbong, the same preacher who had led the revival that healed her mother decades earlier. That night, Choi herself began speaking in tongues. From that point on, Choi spoke in tongues regularly. For her, glossolalia was a secret (ŭnmilhan) conversation between her and God. Through glossolalia, she wrote, her soul (yŏnghon) was able to breathe.[12]

Shortly before Choi's mother's death, her mother had told Choi, who at the time was the CEO (sajang) of a successful company, to become the chŏn'guk sajang—the CEO of heaven. Choi did not follow her mother's advice. However, after Choi's "rebirth" (chungsaeng) at the revival, Choi consulted with Yi Sŏngbong about attending seminary. She intended to enroll in a Holiness Church seminary, but Yi suggested instead that she join the Full Gospel Seminary administered by the Assemblies of God denomination; he told her that she would be kicked out of the Holiness Church seminary for speaking in tongues. So, as woman in her forties, she sat for the entrance exam for the Full Gospel Seminary. That day, "a tall young man with a prominent nose" named Cho Yonggi also took the test.

As a student at the Full Gospel Seminary, Choi prayed in tongues fervently during t'ongsŏng kido. However, the other seminary students were unfamiliar with glossolalia and were bothered by it. Eventually one of the seminary students took her aside to ask her to refrain from praying in tongues during their worship session. She describes the encounter this way:

> "Chŏndobujangnim [head evangelist], when we were praying, what was that sound that you were making, tto tto tto tto? It destroyed the atmosphere (kido punwigi) of our praying time. I am saying this because I care about you. Other students are talking behind your back."
>
> Once again my heart sank. At first, everyone told me that they were saying such things because they cared about me. But when that didn't work, they would finally call me out in front of them and openly ridicule me. I could not understand. During the time of praying aloud in one voice, everyone should not have been able to hear each other's prayers because of their own voice. Had they all been listening to my prayer?[13]

Choi's initial solution was to pray quietly, even silently, under a blanket at her relative's house where she was staying. But this was unsustainable. Eventually she made her way to the empty chapel in the middle of the night and prayed there all night, in full voice. She continued to hold her all-night (ch'ŏlya) prayer vigils in secret (ŭnmilhi).

It was only later, with the help of Cho Yonggi, that she convinced others in the seminary to speak in tongues. Before Cho married Choi's daughter, Cho had already begun addressing Choi as "mother" (ŏmŏni). During their time together at seminary, Cho became deathly ill—one of his many accounts of near-death battles with illness. Choi nursed him back to health and became, in Cho's eyes, his spiritual mother. Cho insisted on addressing Choi as "mother" in private, but in the presence of others (*nam*) they called each other by their institutional status titles in the seminary: she was "head evangelist" (*chŏndo pujang*) and he was "student president" (*haksaeng hoejang*). Choi and Cho kept their close relationship a secret in the seminary, worried about the talk and judgments it might generate. Just as Cho addressed her as "mother" only secretly, she also took care of him secretly, favoring him above other students but hiding her actions so as not to produce jealousy or resentment; once she purchased and cooked a chicken for Cho "without a mouse or a bird knowing" (*chwi to sae to morŭge*).

As head evangelist and student president, she and Cho led other seminary students to the mountain one night to receive the Holy Spirit. Cho first led the men, then Choi followed one hour later with the women. As many Christians recount, mountain prayer is powerful but dangerous. On their way up, suddenly the weather became fierce and rain poured down, forcing them into a cave for shelter. As they kneeled and prayed in the cave, the women received the Holy Spirit and broke into tongues. When they exited the cave, they heard voices carried by the wind crying, "Lord, Lord," and they encountered the men, who also were praying in tongues. The men were uttering the same simple syllables that they had criticized Choi for using. She wrote that after going to the mountain and entering the cave with the other students, her "secret-like" (*pimil sŭrŏun*) all-night prayer sessions in tongues grew as more students joined. Soon thereafter, the collective activity of group prayer at night, which had begun in frustration and isolation, sounded like a "swarm of bees" (*polttae chŏrŏm*).

One of Choi's most important, influential, and secretive activities was the establishment of Osanri Prayer Mountain.[14] It was the supreme materialization of Choi's devotional triad of speaking in tongues, all-night prayer vigils, and fasting. She initiated construction on this prayer mountain against the financial scandal and unrelenting gossip and rumors connected to the construction of the massive Yoido Full Gospel Church. In 1968, Cho purchased land on the sandy island of Yoido on the Han River for the construction of what would be a new church building. In 1961, they had moved from their tent church in Taejodong to a building in Sŏdaemun, which they named the Full Gospel Central Church. With the help of evangelical cell groups, led largely by women, they quickly outgrew the space when the congregation grew from fifteen hundred to eight thousand in just seven years. Yoido was not, at the outset, a logical choice for a new building: it was a sandy patch of earth, with no transportation or bridge, and Cho did not have remotely enough financing to build it. According to Choi, the church building was estimated to cost eight hundred million Korean wŏn, of which the church only had a million.[15] Construction began in 1969 but was beset by financial woes, currency deflation, delayed construction, a rusting and crumbling church shell, infighting, and—crucially—rumors. After years of setbacks, financial and psychological pressure was mounting on both Cho and Choi. Choi collapsed from exhaustion. When she awoke in the hospital, she suddenly had an urge to go to the mountains and pray.

Choi eventually found herself in a graveyard in the mountains northeast of Seoul, near the demilitarized zone; the church had purchased land there in 1968 to create a cemetery for its members. She found a shed and prayed there all night. In the middle of her prayers, she encountered a twelve-foot-tall demon and cast it away. She returned every night thereafter. After three months of secret all-night prayer in the graveyard shed, a widowed deaconess joined her. Their combined prayers were so loud that soldiers from a nearby military base told them to stop. The two women decided to bring tools to dig a prayer cave in the side of the mountain, which they covered with branches for soundproofing. As they continued to visit the mountain cave for all-night prayer, their activities, like Choi's vigils years before, began to attract more and more people. Choi wanted to establish a prayer house on the land, but the elders of the church were opposed to using the land for prayer. They objected to its location near a graveyard, and desired instead to establish one south of the Han River where Seoul was destined to expand. Nevertheless, she persisted. As she explains it:

> **Mollae mollae** kudŏngi rŭl hanassik tŏ p'atta. **Nammollae** hamyŏn tŏ chal toendago **ŭnmilhage** moyŏdŭnŭn sŏngdo tŭl kwa hamkke ssannŭn kido ŭi chedan ŭn pul kach'i ttŭgŏwŏtta.[16]

The translators of the book into English render the sentence as follows:

> I **secretly** continued to dig more holes, one by one. There is a saying that a **secretive** business prospers more, and this **secret** activity of constructing the altar of prayer with other members burned like fire.[17]

In the passage above and throughout her autobiography, Choi uses a number of different Korean terms that her translators render as "secret," "secretive," or "secrecy" in English. In the passage above, she uses derivations of the native Korean verb "do not know," morŭda, to describe the act of digging holes in the mountain. The reduplicative mollae mollae can be glossed as "clandestine," "furtive," or "surreptitious"—"without anyone knowing." And *nammollae*, combining the Korean word for human "others" (*nam*), yields something similar, but emphasizing "others" as outsiders to the activity, pointing out specifically the hiding or active concealment involved.[18]

However, the passage above also contains the Sino-Korean term *ŭnmil* (隱密), which is by far the most frequently used of this lexical group throughout the book.[19] Although *ŭnmil* can technically stand alone as a noun, it is more widely found in the descriptive verb form (what we call an adjective in English), *ŭnmil hada*, or the adverbial form *ŭnmilhi* or *ŭnmil hage*.[20] The noun form is closer to "secrecy" in English. People do not exchange *ŭnmil*; rather, *ŭnmil* characterizes an act. The adjective or adverbial forms can be glossed as "covert" or "undercover." My Korean interlocutors sometimes described *ŭnmil* as "even more secret than the secret" because of the explicit intentionality that is invoked. *Ŭnmil* is deliberate (the Sino-Korean character for *ŭn*, 隱, means "hidden," *sumgida*). Choi uses this term to describe everything from sneaking across the border from North to South after liberation, to praying with God in the mountains, to the early days of her all-night prayer vigils, to the character of glossolalia as a secure, private, exclusive conversation with God.

The most straightforward translation of secret is *pimil* (秘密), which operates as the unmarked noun equivalent of a secret in English. This is the word that Cho Yonggi uses to describe speaking in tongues as a language of secrets. People can exchange *pimil*. Occasionally, Choi uses the morphological derivation of this word to describe something carried out "in secret": *pimilhi* (secretly) or *pimil sŭrŏun* (secret-like). But its most unmarked usage is a count noun: one can have, give, share, tell, exchange one or many secrets. Unlike Cho's insistence on glossolalia as a medium for sharing a secret (*pimil*), Choi's Christian practices more generally, of which glossolalia is emblematic, were often carried out in secret (*ŭnmil hage*). For Choi, it is not secrets per se—as sensitive or explosive information awaiting a communicative vehicle for revelation—but rather a more general feeling of secrecy that pervades glossolalic practice. Where Cho Yonggi emphasizes the secret as something that is denotationally renderable and which can be obscured by glossolalic unintelligibility, Choi's account shows how the actual self-reflexive metapragmatics of contact and concealment go well beyond the prototypical secret to a more diffuse and immersive secrecy of spiritual intimacy.

Choi's secret activities were eventually revealed and broadcast to the church and beyond. And in her account, it was ultimately their secrecy that made these activities successful. Choi explains that she felt the need to carefully shield her activities from the prying eyes and ears of others. Her all-night prayer vigils, personal fasts, trips to mountains and caves, and glossolalia were removed entirely from view until others were ready to join. And join they did—the Osanri Choi Jashil Memorial Fasting Prayer Mountain is now visited by thousands of Christians every year. And, like glossolalia within the doctrine and practice of the Full Gospel Church, the prayer mountain offers the masses the same social exclusion afforded by Choi's early clandestine actions. Choi began by digging a cave into the mountain to prayer. Today there are more than two hundred small prayer caves or grottoes (*kido kul*) carved into the mountain, where individuals can be alone with God, praying in privacy, intimacy, and even secrecy whenever they want, for as long as they desire. The caves make spiritual isolation physically possible, and the mountain makes this isolation socially acceptable. And yet the isolation is acceptable, in part, because it remains observable: the caves are organized into separate sections for men and for women, and the sounds of vocalization are still often audible even with the doors closed. On the prayer mountain, the isolation of the caves, like the isolation of glossolalia, draws no special attention, in part because it is not complete.

Transparency and Trust[21]

Although some Christians described glossolalia explicitly as a form of prayer allowing them to tell secrets to God, many were hesitant to describe their prayer in terms of secrecy. While they readily admitted that everyone had things they wished not to discuss, they resisted labeling these things "secrets" if they accompanied glossolalic prayers. Explicit mention of secrets and secrecy can quickly take on a negative ethical charge, and not everything one wishes to keep private rises to the volatile level of a secret.[22]

The broader concern was with the pervasive, often stifling pressures of verbal participation that were expected of Christians at church. As much as they spoke of the church as a space of comfort, love, compassion, and understanding, they also described it as a space of social pressure (*amnyŏk*), with overwhelming responsibility (*ch'egim*) to participate. For some, the church was an institutionally extreme form of social surveillance.[23] It was a space in which a person had to be careful (*chosim sŭrŏpta*) with speech and actions more generally. Under the amplified pressure to display signs of active, sincere participation, as Christians consistently pointed out, one must give enough to be present, but never so much that one becomes the object of attention. Attention is quickly converted into gossip. To provide personal or sensitive information is to potentially produce circulating stories. So even simple prayer topics and testimony, let alone confession and repentance, must be delicately obscured. Group prayer, testimony, and confession produced especially heightened feelings of danger and anxiety. The common caveat was that these feelings were more oriented to self-protection before other Christians than guilt before the deity: shame, not sin, was the central problem. Because it was often felt that any personal detail, however inconsequential, could potentially become a source of stigma in the wrong hands, talk in church required careful attention to both the management of information (and its potential for circulation) and the management of interaction (and its potential for failure or contamination).[24] It was common to confess and repent while speaking in tongues, because glossolalia could obscure the contents of their utterances. For some, glossolalic concealment became a way of controlling chatter rather than actually protecting denotational content (which was often quite banal).[25] In this way, glossolalia fit within a much wider variety of speech strategies aimed at concealing or avoiding certain topics.

As one tongues-speaking Presbyterian seminarian put it, the church is an institution that runs on speech.[26] It is a "group where there are many utterances" (koengjanghi mal i manŭn chiptan), where "talk gives birth to talk and talk gives birth to talk" (mal i mal ŭl nak'o mal i mal ŭl nak'o). By sharing news about one's life or one's concerns, one produces talk about oneself that can result in the circulation of false information. It is especially important to ensure the limited circulation of personal information in a place like the church, where mere attention and talk could cause great damage. Someone might make information about a person "open" (op'ŭn)—intentionally or accidentally—which would enter circulation and transform into a "knife" (k'al) that would ultimately return to hurt the person.[27] People end up speaking behind others' backs (namyaegi rŭl twi esŏ), especially if the stories are very amusing or stimulating. Whether or not the facts are true, whether or not the details are juicy, one simply should avoid being the object of too much talk and attention.

Many Christians, especially younger ones, were candid about their concerns and fears of exposure and gossip in the church. Omission and avoidance were commonly listed strategies for self-protection. In testimony they avoided sharing details about their families. Although members of their families might be troubled, they did not trust their Christian compatriots with that information. When leading prayer, they avoided expressing progressive political views at odds with their conservative churches. Rather than saying, "Let us pray for our president," as others would expect, a person might say, "Let us pray for the peace of our country."[28] In group prayer, they avoided uttering anything too specific, lest someone might be listening. Their decisions regarding what to reveal during prayer or testimony at church depended, predictably, on who else was present. At church and beyond, these Christians carefully revealed information about themselves according to a social gradient of intimacy and trust. The gradient usually began with God, and then moved on to certain members of the immediate family or romantic partners, to other friends, and finally to a group of "trusted" people. "Trust," in these instances, was often rendered with the same verb used for "belief" (*mitta*).[29] Along this social gradient, there was also a gradient of potency. The most intimate of these, God, was often (though certainly not always) viewed as being able to "work" (*yŏksa hada*) through them and others to solve or address problems in a person's life.

Glossolalia figured directly into this bigger problem of talk and participation at church. As Christians stressed the responsibility and pressure they felt to participate, visibly and audibly, in church activities, they also described managing the pressure through a gradient of transparency between explicit denotational clarity and outright silence or evasion, of which glossolalia was one extreme form. This was especially clear for ubiquitous *t'ongsŏng kido*: vocalized, individuated prayer in groups. While people did not always say they had to report their thoughts, feelings, or transgressions to God in prayer—they understood the deity to be omniscient—they still acknowledged the necessity for prayers of confession to deal with personal, individuated information and concerns.

Consider the accounts of two educated, politically and socially progressive Christian women in their twenties in Seoul, who as college students had been involved in feminist and labor activism on campus. The first woman came from an affluent family and was raised in an extremely conservative Presbyterian church in Seoul. She described the way Christians like her had developed prayer tactics to avoid revealing personal details. She pointed to the widespread practice of using jargon or vague speech forms when speaking in church. Such fixed forms allow church members to participate enthusiastically without revealing sensitive or stimulating information among small groups of others. She explained that when one is not prepared, or speaks without an arsenal of fixed phrases, one can accidentally reveal one's more sincere stances. She described these speech forms as a kind of "church dialect," using the "native" Korean word *sat'uri*, rather than the Sino-Korean *pangŏn*, which, in this context, would have denoted glossolalia. Certain figures of speech "stick" (*susa rŭl chom puch'ige*), can be used repeatedly, and become the "ambiguous" (*aemaehan*) phonosonic substance for sincere-sounding group participation. She laughed as she performed examples: "Please bend down and look upon me" (*Kubŏ salp'yŏ chuseyo*) or "I pray that I will not act according to my will" (*Chŏngkŏndae che ttŭttaero haji masigo*) or "But if it can be, please fill this cup" (*Hajiman toel su itkŏdŭn i chan ŭl ch'aewŏ chuseyo*).

She explained that such phrases are uttered "so that even if by chance this voice enters another's ears, that person cannot infer what the contents are" (*haengyŏ i ŭmsŏng i tarŭn i ŭi kwi e tŭrŏkadŏrado kŭ saram i ŏttŏn naeyong inji yuch'u hal sun ŏptorok*). The church dialect was continuous with other "habits of speaking" (*mal ŭi sŭpkwan*)—"idioms and common words" (*kwanyong ŏgu na chaju ssŭnŭn mal i*), for example, from scripture or hymns—as a way to participate with appropriate prayers without revealing too much of oneself.[30]

On the one hand, she emphasized her desire to live up to her social responsibility at church. Her social life was largely linked to her church, and she rarely missed a Sunday service. She even volunteered to serve the teenagers at her church (*chunggodŭngbu*) as a teacher. On the other hand, she did not want to reveal her true thoughts or feelings about many of the prayer topics assigned by church leaders. She described participation in her church in terms of danger and risk (*wihŏmsŏng*). She used uncommon phrasal compounds to refer to the feelings of caution (*chosim kam*) and burden (*budam kam*) that accompany a "heart-mind that does not want to make itself known" (*alligo sipchi ant'anŭn maŭm*). So she omitted her sincere prayers from the verbal space and filled it instead with "church dialect" to avoid being viewed as a stubborn or obstinate person (*monan saram*), who might become the subject of talk and reflect negatively on her family. She provided an example, in which she shifted from her ambling pace of speech to the rapid-fire, chanted, fixed-pitch recitation of a common phrase, "Lordwhoisfullofloveandgrace" (*sarangkwaŭnhyekach'ungmanhasinChunim*), and then back to the ambling pace of conversational speech, adding, "It's that kind of feeling" (*Kŭrŏn chongnyu ŭi nŭkkim*).

Across Christian communities, these rapid, repetitive utterances were useful for generating feelings of group stimulation and excitement.[31] Sometimes the intensification of repetition could be literalized denotationally, as when people repeated the intensifier *chŏngmal* ("truly," "really," or "very") multiple times before arriving at a point. Sometimes speakers never quite resolved the intensification and simply repeated the intensifying form until their breath ran out. For this woman specifically, the ubiquitous pressure to contribute to group feeling, which was incited by pastors and other group leaders, led her to produce glossolalia as a junior high student. She recalled that she began to produce sounds in a loud voice as instructed by the "revival pastor" (*puhŭng moksa*), who said to her, "You received tongues!" She herself did not believe at that time that she had received the gift. She said it "was not the feeling of prayer"; it was merely a "feeling of producing sound," not a spiritual language. She even wondered aloud if the ubiquitous cries of *abŏji!* (father!) could be considered a kind of glossolalia.[32] She described glossolalia as a trend during her junior high and high school years, when people at church spoke of "hoping for tongues" and encouraged one another to "pray like fire" to achieve a fervent state of group worship.[33] She explained that there was much talk at that time about the "utility" (*yuyongsŏng*) of glossolalia as a way to become "extremely close" (*kajang kakkapke*) with God by creating a flow (*hŭrŭm*) of prayer. However, she added, such feelings of revival from her childhood had largely abated (*sagŭradŭrŏtta*) in her adulthood.

Still, in adulthood, she did speak in tongues. Although she might have preferred to remain silent during group prayer, it was difficult to be silent in small groups. Glossolalia often served the same function it had when she was a teenager: it was a way to participate when there was a "responsibility to make sound." She did not use tongues to share secrets with the deity, finding that confiding in friends actually provided more emotional relief. She emphasized that her prayer, glossolalia or not, was not comparable to gossip or "chatter" (*suda*). Rather, speaking in tongues was a comfortable way to participate both enthusiastically and safely.

The second woman came from a working-class family that provided almost no financial support for her education. She was raised in a provincial city in the southern part of the peninsula, and her family attended a Presbyterian church that was theologically conservative but relatively politically neutral. She gave an extreme example of the role of glossolalia in managing the balance between participation and privacy: silent glossolalia. Although she spoke in tongues, it was not audibly verbalized. She was repulsed by Pentecostal churches, where, as she put it, "extremely enthusiastic" (*toege yŏlgwang*) worship caused people to "expose themselves" (*chagi rŭl mak tŭrŏnaego*). She explained that at such churches, people think they will receive salvation if they merely have the gospel, and that she hated when they put absolute trust in simply receiving a blessing (*poksa e taehan chŏltaejŏk in silloe*). Her resistance extended to her own participation style in Presbyterian and Methodist churches (between which she found little consequential difference): she preferred extremely large but not charismatic churches, where less attention was given to new members. Overall, she was repelled by the pressures of participation that churches placed on their members and actively sought out spaces where she could remain anonymous. She disliked *t'ongsŏng kido* and criticized the way group prayer a church became a site for boasting and competition. There she overheard others asking for earthly rewards, like God's help to pass various entrance exams (she herself had passed civil service exam, and once she had secured a stable position in the central government, began supporting her parents financially). She also criticized the atmosphere of Christian "training" retreats (*suryŏnhoe*), where she observed too much emphasis placed on speaking in tongues, especially the sound of tongues, such that its purpose became twisted, warped, or distorted (*pitturŏjige*). These environments, she said, quickly make Christians feel like their faith is lagging behind others'.

As a child, she had participated church retreats, where other children often experienced the overwhelming feelings of the fullness of the Holy Spirit. But she herself did not. A Christian with "faith from the mother's womb" (*mot'ae sinang*), she lacked "fervent belief" (*yŏllyolhan midŭm*). But then suddenly, one day, in her second year of high school, while she was deep in thought and full of doubt, she began to feel something. It was God's anger at her for being a superficial Christian, for not putting in effort. The feeling was both frightening and good. And with these feelings came the gift of tongues. At first she could not control the gift, but over time she gained more conscious control (*ŭisikchŏk in chojŏl*). Her glossolalic speech sounded to her like a European language. Occasionally she heard hymns in glossolalia. And she, like so many others, wanted no one to overhear either the sound or the denotation of her prayers, whether in Korean or in tongues. She stressed that she did not want to be listened to. Silent tongues helped her avoid intimidating others or being seen as one of the many who use their tongues to boast.

She prayed best when speaking was extremely difficult. She spoke to God when there was no one else to speak to. She did not want to burden others with her own problems if they could not solve them. God, to her, was limitless in power and concern. If her silent tongues emerged in prayer "naturally" (*chayŏnsŭrŏpke*), without her effort, it felt as if God was trying to communicate (*sot'ong*) with her. She would become immersed in prayer, feeling unable to stop the words or disconnect (*kkŭnta*). Her silent glossolalia became a way to maintain contact with God, to focus on the connection to God, and to maintain that connection not as an active church member but through her personal, private relation. She was frustrated, however, by the fact that she could not understand the meaning of the sounds.

The nature of the relationship was profoundly private. She prayed with silent glossolalia so that others could not hear her prayers, and so that others would not know of her gift or her sincere spiritual devotion. In contrast to many people who gain extroverted confidence by speaking in tongues, she was afraid of being known as a sincere believer (*sinsil han sinja*), because that inevitably meant she would need to involve herself more deeply in the social life of the church. The pressures of participation would be burdensome and time-consuming, and also would threaten her very private relationship with her deity. She explained that she could use church as place for "training" (*hullyŏn*) toward spiritual maturity, participating and serving in many ways, but was extremely withholding about the nature or character of her faith. She was so controlling that no one outside of her family knew that she spoke in tongues. Her glossolalia was not a language of secrets; her glossolalia itself was a secret.

Contact and Concealment

The characterization of glossolalia as a medium of personal communication with God is continuous with a less conspicuous, but no less crucial, dimension of Korean Christian sociality: the "small group" (*sogŭrup*). Like glossolalia, small-group worship promises to allow Christians to say what elsewhere would be unsayable. Just as the bidirectional, conversational notion of glossolalia is linked to feelings of intimacy, closeness, and exclusive dialogue, small groups are intimate, contained, carefully orchestrated, and enclosed social groups that mediate between micro-interaction and mass society, between face-to-face intersubjectivity and membership in larger scales of institutional belonging. Against the anonymizing scale of the megachurch, small groups are settings for the cultivation of personal relations, recognition, and responsibility.

These contexts of intimate and personal communication and socialization recruit Christians to specific roles, forge lasting relationships, make ethical order explicit, and provide a surveillance structure for large organizations. They are supposed to bring adherents closer to the deity through shared fellowship and close, collaborative encounters with the gospel. Hyejin's church, for example, describes its small groups as a "warm and intimate community of sharing" (*ttattŭthago ch'inmilhan nanum kongdongch'e*), where "recovery and healing" (*hoebok kwa ch'iyu*) are possible. Members are also encouraged to testify, confess, and repent in a more personal fashion than they otherwise would in a larger worship service. Ideally, small groups are social spaces for sharing personal information that might not be appropriate or even advisable in other church settings. That is, the small group by design promises a particular nexus of increasingly personal information, private communication, and intimate social relations, where members can say things in safety without the threat of wider exposure.

For example, the "restoration" or "recovery" small group (*hoebok sogŭrup*) is a regular Friday-evening meeting at a prominent Presbyterian church in Seoul of approximately seventy-five thousand members. Offering spiritual and emotional support (*yŏngchŏk, chŏngsŏjŏk huwŏn*), this small group aims to address members' need for a "safe situation and people to confess and share failures [*silp'ae*], weaknesses [*yakchŏm*], wounds [*sangchŏ*], and secrets [*pimil*]." The structure of the restoration small group is designed for the safe exchange of sensitive personal information, with precautions in place to prevent the illicit use of such information outside of the group. The participants are told:

1. Everything that is heard and shared here is left here.
2. Every participant is expected to speak about themselves.
3. To share their heart-mind [maŭm] as it is now, and even those things from the past that are felt in the present.
4. To support one another with active listening and eye contact, but not to ask questions or offer advice on what others have shared.
5. To raise their hand before sharing and to share for about 3 to 5 minutes.

These strict rules for participation include an insurance policy to protect its members: anyone who tells a secret is also privy to others' secrets. The poetics of participation are organized like Gricean maxims of controlled revelation: (1) confidentiality, (2) the evenly distributed expectation to participate, (3) the sincere expression of feelings and thoughts, (4) phatic presence, recognition, and acceptance without the threat of verbalized judgment, and (5) an ordered process for the sequence and amount of participation.[34] If a secret should circulate outside the group, the participants are likely to know which members would be responsible the leak—and they would have information about any potential leakers. Among its various spiritual and therapeutic functions, the recovery small group is designed for the balanced reciprocity of information, with safeguards to prevent the threat of negative reciprocity, such as the misuse of others' secrets for personal social gain.

As with these small groups, where the risks of exposure are managed through the reciprocity of self-revelation, glossolalia can operate as a medium of secrecy and fellowship, privacy and participation. In treating glossolalia as a mode of communicative exclusion—whether for the furtive, covert sharing of secrets or simply a more private, encrypted medium for transmission of sensitive thoughts and feelings—the supplicant takes a position relative to God and to others, excluding others and magnifying the relationship with the deity. It is like a small group with God; a portable, adaptable, private prayer chapel; a personal confessional box. It is here, in this interactional framing of glossolalia, that denotationally unintelligible speech and phatic contact with the deity can be scaled up from an individual calculus of information, form, and social relation to the institution-level dynamics of formal vehicles of information, routes of communicative circulation, and forms of social organization.

It is crucial for small groups to have private, secure places to gather. *Kidowŏn*, for example, are socio-spiritual getaways for urban Christians. Akin to retreat centers for the "membership training" activities of other kinds of institutions, prayer centers in South Korea are often located in the mountains, with campuses that provide spaces explicitly tailored for the intensification of individual relations with the deity and social relations among church members. These activities are often called faith-training events (*sinang suryŏnhoe*). Prayer lies at the heart of these activities, and it is there—away from the church building, Sunday services, and other more public dimensions of church life—where *t'ongsŏng kido* is amplified and glossolalia is more likely to arise. Just as I would realize how widespread glossolalia was even among those who distanced themselves from Pentecostal worship, churches, and populations, I would realize how the seemingly peripheral site of the prayer center was actually a fundamental ritual center for the shape of Korean Christianity specifically because it could serve as a space of exception and extremes.

"The Garden" is a Christian retreat center located one hour northeast of Seoul. Close to the demilitarized zone, the Garden hosts churches, businesses, families, or any group looking for a space of prayer, reflection, and fellowship outside of the city. More than a mere garden, it is a forested compound with various buildings for sleeping, eating, gathering, and worshipping. Trails throughout the compound display inspirational messages from Christian and other spiritual leaders. And it is a zoo, with dogs, horses, ducks, rabbits, even small black bears for Christians to observe, pet, and feed.

I visited the Garden with a group of deacons, deaconesses, elders, and musicians from a large Presbyterian church in Seoul. The proprietors of the Garden were senior members of the church who had married and raised their family on the retreat center grounds. We toured the grounds and then dined together. At dinner they discussed the history of the church, with a few very early members telling stories of the old days when it began in the late 1970s as a small prayer group in one of the new apartment complexes south of the Han River. They spoke with ambivalence about the way their church had grown rapidly and lamented the fact that they rarely recognized other faces on Sunday morning. They expressed concern over the feeling that their church was now home to so many strangers and even worried about some of the stranger types that regularly frequented their services. They stressed the necessity to better monitor the church because of how some of the new members seemed to exploit the church. The church was known for being very wealthy and politically influential. Some even suspected that one of the guests that evening was a charlatan, posing as the head of a nonexistent cultural exchange program and using the church to gain access to investors. Their suspicions were aroused for various reasons, high among them being the way the man insisted on saying "hallelujah" frequently and loudly after some of the more prominent leaders spoke.

The proprietors of the Garden had an uncommon vision for their prayer retreat. They explained to me that Christian retreat centers should facilitate fellowship organized around the Word, but they were aware that retreat settings could be stressful. In Korea, the cosmopolitan proprietors said, being a member of a group is both desirable and burdensome. They understood that, after hours of fellowship-building activities, some members might want some time alone. But they also understood that it could feel conspicuous or awkward for members to actively separate from the group—to walk away by oneself. Others might conclude that such a person was lonely and in need of company (and bother the person), strange and not wanting company (and ostracize the person), or arrogant and not needing company (and develop ill will toward the person). The last conclusion, arrogance (*kyoman*), is one of the most common invectives for a person who appears not to need others because they feel superior to others. It is a dangerous accusation that develops a social life of its own once put into circulation. The proprieters also understood that smaller, more intimate groups might want to spend time together, away from the larger group. For friends, the danger was explicit: to actively separate from the group, out of the ordered hierarchy and away from the group activity, was to send the signal of cliquishness, even factionalism. It was socially dangerous for Christians to show or act on certain tie signs during church events.[35]

The proprietors of the Garden created a solution to prevent charges of arrogance, gossip about romance, or accusations of factionalism. They built a tiny sanctuary, a microchapel (*chagŭn chŏn'guk*), explicitly for individuals, married couples, and very small groups to gather in limited privacy.[36] Ideally, anyone should feel comfortable entering the chapel, in full view of the others, without shame or explanation. The microchapel stands at the entrance of the Garden, near the threshold between the parking lot and the opening lawn. With its tall steeple, the small structure—big enough for only a few people to enter—is one of the first things one sees as one enters and exits the compound. Just as a sanctioned fellowship retreat to the Garden is an acceptable form of exclusion from the church as a whole, where social relations among participants could be clarified in acceptable terms, so too is the microchapel offered as an acceptable form of exclusion from the church group: on display and yet private, visible and yet concealed. The chapel offers the opportunity to worship in a space of exclusion that should be, in principle, unthreatening to the fellowship of a larger group. The interior of the chapel is furnished modestly, with a cross, a Bible, a table, and a few stools, and walls adorned with stained glass depicting a European, golden-haired Jesus. Above the cross is the same

Korean verse that appears on the balcony of the main sanctuary of the proprietor's church. It is a scriptural example of a spiritual intimacy with the deity promised by the Bible: "And surely I am with you always, to the very end of the age" (Mark 28:20). Outside the chapel, prospective entrants encounter a sign that reads prominently in English capital letters, "LOVE ONE ANOTHER (John 13:34–35)" (see chapter 4), and below and to the left, in smaller writing, "PRAY continually." In the microchapel, the communicative channel of divine relation—prayer—would mediate other sanctioned social relations.

The structures and arrangement of the grounds of the Garden—from meeting halls to dormitories, from bathrooms to the cafeteria—form a life-size diorama of acceptable social activities and intimacies in South Korean Christian society. This diorama traces a delicate balance between scales of Christian belonging. The management of scales of belonging is an object of persistent reflection and often stress, and it is highlighted in a Christian context by the particular religious frames through which social relations are characterized. Fellowship (*ch'in'gyo*) is a macro-oriented, ecumenical, massifying teleology that aims to unite Christians. Although the church is replete with internal structures of hierarchy and exclusion, in principle all Christians should be brothers and sisters.[37] The microchapel is a counterbalance to this. It promises a micro-oriented, individuating, fragmenting space for Christian intimacy.

The microchapel is intended to control and sanitize the threat of intimacy. Intimacy is a necessary ingredient for the Christian community, both for the fellowship of the community, and, in its most extreme form, for the intimacy that each Christian should share with their deity. But intimacy is also a volatile substance and must be carefully managed within groups so as not to produce the appearance of factionalism, elitism, arrogance, or any other antisocial attribute. Intimacy, as much as it is celebrated, can quickly become a threat for the way that it seems to undermine the lines of authority that are expressed in terms of institutional status. Intimacy is potentially radical.

For this reason, few of the people I spoke to had actually used the chapel for prayer with others. When I encountered church members who had been on retreats at the Garden and asked them about the microchapel, nearly all said that they noticed the chapel and had been informed about it, but never thought of actually using it to pray with others. Although they praised the chapel and the Garden more generally, and commented on the chapel's cute appearance and the good intentions behind its construction, they thought it would be too embarrassing to use. They thought it would call attention to themselves. They asked aloud, "Why would you go in there with someone?" These respondents were not worried that someone would suspect something untoward taking place in the chapel. Rather, the problem was the attention that would be drawn to the act of social intimacy through social separation—an overt tie sign—which, they were certain, would generate talk.

I discussed the Garden with Insu and Minha, a married couple whom I had known for many years. The two had visited the Garden for church retreats and laughed about the possibility of using the chapel. They had heard of weddings that used the chapel as a backdrop, but they thought it too awkward to use for prayer. For them it was too visible. They saw such retreats as a necessary activity for building fellowship and appreciated the chance to leave the city and relax outdoors. But they also admitted that it could be a burden to attend them, to follow the strict worship schedule, and to have to stay with the same people for days. In this sense, the chapel did seem to them like a possible escape—a space of exclusion, where true intimates could get away together and pray. But the acceptable intimacies that would be on display by entering the chapel depended fundamentally on status. Married couples, members of the same demographic, carrying the same rank, of the same activity group, etc., might be encouraged to enter the microchapel. But those without a status-based reason to gather and exclude others would, again, be conspicuous, awkward, even sensational targets of gossip. They acted out possible reactions to church members voluntarily entering the chapel together: People might say, "Oh, they must be very close since they are going to pray together." Such intimacies were best left outside of church context of fellowship. They joked that outside of church, not inside, was the time to meet other Christians who were really "close" (*kakkapta*). And that was also the time to gossip. Gossip, here, was the communicative manifestation of intimacy's disruptive potential among Christian communities.

The microchapel invoked an ambivalent intersection between two kinds of intimacy. The first was a pan-Christian intimacy based on the circulation of the gospel and its performative enactment through prayer. The second was a more fragmented intimacy built on small-scale social relations. As Insu and Minha pointed out, these smaller-scale relations were involved in the circulation of the gospel's inverted, negative twin: gossip. The gospel is an evangelistic model of speech that links each interaction to a broader institution founded on the notion of the movement or circulation of the Word. The cultural model of the circulating Word fuses propositional truth with ideal social relations and aims to generate the massifying effect of spiritual sameness across all contexts of action and interaction. Whatever debatable truth propositions it may further, the Word as a medium coordinates reference, relations, and ideation, thereby stabilizing a community in terms of the pragmatically realized conception of a deity. Different denominational perspectives on this movement, and on the nature of the Word, produce different accounts of glossolalia and of Christian speech and speakers more generally.

Whereas the gospel orients speakers to a transitive "principal" of evangelism, gossip focuses on the social relation of exchange itself. Whereas the gospel is supposed to unite all Christians in fellowship, gossip fractures Christian communities, forming intimacies that undermine both the general status of universal Christian siblinghood, as well as the lines of hierarchy and authority through which the church controls its members. For this reason, preachers regularly characterized gossip as a kind of counteractive centrifugal force against the condensing, centripetal work of the gospel; it was the work of Satan, a negative dimension working against the unifying promise of the church. And preachers had good reason to fear gossip, for they were so often found guilty of un-Christian violations against their own explicit morality systems as well as their own congregations.

Insu's and Minha's consciousness of the countervailing forces of the gospel and gossip came out clearly in our discussions of glossolalia. Both Presbyterians had been around glossolalic practice since their conversions in their late twenties (they were in their early forties at the time of our conversation). Insu called glossolalia scary and said he had not yet produced it. Minha said she had spoken in tongues on some occasions when she was praying fervently among others who spoke in tongues. Insu joked that maybe Minha was a shaman. He looked at me and said, in his characteristic deadpan, "When she is speaking in tongues, I wonder what she is saying. Is she talking about me?" Minha, ever quick to respond, said: "It is a secret (*pimil*) between me and God." And they laughed. The fracturing force of gossip against the uniting force of the gospel had been reformulated as glossolalia—the sharing of private, intimate secrets with the divine.

Conclusion   Glossolalia's threefold capacity for saying the unsayable—through excess signification, phatic endurance, and socio-communicative enclosure—lends itself to association with secrets. While many Christians conceptualized their glossolalia in terms of secrecy, others resisted the characterization of their prayers as secrets, instead preferring labels of intimacy or closeness, sometimes privacy (although that too was complicated). However, glossolalia and the secret emerge together as limit cases for the verbalization of intimacy in the Protestant Christian context. The secret, like glossolalia, is oriented to denotation, even as it resists it. To exchange secrets, like speaking in tongues, is to emphasize the phatic dimension of a social relation. And with the secret, as with the nontransparent speech sounds of glossolalia, excluding others through opacity and concealment can produce feelings of intimacy between interlocutors. A Korean Christian sociology of secrecy emerges in relation to glossolalia's production at the conjuncture of three intersecting paradigms of contact and concealment. The first is the competing pressures of communication with the deity and participation with others, the contradictions between which are heightened in settings of group prayer. The second is the broader models of semiotic circulation that are invoked by these pressures: the gospel and its negative twin, gossip. Finally, the third is the range of strategies people employ to deal with these challenges; these are formed by two intersecting gradients: transparency and trust.

Glossolalia links speech and social relations to a much broader range of activities that are dependent on deliberate underdeterminacy. Specifically, through opacity, phaticity, and exclusivity, the valued intimacy of Christian communicative forms inevitably invokes secrecy. Through strategic nontransparency, a person can participate in an institution that promises intimacy, comfort, and love, but is also known for producing feelings of social caution, danger, and risk. Saying the unsayable becomes possible when speaking in tongues carves out a spiritual safe space for speech. The ambiguous directionality of communication in glossolalia—from the deity to the prayerful, or from the prayerful to the deity—is a functional admixture that reflects its location at the intersection of competing regimes of revelation. Glossolalia's intimate enclosure appears to be a spiritually sanctioned space for the controlled revelation of sensitive information, even as it promises revelatory broadcast of the speech of God directly from a person's mouth. And at the boundary between the authoritative and the subversive is glossolalia's nondenotational capacity to produce mass gatherings of civil inattention.

The pragmatics of contact and concealment intersect in glossolalia to amplify the intimacy of secrecy for Christians and the deity. Glossolalia is continuous with other genres, settings, and spaces in Christian social life, such as small-group worship, prayer retreats, and prayer chambers. And these genres, settings, and spaces are formed explicitly to direct Christians toward the gospel and away from gossip. To understand how glossolalia invokes both the gospel and gossip, as inverse functions of concealment and revelation, we expanded from the secret (*pimil*) as denotationally reportable information to secrecy (*ŭnmil*) as self-reflexive metapragmatics aimed at concealment itself. Certainly it has a prototype—the unsayable secret—but the practice of secrecy is far more widespread and varied; the secret is a limit concept for a wide variety of pragmatic behavior aimed at curtailing circulation. Secrecy has a gravity, the extreme form of which must be something like a black hole, drawing into its unknowable, unviewable, unsayable center anything that could shed light on it.

Avoidance and vagueness, silence and distraction, indirectness and encryption, gossiping and passing, and all the metaphors of surface and depth, opacity and transparency describe semiotic complexes in which the social viability of a secret and the cultural value of secrecy depend on the underdeterminacy of salient sign phenomena in multiple modalities, whether verbal or nonverbal, relatively ideational or material. Moral systems of secrecy regulate not merely what is or should be a secret, but also who may have access to it, how this access is achieved, the mechanisms by which access is controlled, the routes and extent of circulation, and so on. The moral determination of secrecy—from the disclosed but unmentioned (and carefully regulated) "open secret" to the mentioned but undisclosed (and jealously guarded) "divine mystery"—depends fundamentally on the semiotic feature of underdeterminacy. That is, in these highly determined complexes of secrecy, semiotic underdeterminacy is the very arena in which the capacity and privilege to discern and interpret are unevenly distributed. Glossolalia belongs to a group of Christian practices of sanctioned concealment that bring acceptable forms of secrecy and enclosure into the open.

6

Deception

I come to the garden alone
...
and the joy we share as we tarry there,
none other has ever known[1]

Nim iranŭn kŭlcha e chŏm hana man tchigŭmyŏn nam i toenda.[2]
If you add just one dot to the word *beloved* (님), [it] becomes *stranger* (남).

Danger in Isolation

Ansu kido refers to the laying on of hands during prayer. It is a common practice across Christian communities, in which bodily contact serves as the phatic channel of communion among humans and the spiritual conduit for the Holy Spirit to travel among them. *Anch'al kido* is a more extreme, violent form of *ansu kido*. It often involves beating, slapping, kicking, or otherwise harming a person's body to expel spiritual impurities or exorcise demonic presences. The recollections of informants who had witnessed *anch'al kido* as children or young adults, at the height of its underground heterodox popularity in the 1980s and '90s, emphasized the vividness of the actions, sounds, and visible traces of violence. They saw hands raised in the air before striking a body. They heard yelling and groaning and high-pitched sounds of skin making quick contact with skin. They recalled that, while the person performing *anch'al kido* could be a man or a woman, the recipient of the violence was usually a woman; sometimes it was a family member, occasionally the speaker's own mother. They remembered seeing the bruises on these women's bodies. The arms and torsos and backs and shoulders of their mothers and aunts were covered with the signs of trauma.

Anch'al kido has led to a number of high-profile incidents in which Korean Christians have brutally, sometimes fatally, injured other Christians. An extreme and violent form of human interaction, it is generally carried out in secret—away from the ritual centers of Christian practice—at prayer centers (*kidowŏn*), hotels, and homes. These spaces are attractive for the isolation they can generate. For that reason, they are also dangerous. And although they are set apart from the most visible centers of activity, they are not entirely peripheral or marginal. They have a gravity of their own.

Large churches sometimes make spiritual isolation chambers available to their members. They are called individual prayer rooms (*kaein kidosil*) and resemble the prayer grottoes of Osanri Prayer Mountain. Containing only a mat, a small stand for a Bible, and a cross on the wall, they are physically exclusive, allowing for focused, prolonged, private interaction with the deity. Individual prayer rooms are designed to enhance a sensation of spiritual intimacy and dependency. And they are carefully regulated. Notices on individual prayer rooms explicitly prohibit turning off the lights or blacking out the windows while using the room. They announce that two persons may not enter the room at the same time.[3] Consider the following notice on the individual prayer rooms in one prominent Presbyterian church of more than seventy-five thousand members in Seoul (the portions in bold appeared in bold red font on the notice):

Excerpt 6.1

ALLIM ŬI KŬL

*Pon kyohoe esŏ nŭn **p'yŏngsindo ŭi ansu mit anch'al haengwi** rŭl chŏltae kŭmhago issŭmnida. I il ro inhae palsaeng toen p'ihae e taehayŏ pon kyohoe esŏ nŭn ch'aegim ŭl chiji ansŭmnida. Ttarasŏ sŏngdodŭl **ŭn p'ihae rŭl ipchi ant'orok** yuŭi hasigi paramnida.*

NOTICE

In this church, *ansu* or *anch'al* **activities by lay believers** are **strictly forbidden**. The related injuries that occur from the compounding of this [activity] are not the responsibility of this church. Therefore, we ask believers to be cautious **not to suffer any harm**.

There are predators—sometimes ordained clergy, sometimes lay members—who target other members for private prayer, study, and worship as a cover for more nefarious, often sexual or abusive activities. *Anch'al kido* was sometimes associated with these schemes. Persons claiming have spiritual gifts would hold "altar of prayer" meetings (*kido ŭi chedan*), during which participants would "construct" (*ssat'a*) an altar of prayer that produced stimulating, powerful experiences and the feeling of direct access to spiritual gifts. Participation often required *chemul*, offerings or sacrifice, which could be something as simple as money (*hŏn'gŭm*) or the pain of bodily violence. Although such meetings offered hope for Christian revival that would draw participants closer to the deity, many of my tongues-speaking interlocutors found them suspicious for their off-the-books, unofficial character, their political potential to create factions or even new churches, the likelihood of false or sham (*saibi*) prophets to take advantage of people, and the deliberately private, secret, isolated way in which these gatherings took place.

Individuated and peripheral spaces of Christian practice are both attractive and frightening. While they are designed to produce heightened experiences of the deity, they sometimes lead people to suspect other sources for their spiritual experiences—whether demonic, social, or self-induced. Moreover, while they contain the potential to produce overwhelming, even terrifying feelings of encounter with the sacred, they also have the capacity to produce the sudden, disorienting recognition of an underlying profanity. Peripheral and private worship demand careful discernment (*punbyŏl*), so that that the diverse qualia of spiritual encounter can be differentiated, amplified, or avoided.[4]

Glossolalia produces a similar set of problems. On the one hand, as we saw in the previous chapter, glossolalia promises a private, isolated space of worship. For example, one Presbyterian man's initial experience of praying in tongues was a great happiness that came with being completely alone with God. To explain this happiness, he drew on an image that is familiar to Korean college students: the *tongari*, or student club. He compared praying in tongues to entering the room of a club by oneself to pray—an inherently social space of focused activity that one could have all to oneself. In this socially isolated space of glossolalia, it felt to him as if even an ant crawling through the room could understand what he was saying, as if he and the ant were praising God together. If a flock of birds alighted to the windowsill of this private room of glossolalia, there was a feeling of being with God, of praising God with all of creation, or communion with God. He experienced a similar feeling when praying in tongues while hiking in the mountains: "With the trees being blown about by the wind, squirrels passing by, gazing upon ants, I feel really happy when I pray in tongues."

But danger lurks in the very space that should be most purified and holy, where a sense of the deity is most proximate and intimate. A seasoned elderly Methodist glossolalist described the dangers of glossolalia, especially when practiced alone in the mountains, where a person is most at risk for spiritual deception. With its resonances with Buddhist mountain temples and shamanic mountain spirits (*sansin*), mountain prayer is at once among the one of the most spiritually powerful and productive practices as well as one of the most dangerous and spiritually vulnerable. She explained that if a person doesn't have the ability of discernment (*punbyŏllyŏk*), the person cannot, for example, hear the footsteps of demonic spirits following behind. The person cannot tell that Satan has been whispering (*soksakkŏrida*) in her ear. Although people sometimes described glossolalia as happening suddenly, sporadically, spontaneously, uncontrollably, and so forth, there were many warnings against yearning (*samo hada*) for such a radical break into tongues all at once. A person should avoid praying recklessly (*hamburo*). Instead, one should gradually develop one's glossolalia, always cautious of the forces that one encounters, whether in one's own tongues or in the tongues of others around them. If a person with a "bad spirit" (*nappŭn yŏng*) prays for a spiritually weaker person, the bad spirit will enter the weaker person. Similarly, if a person receives glossolalia incorrectly, they end up as "food for Satan" (*sat'an ŭi pap*).

This final chapter returns to the profound ambivalence of the gift of glossolalia. In the previous chapter, we saw how spaces of intimacy and privacy were risky for the outside talk they could generate. Here, the focus of the danger is on what comes from the inside—specifically, the ruptures of intimacy that threaten to occur. Glossolalia, like the individual prayer room or the altar-of-prayer meeting, promises a close, even fusional relationship with the divine. But dissolving the dyad is risky not merely because of a loss of agency. It is dangerous because it is potentially an alignment with and delegation of agency to a nefarious force, or even to an illusion. Spiritual trust and intimacy themselves become potential sources of deception.[5] Informants gave different accounts of this problem. The secrets that they freely revealed under the mask of unintelligible vocables could be revealed to others who have the gift of interpretation. The free-flowing, sonorous prayers that seemed to be placed into their mouths by the Holy Spirit could turn out to be mere mimesis, simple copies of others' sounds. The spiritual isolation that people imposed on themselves to reach their deity actually brought them face to face with evil spirits. In the worst case, a total fusion with the deity—where not only the "I" and "you" of exchange, but all the familiar signs demarcating relations and boundaries the speaking persona—produces an unstable state of permeability that could let Satan into one's heart.

Glossolalia's relation to the problem of language produces feelings of both semiotic transcendence and disorientation. Spiritual intimacy is supposed to provide an anchor in this disorientation; in practice, it often fails. To explain the consequences of this failure, I begin with an account of glossolalia at a *kidowŏn*, or prayer center, where doubts about the practice emerged. I follow these doubts in terms of the forms, the feelings, and the forces associated with them. Finally, I turn to some more-high-profile examples of spiritual deception to locate glossolalia within a broader context in which anxieties about deception, intimacy, and isolation are voiced. In the previous chapter, one person described speech in the church being circulated as gossip, transforming into a knife, and returning to hurt a person. In the present chapter, as the seasoned glossolalist above put it, glossolalia itself is dangerous like a knife—especially for those who do not know how to use it.

Doubting Real Glossolalia

There are many degrees to the problem of discernment. When speaking with God in tongues, the prayerful must be sure they have the correct interlocutor; it could be Satan. When longing for tongues, the prayerful must be aware of the nature of one's own desire; it could be temptation. When praying in tongues among others, the prayerful must be careful about their orientation to sounds around them; they could be just copying the sounds of others. When evaluating glossolalia, they must be both firm and humble in their judgment. The problem, at its most basic, is the simple discernment between glossolalia that is real and that which is not. Like a social relation, if it is not real—i.e., if it does not live up to what it promises to be—then it is a source of risk, possibly deception, and even danger.

My first encounter with doubts about glossolalia by those who practiced it came at a visit to a prayer center (*kidowŏn*) with Presbyterians in 2008. The members of the choir had gathered on a Saturday in early March for a faith-training retreat (*sinang suryŏnhoe*) at a prayer center just south of Seoul. Much of the day was like any other day at the wealthy, conservative Presbyterian megachurch: a sermon, Bible reading and discussion, music rehearsal, and lots of eating. However, the afternoon prayer session took on a more fervent character. Away from the formal sanctuary of the church building, the prayers became wilder, the emotions more elevated.

An evangelist (*chŏndosa*) stood beneath a cross made of two varnished logs.[6] He divided the group into men and women. He asked us to pray for our leaders. The women formed a circle around the *taejang*, or senior representative who spoke on behalf of the choir to the elders of the church. She was a *kwŏnsa*, or senior female deaconess, a woman in her late sixties and one of the founding members of the church.[7] The men formed a circle around the *ch'ongmu*, or manager of the choir. He was a *chipsa*, or deacon. A man in his late fifties, he had tried and failed many times to be elected as elder. Both had converted to Christianity in adulthood. The evangelist, a man in his thirties, asked the *taejang* and the *ch'ongmu* to kneel. I watched the *ch'ongmu* place his hands on his knees, turn his palms toward the sky, and lower his head. The rest of us placed our hands on his head and back, preparing for *ansu kido*. The women did the same for the *taejang*.

The accompanist improvised on the piano, following the chords of the Korean praise song we had just sung, "God Is Your Protector" (*Hananim ŭn nŏ rŭl chik'isinŭn cha*) by Chŏng Sŏngsil. The evangelist began to pray over the choir; the choir members followed by praying over their leaders. The room broke into *t'ongsŏng kido* that sounded like a collective, urgent hum. It lasted for two minutes until the evangelist stopped us.

Then the evangelist asked the choir to pray for the conductor and the accompanist, both of whom had been raised in devoutly Presbyterian families. The choir conductor, a mother of two in her early thirties at the time, was encircled by the other women. The accompanist, a woman in her midtwenties who had a recently received a master's degree in music, left the piano and was encircled by the men. The men cautiously placed their hands on the young woman's back. The evangelist picked up his guitar and began playing the same chords. As he played and yelled, the group again began to pray.

The pulsating chords of the evangelist's guitar, along with his impassioned calls, elevated the mood of the prayer. The two women at the center of each circle began calling out in a way the older *taejang* and *ch'ongmu* had not. Their prayers were louder, their cries more full-throated. I could feel the organist's arched back heaving upward against our hands as she took deep breaths between her prayers. A baritone next to me began to pray loudly above others, his voice rising in pitch and amplitude. Earlier he had told me that it was his personal dream to introduce Kim Jong-il (Kim Chŏngil), then still the leader of North Korea, to Jesus (he was not aware that Kim Il-sung [Kim Ilsŏng], Kim Jong-il's father, had been raised a Christian). Now from his mouth flowed repetitive vocables, occasionally punctuated by vocatives to the deity: *Chunim!* (Lord!). *Babababababa. Abŏji!* (Father!). *Lolololololo. Hananim!* (God!). *Dadadadada.* The other men's vocalizations grew more fervent, swelling collectively. The voice of the accompanist was higher in pitch and cut through the lower male voices around me. Except for her calling out to God, I could understand nothing of what she said. And then, as before, after just two minutes, the evangelist began to slow his tempo and stridency and transition the group back into normal speech. When the organist and choir conductor stood up, their faces were wet with tears.

Glossolalia had taken place in what seemed at the time an unlikely place. The church was not known for glossolalia. If anything, among South Korean protestant denominations, this church was seen as a kind of antiglossolalic institution, if not explicitly in doctrine then at least implicitly in practice. Its members generally looked down on and distanced themselves from congregations where glossolalia was the norm. During the year that I would spend at that church and the many follow-up visits, I heard tongues mentioned only once in official church communications, when it was announced in a regular church news update that a prominent young performing artist and member of the church said she had received the gift of tongues. After the prayer session, as we sipped sweet instant coffee and snacked, I mentioned to some of the others how new the experience of group prayer had been for me. Many of them expressed empathy. Older members found the praise-and-worship style unbefitting the status and character of their community. This sense of propriety revealed the presence of class anxieties and, in this specific case, generational differences that mark out different religious practices and ideologies across Christian congregations. Some had converted to Christianity as adults—a few very recently—and were still getting used to prayer itself. Others, despite their Christian upbringing, were uneasy with the more fervent styles. They pointed to other churches, especially the mammoth Yoido Full Gospel Church, as more exemplary of this kind of prayer. They used words like "scary" (*musŏpta*) or "noisy" (*sikkŭrŏpta*) to describe it. Others, however, said they liked it and wanted more of it.

Some years later, as I sought to better understand the widespread practice of glossolalia across Korean churches and denominations, I broached the subject with some of the people who had participated in the faith-training retreat in 2008. Both the choir conductor and the organist had become close friends of mine. Recalling that day, the choir conductor revealed that she had probably spoken in tongues as the others prayed over her. She could not remember for sure, but she thought it likely because glossolalia came easily to her, especially in settings of fervent group prayer. In contrast, the organist was very sure that she had prayed in tongues on that day. Her doubts, however, focused on whether the glossolalic vocables she had uttered counted as "real glossolalia" (*chintcha pangŏn*). She explained that she often produced sounds that were unintelligible to her and to others. When she prayed hard, fast, and fervently, she found that her words simply moved more slowly than her thoughts (*mal i saenggak poda tŏ nŭrida*). Her solution was to focus on her prayerful thoughts and just let her mouth run, allowing long streams of unintelligible sounds to keep her prayers going. By allowing herself to utter sounds without making them into words, she could focus on her thoughts, her relationship with the deity, and the emotional urgency of her expression, all while responsibly contributing to the group. Although she called this *pangŏn kido*, she admitted her doubts that it was "real." To her, real glossolalia was the full possession of one's speech faculties by the Holy Spirit—not trance, but rather a kind of verbal possession. And this had happened to her only a handful of times.

During these conversations, I revealed to them my own experience of prayer and worship during that retreat. I explained that I had tried to participate, but that I had little experience with prayer, especially the style of fervent prayer we were encouraged to produce. I told them that I had tried to say kind, hopeful things. I wished the leaders well. I wished the others well. I wished the choir well. And I tried to do so sonorously and quickly to match the others. I began repeating myself. When I could not keep up with the rapid-fire utterances of those around me, I began uttering simple sounds—any sounds, streams of sound. I moved my lips and tongue, my articulators, and phonated long streams of sound. They both acknowledged that this is much of what people do; they themselves often did something similar. In such prayer settings, they both said, one cannot pray quietly or only for oneself. The responsibility to participate meant that one had to make sound. The coercive force of participation made the problem of real glossolalia a persistent source of concern.

Forms, Feelings, Forces[8]

Questions about "real" glossolalia emerged in different ways around three consistent targets: the forms, the feelings, and the forces associated with tongues. The glossolalic forms are empirically closest to the problem of speech qua syllables as a brute realization of language. Here, the feelings are the personal sensations and impressions that are generated in relation to the linguistic forms. These feelings are at once seemingly the most indisputable but also regularly called into question. And the forces are inferred from the forms and the feelings. Leading directly to questions about the true motivation of behind glossolalia, the problem of forces was most central to theological debates.

In contrast to the stereotype of a sudden glossolalic takeover by the Holy Spirit, many practitioners and aspirants described long periods of indeterminacy, when they were unsure whether they were really speaking in tongues. As is widely attested in the scholarly literature on glossolalia, they described beginning with simple, repetitive vocables and praying fervently with the hope of transitioning into the speech of the spirit. Pastors and churches held revival seminars to instruct Christians on effective ways to receive tongues, often emphasizing "starter" or "elementary" tongues (*chʼobangŏn*). Sometimes they cautioned novices against trying too hard—i.e., asserting their own agency. Sometimes they suggested the opposite, instructing people to pray hard (*sege*), with passion (*yŏlchŏng*), to increase their speed and amplitude. Sometimes they directed Christians to raise the pitch of their prayers to approximate the sound of a buzzing bee (*pŏl sori*; see chapter 5). Sometimes they asked Christians to pray until they could no longer breathe. For some, this develops into elaborate speech-like behavior. For others, their ability might reach a level satisfactory enough to practice and participate with intensity and focus. Still others are not so lucky, and turn to books and other sources for guidance.

One of these books is *The Hidden Secret to Praying in Tongues* (*Pangŏn kido e sumŭn pimil*), by Kang Yosep. The book promises to reveal the mysteries of speaking in tongues, to help readers receive the gifts of tongues and interpretation, and to develop deep spirituality. Like water, breath is one of the central metaphors of the spirit. Kang literalizes the metaphor of breath, using respiration for inspiration, and focuses directly on the breathing body. His method bypasses even the simple syllabic composition of glossolalia. He prescribes exercises that appropriate the inhalation and exhalation of breathing as interpenetrative processes that open up the body and its interiors so that the spirit may "work" (*yŏksa*) within a person. Through these exercises, the breath of the person intermingles with the breath of the spirit, entering and exiting a person like amniotic holy water, producing heavenly speech by dissolving earthly language.

Parŭn chase ro anjasŏ chŏnchŏnhi sum ŭl kip'i tŭrimasimnida. I ttae konggi rŭl masinŭn kŏt i anira saengmyŏngch'e isin Sŏngnyŏngnim ŭl masindago saenggak hasipsio. Kŭrigo naeshwimyŏnsŏ pangŏn ŭro kido rŭl hamnida. Ye rŭl tŭlmyŏn irŏk'e hamnida.

Sit in an upright posture and slowly drink in a deep breath. At this time, do not think that you are drinking air but rather that you are drinking the living body that is the Holy Spirit. And as you breathe out, pray in tongues. For example, do it this way.

1. *(Tŭrishwinŭn sum) Sŏngnyŏng ŭi kamdong ŭl patsŭmnida.*
   (Inhaling breath) Receive the feeling of the Holy Spirit.
2. *Sum ŭl mŏtsŭmnida (1–2 ch'o kan).*
   Stop the breath (1–2 seconds).
3. *(Naeshwinŭn sum) lallalla~ lallalla~ Pangŏn ŭro kido hamnida.*
   (Exhaling breath) Lalala~ lalala~ Pray in tongues.
4. *Sum ŭl chamsi mŏmch'um (1–2 ch'o kan).*
   Pause breathing (1–2 seconds).
5. *(Tŭrishwinŭn sum) Maŭm esŏ ttŏorŭnŭn kamdong ŭl mal hamnida. Ye rŭl tŭndamyŏn "Nae ka nŏ rŭl sarang handa."*
   (Inhaling breath) Speak the emotion that comes to mind. For example, "I love you."
6. *Sum ŭl chamsi mŏmch'um (1–2 ch'o kan).*
   Pause breathing (1–2 seconds).
7. *(Naeshwinŭn sum) lallalla~ lallalla~ Pangŏn ŭro kido hamnida.*
   (Exhaling breath) Lalala~ lalala~ Pray in tongues.
8. *Irŏk'e kyesok panbok hamnida.*
   Continuously repeat like this.

> *Hohŭp ŭl kip'i tŭrishwimyŏnsŏ sŏngnyŏng ŭi kamdong ŭl pannŭn kŏt ŭl kyesok panbok ham ŭrossŏ uri nŭn Sŏngnyŏngnim ŭl kip'i pada tŭrige toemnida. Sŏngnyŏng ŭi him i hohŭp ŭl t'onghesŏ uri mom e kadŭk sŭmyŏdŭlgo naomyŏnsŏ yŏrŏ kaji yŏngchŏk in hyŏnsang i nat'anamnida.*

By continuously repeating [the act of] receiving the moving feeling of the Holy Spirit while breathing in deeply, we come to receive the Holy Spirit deeply. As the power of the Holy Spirit permeates, fills, and comes out of our body through our breath, many spiritual phenomena appear.[9]

Despite such guidance, advice, and concrete exercises, many Christians found that they simply cannot speak in tongues. For some, this was painful, as their congregations and the groups that they belonged to were organized according to the public display of these spiritual gifts. Some pastors discriminated against those who did not speak in tongues by separating them from congregants who could, refusing to lay hands on them, or simply asking them to leave. For others, the frustration came from assuming their lack of tongues meant they had insufficient faith. They confronted this frustration with methods designed to increase the strength and foundations of their faith. For instance, the accompanist, mentioned above, who distinguished between her everyday practices of glossolalia and a few instances of "real" glossolalia explained that she was trying to raise the level of her faith through a new, more mature approach to prayer. This, she hoped, would help her produce real glossolalia more frequently. Raised as a Presbyterian, she had begun attending a Methodist church when they advertised a need for an accompanist. There, she found the pastor's sermons moving and helpful for developing her spiritual maturity. Over a lunch of beer and grilled pork belly in 2018, ten years after we first met, she pulled out a notebook that was filled with notes from her pastor on how to pray, studiously color-coded in red, blue, and black ink. The pastor's guidance stressed three things: fervor, stamina, and individual feelings of contact with the deity.

Often, however, their frustration is not with their own inability to speak in tongues, but with the church leadership's insistence that they should speak in tongues. Even more confusing was when leaders—contrary to a person's own feelings—insisted that the person was already speaking in tongues. It was not uncommon to hear stories from informants about being pressed to produce a stream of vocables and then being told by church leadership, "You are speaking in tongues!" In these cases, the informants generally disagreed with the assessment. They said things like: "The pastor told me I was speaking in tongues, but I did not think I was." "How could it be tongues? It doesn't sound like another language." "I didn't feel anything. This can't be it." Despite numerous claims by glossolalia enthusiasts that speaking in tongues often begins with the simplest of syllables, these Christians had their own linguistic and sensuous standards of what should count, formally, as glossolalia. Their standards were higher and stricter than those of the church leadership. They were not convinced that glossolalia—"real" glossolalia—was distributed equally among all. They asked themselves: "Didn't God assign different talents to different people?" "Didn't St. Paul explain that different people had different spiritual gifts (*ŭnsa*) and that glossolalia was the lowest among them?" Often, the overt pressure from church leaders to speak in tongues, combined with the coercive force of participation, led them to think critically about the examples they had encountered and to have doubts about the whole genre of glossolalic prayer, even as they practiced it.

Their doubts came from empirical observation. They compared the everyday sociolinguistic facts of speech in South Korea with their observations of glossolalia. They noticed what appeared to be patterns of sociolinguistic variation among different groups, which, they surmised, might be a sign of earthly influence. They noticed that different Christian groups seemed to have, collectively, different styles of tongues. These styles were differentiable not merely by the normal congregational or denominational differences (e.g., loud versus quiet; raucous versus calm), but also, and specifically, by the particular phonetic patterns that defined the glossolalia of the different groups. For the two tongues-speaking Presbyterian men mentioned in chapter 5, the glossolalia of the "entire community" (*kongdongch'e chŏnch'e*) of the InterVarsity Christian Fellowship (Kidok Haksaenghoe) sounded like "*ŏbŏbŏbŏ*," with "a lot of nasal sounds entering" the speech (*isanghage piŭm i mani tŭrŏgada*), whereas Youth with a Mission (Yesu Chŏndodan) sounded more like "*riŭl riŭl*" or "*lalalala*," as well as "*mŏsŏmŏsŏ*," "*mŏsŭmŏsŭ*," "*mŭsŭ mŭsŭ*." They described the daily early-dawn prayer (*saebyŏk kido*) at their seminary as extremely noisy, full of people praying in tongues, often with aspirated consonants such as "*p'ŭ, t'ŭ, k'ŭ*," which they characterized as angry tongues (*hwanan tŭthan pangŏn*). These group-relative variations in form (*hyŏngt'ae*) were "evidence" (*chŭnggŏ*) that the sound of glossolalia one speaks comes from the sound of glossolalia that one hears. For these glossolalists, glossolalia was evidently a "learned result" (*haksŭp toen kyŏlgwa*).

Certainly, South Koreans are well aware of the absorptive power of the institution or social group to produce the appearance conformity among its members. They are not naive to the overwhelming force of trends or fashions to produce rapid change and variation in behaviors—whether it be speech, clothing, plastic surgery, restaurant choices, or health remedies. So it was not surprising to my informants that social forces would pervade even the sincere, individuated glossolalia of Christians. However, the group-level predictability of the variation raised an uncomfortable issue: If glossolalia is really supposed to be the language of heaven, if it is to be individuated and personal for each individual, then why should it be so easily shaped by human processes and subject to the same human limits as other linguistic forms? They understood human language to be a fundamentally social phenomenon. Was glossolalia also such a phenomenon?

With the reliability of linguistic forms alone in doubt, many glossolalists turned to the feelings generated during tongues for guidance toward "real" glossolalia. Consider, for example, the following list of the most common "symptoms" (*chŭngsang*) Kang Yosep has noticed regarding his oxygenating approach to glossolalia. They are supposed to be the felt sensations of the Holy Spirit working in a person as that person speaks in tongues.

1. *Mom i iwan toemnida.*
   Your body relaxes.
2. *Mom i ttŭgŏpkŏna chŏllyu ka hŭrŭnŭn kŏt katsŭmnida.*
   Your body feels hot, or it feels like electric current flows [in your body].
3. *Mom i much'ŏk ap'umnida.*
   Your body aches very much.
4. *Momsok e imulgam ŭl nŭkkimnida.*
   You feel the sensation of a foreign body in your body.
5. *Sŏnŭrhan kiun ŭl nŭkkimnida.*
   You get a chilly feeling.
6. *P'yŏngan hago mom i kabyŏwŏ chimnida.*
   You feel peaceful, and the body becomes light.[10]

The phased sequence of relaxation, stimulation, overstimulation, penetration, cooling, and lightness aptly accounts for many of the experiences that informants described. Some practitioners were confident in their ability to discern the source of their glossolalia by feelings like this. Glossolalia might produce a feeling of power (*him*) in the stomach, accompanied by courage, strength, and boldness. If a person felt happiness, joy, love, gratitude, and security, then it was a sign of the Holy Spirit. If a person felt insecurity, anxiety, jealousy, hatred, anger, or any sensation of destruction, death, or killing, it was a sign of Satan.[11] Some informants claimed to know straight away—in the manner of a witchcraft accusation—whether others' glossolalic prayers were pure or impure, heavenly or satanic, both by the sound of the utterance (e.g., shrieking or wailing) or by the strange feelings they had simply by being near the person. In some cases, they explained, the Holy Spirit took over their own glossolalia as a form of intercessory prayer to defend their neighbors' "weak spirits" and battle directly against the satanic or demonic forces at work in them. When practiced correctly, glossolalia was said to have a purifying function on the rest of a person's prayer, like cleaning a bowl before eating from it or removing impurities from the surface water of a well before drinking from it. One purified oneself for immersive prayer through confession and repentance—intimately, privately, and secretly in tongues. Without this process of purification, glossolalia was at risk for becoming contaminated.

However, as much as some insisted that a person could feel the difference between holy and unholy tongues, there was widespread distrust of using feelings more generally as a guide to spiritual discernment regarding the forces motivating the forms. Although it is often reported that tongues speakers celebrate the beauty of speaking in tongues, many informants stressed the danger of orienting to enjoyment or beauty as a gauge for the holiness of glossolalia.[12] They explained that if even for a moment a person is thinking about the sensuous enjoyment of the practice and not about God, the person is already intoxicated (*ch'wihada*) by these feelings and will have vain or selfish thoughts in their hearts.

The problem emerged in discussions about the sonorous flow (*hŭrŭm*) of glossolalic prayer. On the one hand, flowing glossolalic speech is the ideal form for a person to repent their sins and purify their hearts in a space of privacy; through this purification they open their mouths to be filled up by the flowing speech of the spirit. On the other, if the free flow of glossolalic utterances is achieved too easily or produced with too much pleasure, it can constitute a dangerous route away from the deity. They were skeptical about emotions as such as a reliable tool for spiritual discernment. This skepticism extended from the murky and disorienting practice of glossolalia itself to the music-filled settings of group prayer in which it often took place. Many commented on the confusion that arises from mistaking the emotional climaxes of collaborative group intensity for the presence of God "working" (*yŏksa hada*) in a person. They stressed the caution one must take, especially in a place like South Korea, where they saw what they described as a widespread culture of "emotional release" (*kamjŏngjŏk in haeso*), or, as Hyejin put it, "stimulation" (*chagŭk*). The cathartic experiences that Korean churches excel at generating are also dangerous, because, as one person put it, a person can be "completely immersed in a world of one's own" (*ponin manŭi segye e ppajyŏbŏrida*). That is, both the collaborative activity of prayer and the fusional feelings of intimacy with the deity can produce the unintended effect of isolation.

The democratization of glossolalia as a spiritual gift potentially available to all caused many Christians, even regular practitioners of glossolalia, to worry about the risks to which they would be exposed if they took the phenomenon too lightly. Beyond the more specific accusations of charlatanism or even heresy for some glossolalia-promoting pastors, there was worry that in promoting glossolalia, many church leaders were guiding Christians to engage in a spiritually charged activity for which they were not prepared. Although many informants claimed that glossolalia could help Christians block out the devil (and other eavesdroppers) in order to share their secrets with God, others cautioned that Christians were potentially being sold a defense against the devil that was actually a medium through which they could invite demonic agents into their devotional practices.

In this regard, Christians who were surrounded by glossolalic prayer practices reflected on the uttered forms and sensuous feelings they encountered in order to make inferences about forces and the sources behind these forces. Many were familiar with possessions and exorcisms as a common outcome of focused prayer gatherings. Some had even participated in exorcisms. And in familiar, predictable terms, they spoke of certain kinds of speech forms that seemed to emerge from demonic sources, such as raspy voices, hissed voices; the sounds of souls in torment, such as shrieking and moaning; and the sounds of wailing beasts in spiritual warfare.

More often, however, the presence of demonic forces was not as obvious. That is not how the devil's seduction works, they explained. The devil tends to whisper and work in other effectively deceptive ways. In response to this threat, many emphasized the need for a gradual, cumulative building up of discernment in relation to glossolalia, because through glossolalia one is subject increasingly to states of socio-semiotic isolation. One must become accustomed to finding one's orientation to faith in moments of extreme disorientation.

It is important to pause here and note that the familiar skepticism about emotionalism or enthusiasm in Christianity is not aimed at emotionality or bodily feeling per se.[13] Moreover, as practically everyone stressed, rituals of group enthusiasm (e.g., for collective labor, national celebration) are common to Korean sociality more generally and have been treated as a key factor in Koreans' widespread religiosity and enthusiastic conversion to Christianity. The central problem is how to triangulate feelings with linguistic forms and inferences about spiritual forces in order to find safe, pure, holy modes of orientation and stabilization within a practice that was fundamentally disorienting. The problem is that the very medium that enables positive spiritual contact was consistently an object of suspicion and doubt for the feelings of risk it provoked.

The Devil Next Door

A most striking example of this anxiety of deceptive intimacy projected onto an entire religious movement is the case of Shincheonji (Sinchŏnji), or "New Heaven and Earth," that most Protestants view as heretical.[14] Its members are known to infiltrate churches in order to "harvest" unsuspecting Christians. They are said to deceive these Christians by posing as friends, confidants, and helpers, only to lead them away from God and to the cult of its founder, Lee Man-hee (Yi Manhŭi).

In the autumn and winter of 2013, I stayed for some months in Pogwang-dong, a hilly neighborhood in the Yongsan district along the north bank of the Han River. Bordering It'aewŏn to the north and just steps from the US military base to the west, the neighborhood had once been a postwar shantytown. Near my rented apartment was a small Presbyterian church of approximately three hundred people that was established in 1960. I often walked up the small alley to this church to listen to their worship. On the front doors of the church, next to the notice prohibiting mobile phones in the sanctuary, were posted warnings about the threat of Shincheonji. I had seen variations of these warnings displayed in churches throughout South Korea. The posters depicted a person wearing a large smiling white mask with a cross on the forehead; from the person's rear protruded the long, red pointed tail of a devil. The threat was clear: deception and danger in the form of people who appear to be Christian but in fact are agents of Satan.

Just down the small alley from the Presbyterian church, a new church had opened the year prior in an empty storage area above a small food market. The church was a branch of the Nigeria-based Mountain of Fire and Miracles Ministries, established by Dr. Daniel Kolawole Olukoya, and was ministering to Nigerian migrant workers in Seoul. Local Korean workers at the "Harmony Mart," which rented the space to the church, explained to me that neighbors had complained about the loud noises they heard from the church late at night. The congregation's late-night prayer sessions involved stomping and yelling until the early hours of the morning.

Late one evening I heard the raucous sounds coming from the Mountain of Fire and Miracles Ministries outpost and decided to attend the service. I climbed the outdoor steps to the second floor, entered, and sat in the rear pew of the small upstairs gathering. Approximately twenty people, aged in their twenties and thirties, stood, shouted, and prayed out loud. I sat for an hour as an officiant paced before the audience and roamed the aisle that separated the two sides. He cried out intercessory commands on behalf of the congregation: "Leave those evil spirit fetuses behind!" "Smash any spirits that have followed you from the forest!" "Let this time in Korea not be in vain!" I left after the pastor had finished his sermon and the congregants transitioned to quietly uttering their individual prayers.

After that evening, I went back to the small Presbyterian church, curious what its members thought of the Nigerian Pentecostal church and its noisy midnight prayer sessions nearby. It was a weekday afternoon, and I found no one but an older woman scrubbing surfaces in the kitchen. I asked if she knew anything about the second-floor church down the alley. She said she didn't know much. I told her that I had heard they make a lot of noise. She agreed that they were noisy and volunteered the additional information that they were foreigners—and Christian. Then I asked about the Shincheonji warnings on the front of the church. She told me that they were extremely dangerous. I asked why they were so dangerous. As she scrubbed, she said that they look like Christians and could even act like Christians, but they were not Christian. This made them extremely dangerous.

To her, the loud midnight- prayer sessions, with shouts and cries and stomping in another language, was not an immediate threat. They were foreign, and therefore other, but they were Christian, and the neighborhood was increasingly used to these kind of others (widespread racialized xenophobia notwithstanding): Pogwang-dong, next to It'aewŏn, has long been one of the most international areas of the city. Rather, the terrifying ones were those who appeared to be Korean Christians but were heretics, who presented themselves with the cross but had tails of the devil, who appeared to join in fellowship but were covertly harvesting souls for their own cult. Lurking in familiarity was strangeness; in intimacy, deception. A person required the powers of discernment to remain safe.

The threat of the nefarious masquerading as the familiar is keenly felt in Korea. It is the stuff of popular dramas and sensational news reports. One of the first glossolalists I met in South Korea, a Presbyterian convert, explained that in contemporary Seoul, it was almost impossible to know if someone was true, honest, and sincere or lying, deceptive, and manipulative. She insisted that the older generation used to be able to see right away—in someone's face, speech, or behavior—whether or not the person was trustworthy. But the ability to distinguish at first sight among people had become almost impossible. The subjective skill had been lost, and the object of scrutiny had fundamentally changed. People could transform their faces as easily as they could transform their clothes. Indeed, face readers and phrenologists (*kwansang*) sometimes advised their clients to change their faces precisely to avoid the effects that the original might have on employment or romantic prospects. In a city like Seoul, people could hide or fabricate their pasts and social relations. They could appear and disappear without a trace. She told this to me as she revealed that her recent marriage, which had taken place quickly, was already dissolving. Although they had met through a matchmaker, and although he was a Christian, she had been deceived. I never learned exactly how she had been deceived. She told me only: "He is not the person I thought he was."

The Republic of Korea experienced a deception of intimacy in 2016, when a few key revelations instigated the impeachment, arrest, and trial of President Park Geun-hye (Pak Kŭnhye). Park is the daughter of the former autocratic leader Park Chung-hee, who ruled the country from 1961 until his assassination in 1979. The country watched her grow up in the presidential residence and become a leading conservative politician South Korea's post-1987 democracy. Her mother, Yuk Young-soo (Yuk Yŏngsu), was killed in an attempt on Park Chung-hee's life in 1974. After her mother's death, Park Geun-hye held an official position as honorary First Lady in her father's government. She held this position until her father was assassinated by his own head of intelligence in 1979. With the support of older voters and conservative Christians (who had supported her predecessor, Lee Myung-bak [Yi Myŏngbak], who was sentenced to seventeen years in prison for corruption), she won the presidential election in 2012 in part due to a nostalgia for a combination of her father's era of economic development, anticommunism, and social order, as well as sympathy for her having lost both parents to murder.

Park encountered considerable trouble and conflict during the early years of her presidency. Shortly after she assumed the presidency in 2013, it was revealed that the National Intelligence Service, under the direction of Won Sei-hoon (Wŏn Sehun), had actively tried to sway the 2012 election in her favor by producing misinformation online about opposition candidates. This was followed by the awful *Sewŏl* ferry tragedy of 2014, in which 304 passengers and crew members—most of them high school students on a school trip to Jeju Island—drowned due to negligence and profit-oriented cost cutting that put the vessel at risk. President Park's whereabouts for the seven hours after the first reports of the sinking could not be confirmed, leading to various, and often misogynistic, rumors about her secret preoccupations (e.g., Botox and stem cell treatment for youthful rejuvenation). The vessel was owned by a company under the direction of Yoo Byung-eun (Yu Pyŏngŏn), the leader of a heterodox Christian organization called the Korean Evangelical Baptist Church, or, more commonly, the Salvation Sect (Kuwŏnp'a). After a months-long manhunt for Yoo, his decomposed body was found in a field two hundred miles south of Seoul.

Then, in late 2016, it was revealed that a personal friend and advisor, Choi Soon-sil (Ch'oi Sunsil), without an official position in the government, had not only read but actually edited some of Park's presidential speeches. It was not merely one or two, but as many as forty-four.[15] This particular scandal was preceded by protests by students at Ewha Womans University over the creation of a new academic program that, according to the students, would weaken the rigorous entrance standards of the elite school. This led to escalated charges of favoritism and influence peddling that began to reveal, through a series of linkages, a special relationship between President Park and Choi Soon-sil.[16] Choi Soon-sil's daughter, Chung Yoo-ra (Chŏng Yura), a champion equestrian, became a key figure in the Ewha scandal, again for favoritism regarding her entrance and performance there. In a most captivating twist, Choi herself is the daughter of Choi Tae-min (Ch'oi T'aemin), another leader of a heterodox religious organization, the Church of Eternal Life, who had been an influential associate of Park Chung-hee and a mentor to Park Geun-hye herself after her mother's assassination. The story was that Choi Tae-min had become a personal caretaker and advisor throughout Park Geun-hye's early years, and that he, like a shaman, could channel the spirit of Park's deceased mother. Their close personal relationship and the many hours they spent together behind closed doors led to juicy gossip. Choi Soon-sil went on to become a close advisor to the increasingly lonely, isolated Park Geun-hye. All these relationships would eventually unravel in 2016 to reveal bribery, extortion, shell organizations, and blacklisting involving major Korean conglomerates, with Choi Soon-sil's influence over Park Geun-hye at the center. Hundreds of thousands gathered in protest to call for Park's impeachment. Conservative and Christian groups formed an opposition, protesting in defense of their president. Eventually, Choi Soon-sil was sentenced to twenty years in prison, and Park to thirty-two years.

The unraveling of linkages of influence raised long-standing questions about the integrity of Park's person: Was she a master politician? The rightful heiress of a political dynasty? The tragic, pitiful daughter of murdered parents? An aloof princess? A selfless agent of history expressing the will of the nation? A weak, gullible target of political influence? For many, she was an intimate enigma to be characterized by any nefarious influence, shamanic or otherwise, that people could conjure up. It was ironic that she had been the public face of the Sae Maŭm (new heart-mind) movement in the 1970s, which was a kind of spiritual complement to the Sae Maŭl (new village) movement implemented by Park Chung-hee to facilitate Korea's postcolonial, postwar modernization. Park Geun-hye's own heart-mind, however, was not transparent. In the end, she was viewed not as a sincere leader or a commanding public figure but as an avatar, a puppet being controlled by her "Rasputinesque" master. Accordingly, public protests and digital media sites were awash in 2016 with likenesses of Choi, the marionettist, manipulating Park, a limp, wilted, spineless marionette.

The process of delegitimizing Park's motivations, and thereby her very person, illuminated two dimensions of suspicion that characterized Choi's influence. The first and most obvious was a classic example of corruption: wealthy, powerful players who exerted control over politicians and other officials through bribery, extortion, and institutional maneuvering. The second, and more exciting if less grounded, was the accusation of dark forces, occult personalities, and shamanistic influence.[17] Both of these charges—one secular, one spiritual—illuminate suspicions of influence that are ideologically antimodern. Both are frequently applied to new religious movements and heterodox doctrines as well as to megachurches in South Korea and their charismatic leaders. Accusations consistently tack between two kinds of corruption: fraud and superstition.[18]

The revelations about President Park involved a surprise rupture of intimacy and disintegration of the coherent, bounded person of Park Geun-hye. Unlike Billy Graham and Billy Kim's openly collaborative sermon in 1973, Park Geun-hye's speech sought to hide other authors while orienting to nefarious principals. Graham and Kim depicted an authoritative force that fused the speakers with others, incorporating the speakers into a transhistorical conduit for the movement of the Word and transforming them into composite vessels for the work the Holy Spirit. Park's failures exposed financial and spiritual corruption linked first to Choi Tae-min, through whom the spirit of Park's mother spoke, and then to Choi Soon-sil, who spoke through Park, literally, in forty-four presidential speeches. For Billy Kim and Billy Graham, the evangelical paradigm of delegation and transduction reinforced the broader ideological framing of which it was a pragmatic part. In Park Geun-hye's case, the question of outside influence was precisely what delegitimized her entire public persona. Both examples involved semiotic ruptures of bounded personhood, but to very different effect.

Conclusion In glossolalia as in evangelical oratory as in presidential speeches, the question of influence, power, and agency is highlighted as a problem that is inherent in speech. The problems of discernment that trouble practitioners of glossolalia belong to the same species of questions asked of Graham, Kim, and Park: "Who is speaking?" The difficulty of the question is magnified by the fact that glossolalia's status as speech itself is suspect. Practitioners insist that glossolalia must be language and hope to experience it as such. But as they practice it or observe it practiced, they are regularly faced with doubts about its linguistic integrity. The linguistic forms fail, the overwhelming feelings are suspicious, and the undeniable forces are called into doubt. Denotation can provide a helpful distraction to the complex pragmatics of social action taking place in speech. A focus on "what is being said" can direct attention away from asking "who is speaking." Suppress denotation, however, and we are forced to face the diffuse pragmatics of speech without the service of the uttering "I." The question of "who is speaking" can become even more persistent.

Although speaking in tongues was often idealized as a space of safety from the devil and from eavesdropping others, it was also persistently seen as a site of danger and disorientation. In these highly isolated semiotic spaces of focused interaction with deity, the prayerful could find themselves most vulnerable, most at risk. Their secrets, which they revealed freely under the shield of unintelligible syllables, could be interpreted by their neighbors if the neighbor had the gift of interpretation (which, some claimed, was only given to those who could keep a secret). The free-flowing, sonorous prayers could be revealed to be mere learned behavior. The unintelligibility and narrowed communicative space of glossolalia could produce enough semiotic isolation to cause a person to become "completely immersed in a world of one's own." And the spiritual isolation they imposed on themselves could bring them face to face with Satan.

At the heart of these concerns about glossolalia was a basic anxiety about the socio-semiotic mediation of intimacy and isolation in South Korea. On the one hand, it was through narrowed, intimate spaces of secrecy and privacy that one could repent, cleanse, draw from the well of prayer to produce intimacy with the deity, commune with creation, and feel great joy. On the other, it was precisely in these states that one was most vulnerable—to the work of Satan, to psychological pathology, to self-deception. As one person put it, when praying in tongues, it is important to "carefully examine one's own heart" (*chagi maŭm ŭl chal salp'ida*), to which he added, "I do not discount the possibility that I might be completely deceiving [*sogida*] myself."

Doubt is necessary for the production of faith. And in those very edifying spaces where faith should be most firm—the direct, intimate contact with the deity, produced by the secret speech of the spirit, and complemented by powerful, undeniable sensations and impressions—doubt can also be the most acute. In glossolalia and the fusional spiritual contact that it is thought to afford, there remains the persistent threat of deception. The sense that glossolalists had of engaging in the most intimate of relations with their deity, in the most private of spaces, in zones where the exchange of secrets should produce the security of intimacy, was accompanied by danger. And as much as people practiced glossolalia, they were often suspicious of the real nature of the forms, of the feelings that seemed abundant and incontrovertible, and of the sources or forces behind them. All three—the forms, the feelings, and the forces—were questionable and troubling for the very reasons that they were so desirable. At each stage, in each dimension, the glossolalia complex of speech behavior that is said to contain an ideological core of language, but in fact is produced at the ideological limits of language, condenses and concentrates the doubt that faith requires.

The semiotic space between opening the mouth and letting it be filled by the Holy Spirit is wide, ambiguous, and confusing. In glossolalia, doubts arise with the empirical facts of faith. The disintegration and integration of coherent speakers, along with the different ruptures and fusions of personhood, are highlighted, not resolved, by the suppression of denotation. Glossolalia operates by this logic of ambivalence. And this ambivalence extends to the promise of intimacy and isolation as both desirable and dangerous, where the threat of deception always lurks. How frightening and saddening to be suddenly alone with the evidence and to admit, even for a moment, the possibility that the source of deception might be the most familiar, intimate other of all: the self.

Conclusion

The human throat is a narrow, muscular passageway with three critical functions: breathing, swallowing, and vocalizing. Students of human evolution since Darwin have observed that the anatomy of the human throat which made possible the human capacity for speech also seems to have increased the risk of choking.[1] The evolutionary achievement of speech, afforded by a reshaped vocal tract and lowered larynx in adults, effectively wedged a sophisticated communicative apparatus between the vital functions of breathing and swallowing. The human voice bore the cultural gift of expansive, complex, communicatively mediated social life. Its price was the corporeal threat of individual death. The throat—this miraculous bidirectional conduit of intercourse between the interior and the exterior—is an open system, always subject to interference and penetration despite its anatomical mechanisms of self-containment and defense. Closure is always temporary and unsustainable; full closure is mortal.

The throat's functional trinity materializes in glossolalia as the sensations of inhaling, drinking, and the flowing of speech. Glossolalia exploits the openness of the throat, extending from the throat's functional anatomy, via speech, to the systemic openness of language itself. At the problematic core of glossolalia is the promise of language's most obvious function: denotation. Philosophical and theoretical attempts to close the linguistic system, to purify it for analysis and manipulation, have regularly tried to do so by methodologically purging linguistic features that do not obviously contribute to denotation. They have often confused language's functional uniqueness for its ontological essence. Despite glossolalia's promise of divine denotation, however, it undermines any conceit of linguistic purity. In practice, glossolalia systematically suppresses denotation, focusing pragmatic energy on language's ideological limits, and exposing as fragile any claims to language's autonomy by revealing its inseverable semiotic continuity with the plenum of the social.

For the Protestant Christians of South Korea discussed in this book, the throat anchors a whole transactional theology. Submission, praise, and evangelism are exchanged for sustenance, comfort, and empowerment. Although the New Testament serves as the central inspiration and guide to speaking in tongues, there is a line of scripture from the Old Testament that both invokes this transaction and is associated with glossolalia: "Open wide your mouth and I will fill it." This line anchors the poetics of Psalm 81, which speaks of Israel but could just as well be describing the modern covenant formed between Korean Protestants and their new deity in the twentieth century. The psalm begins with a divine ordinance for joyful singing, shouting aloud, and music making. Denotational unintelligibility marks a transition from voiced celebration to the voice of God, when the psalmist speaks of hearing an unknown language. The psalmist interprets. The voice admonishes Israel, lists her debts and past punishments, and rehearses the monotheistic commandments: "You shall have no foreign god among you; you shall not worship any god other than me. I am the Lord your God, who brought you up out of Egypt." Then comes the crucial phrase: "Open wide your mouth and I will fill it." The psalm concludes with the conditions for protection and nourishment. Those who listen and fear "would be fed with the finest of wheat; with honey from the rock I would satisfy you," while their enemies would be subdued and "their punishment would last forever." For twentieth-century Korean Protestants, grace came to be experienced as both a hard-won achievement and divine destiny. Korean Protestants quote the full psalm to emphasize the labor of faith in receiving the fullness and abundance of the spirit. And at the center of this practical theology, where prayer yields providence, the mouth is open wide.

Glossolalia's contemporary ubiquity as a cross-class, cross-denominational sociolinguistic fact of South Korean Protestantism encapsulates its own history of emergence and diffusion. The chapters of this book have told this story, from the early syncretic Full Gospel congregation at the immediate and impoverished postwar urban periphery; to the spectacular charismatic Protestant massifications that arose under authoritarianism, in the decades before the Cold War would end everywhere except for on the Korean Peninsula; to glossolalia's compulsive, if ambivalent, integration into worship among even the monied, educated, multilingual cosmopolitan Christians of the early twenty-first century. And yet the dynamic synchrony of glossolalia across congregations—the history of glossolalia that is present in the variations of and disagreements over its contemporary practice—prophesies its decline.

CONCLUSION

Despite its utility for comfort and catharsis, prestige and political power, or intimacy and privacy, speaking in tongues exposes communion with the spirit to social interruption, intervention, and confusion. Even among glossolalia's most enthusiastic practitioners, there are feelings of doubt, disappointment, deception, and disillusionment—here and there, a sense of an end to the great arc, the last ripples of a once-powerful wave.

These uncertainties do not apply to glossolalia alone. Feelings of frustration are increasingly directed at the financial self-interest of large churches, the questionable nature of pastoral authority, the suspicious motivations of church members, and the broken promises of personal prosperity that fueled much of Protestantism's growth in the twentieth century. Glossolalia condenses and exposes this broader problem: the fragility of charismatic claims to divine autonomy. But these misgivings are also a predictable effect of glossolalia itself. Glossolalia suppresses the very thing that justifies it. Its experience as language is possible only because it has removed what is fundamentally unique about language. Inspired by its own negation, it sets its own limit. What new spirit will fill the mouth when that limit is finally reached?

Acknowledgments

For some it is easy to speak about speaking in tongues. For others it is not. I am deeply grateful to all who participated in this research, shared their experiences, questioned their faith, and were honest about their doubts.

When I conducted the bulk of the ethnographic work for this book in Seoul in 2013 and 2014, I was fortunate to work with two extraordinary research assistants, Yookyeong Im and Yeon-ju Bae. Some of the discussion in chapter 5, pages 131–137, and in chapter 6, pages 153–159, draws on interviews carried out by Yookyeong and Yeon-ju. In addition to working with me and discussing the ethnographic material, both Yookyeong and Yeon-ju wrote master's theses at Seoul National University based on independent fieldwork carried out among Christian communities in Seoul (Bae 2013, Im 2015). Yookyeong continued to assist me five years later, as a PhD student in anthropology at Harvard, while I prepared this manuscript for publication: proofreading the entire document, fact-finding and -checking, and otherwise insightfully and incisively commenting on my description and analysis. Additionally, Michelle Choi and Vivien Chung, both PhD students in anthropology at Harvard, also provided helpful comments on some of the ethnographic material presented here. Sora Yang, a master's student in Regional Studies–East Asia at Harvard, helped with some of the early transcriptions of my field data. Yunhee Lee proofread the McCune–Reischauer romanization.

Angie Heo and Webb Keane read the entire manuscript and gave me crucial advice on how to improve it. Steve Caton, Constantine Nakassis, Robert Moore, Hyun Kyong Hannah Chang, Paul Manning, and Jeongsu Shin read and commented on portions of earlier drafts. I launched this project while engaged in collaborative research on urban religion in South Korea with the members of the "Seoul Lab," directed by Peter van der Veer at the Max Planck

Institute for the Study of Religious and Ethnic Diversity, including Jin-heon Jung, Juhui Judy Han, Hyun Mee Kim, and Doyoung Song. Around the same time, I was also fortunate to hone some of the key questions and formulations through spirited debate with members of my SSRC New Directions in the Study of Prayer working group from 2012 to 2014, especially Peter van der Veer, Charles Hirschkind, Tanya Luhrmann, Stephen Teiser, Fareen Parvez, and Ruth Marshall.

Michael Herzfeld once asked me about the provenance of the word *glossolalia*. Because of his question, a few footnotes' worth of investigation into early nineteenth-century German theology led to the historical essay appended to this book. Johannes Zachhuber generously responded to my email out of the blue and read and commented on a first draft of my attempt at this historical-etymological reconstruction. And at the National Humanities Center in 2016, Douglas Campbell directed me to some crucial theological resources on glossolalia and the Holy Spirit.

I am grateful for the collegiality and support of the faculty, students, and staff of both the Department of Anthropology and the Korea Institute at Harvard. The initial questions that led to this research began while I was still in graduate school at the University of Chicago, and I remain indebted to my teachers there: Michael Silverstein, Judith Farquhar, Susan Gal, and Kyeonghee Choi. Michael Silverstein died shortly before I received the page proofs for this book. It saddens me that I was not able to present him with the finished product. Michael's influence is present on every single page.

I must also acknowledge another great mentor, Nancy Abelmann, who died just as I embarked on writing this book. Her commitment to the anthropology of Korea and her insistence on clarity, coherence, and ethnographic integrity continued to guide me as I finished it.

Many people have responded over the years to both formal and informal presentations of this material with invaluable comments and questions—in particular, Chris Ball, Anya Bernstein, Niko Besnier, Lucien Brown, Antonella Bruno, Jillian Cavanaugh, Paul Chang, Sukman Chang, Zachary Chase, Lily Hope Chumley, Byung-Ho Chung, Frank Cody, Sonia Das, Erin Debenport, Carter Eckert, Andrew Eisenberg, Omri Elisha, Joseph Errington, Paja Faudree, Richard Grinker, Courtney Handman, Joseph Hankins, John Haviland, Nathan Hesselink, Jacob Hickman, Keith Howard, Miyako Inoue, Judith Irvine, Graham Jones, Hyangjin Jung, Yoonhee Kang, Laurel Kendall, Hisun Kim, Hwansoo Kim, Ig-jin Kim, Jungwon Kim, Kiho Kim, Seong-nae Kim, Sun Joo Kim, Ross King, Nayoung Aimee Kwon, Jung-Min Lee, Michael Lucey, Tom McEnaney, Janet McIntosh, Norma Mendoza-Denton, Elinor Ochs, Si Nae Park, Michael Prentice, Danilyn Rutherford, Franciscu Sedda, Bambi

Shieffelin, Clark Sorensen, Ajantha Subramanian, Nina Sylvanus, Gregory Thompson, Gregory Urban, Hahn-sok Wang, Anthony Webster, Eitan Wilf, Tristram Wolff, Kathryn Woolard, and Alexander Zahlten.

Priya Nelson at the University of Chicago Press early on encouraged me to write this book and was a source of valuable writerly and practical advice as it developed. Jenni Fry, Kyle Wagner, Dylan Montanari, and Tristan Bates expertly ushered the manuscript through final production. Do Mi Stauber prepared the index.

The inclination to write a book like this was nurtured through wide-ranging conversation in childhood and adulthood with my parents, Daniel Harkness and Harriet Hensley. I wrote the final chapters of this book in the Jakarta home of my parents-in-law, Bobby Lee and Darmawaty Yioda, whose generous hospitality allowed for much-needed concentration. The incomparable Lewis Lee Harkness was born in June 2017; I wrote much of the book with him in my arms. And the uncompromising intellectual force of Doreen Lee has had a profound effect on this book; I wrote much of it with her in mind.

Funding and Permissions

The research and writing for this book was made possible by the generous support of a Rockefeller Foundation Fellowship from the National Humanities Center; a New Directions in the Study of Prayer grant from Social Science Research Council (funded by the John Templeton Foundation); a Seoul Lab grant from the Academy of Korean Studies (funded by the South Korean Government [MEST], AKS-2011-AAA-2104), in collaboration with the Max Planck Institute for the Study of Religious and Ethnic Diversity; and a faculty grant from the Asia Center at Harvard University.

Portions of this manuscript have appeared previously in altered form as independently published articles and chapters. Chapter 1 includes excerpts from Harkness 2015c. Chapter 2 is modified from Harkness 2017a. Chapter 3 is modified from Harkness 2010. Chapter 4 is modified from Harkness 2017c. I gratefully acknowledge the permission of the Billy Graham Evangelistic Association to reproduce the photographs and film stills that appear in chapter 4.

APPENDIX

The Nineteenth-Century Invention of Glossolalia; an Etymological Reconstruction

The word *glossolalia* is curious because it does not appear in the Bible as such. It is a modern lexical invention derived from the Greek words *glossa(is)* (tongue[s], language[s]) and *lalein* (to speak), phrasal variations of which appear in the Acts of the Apostles, Paul's First Epistle to the Corinthians, and the Gospel of Mark. I am not aware of the exact person who coined it or the precise moment when it was coined. To the best of my knowledge, the word appears for the first time as *die Glossolalie* in exegetical debates among Protestant theologians and philosophers in early nineteenth-century Germany.

Prior to its coinage, it was common, as it is today, to use the verb phrase *Zungen reden* (to speak tongues), often with the prepositions *in* (in) or *mit* (with). For example, in 1794, Johann Gottfried von Herder published his late treatise on the "gift of languages" (*Gabe der Sprachen*) at the first Christian Pentecost. Throughout, Herder wrote of speaking or talking in "a tongue" or "the tongue" or "tongues," explaining:

> Mit der Zunge sprechen heißt also nach dem Ebräischen Styl nichts anders als im Affect, begeistert, kräftig, und herzlich reden.... Da die Sprache Kunst ward, ward die ganze Grammatik auf das Wort „Zunge" gebauet. Man bezeichnete mit dem Wort Zunge, Ausdruck, Redart, Formel, Wort, Bedeutung; sogar das Geschlecht, die Zahl, die Zeit, die Gattung der Worte.

> Speaking with the tongue in the Hebrew style means nothing other than, in effect, to speak excitedly, powerfully, and heartily.... As language became art, the whole grammar built upon the word *tongue*. By the word *tongue*, one denoted expression, a way of speaking, form, word, meaning; even gender, number, time, and the kind of words.[1]

For Herder, a tongue is not a linguistic code, but rather, according to his philosophy of language more generally, a whole cultural complex of verbal style and thought: "Talking in a foreign tongue means talking in foreign manners of speech [*in fremden Sprachweisen reden*]"; to say "He speaks in my tongue" is to say he speaks "in my way of speaking [*Sprachart*], according to the manner of my thought and land [*nach meiner Gedanken- und Landesweise*]."[2]

In many instances, the verb phrase *Zungen reden* was treated syntactically as a single compound noun, *das Zungenreden*. For example, Martin Luther, in *Against the Heavenly Prophets in the Matter of Images and Sacraments* ([1525] 1589, 42v), used the phrase *Zungen reden* (speaking [in] tongues). By its 1833 reprinting, the same passage (p. 204) features *Zungenreden* as a single compound word.[3] Writing aggressively against another Protestant reformer, Andreas Bodenstein von Karlstadt, Luther addressed the stubborn question, raised by Paul in his First Epistle to the Corinthians, of whether a person may speak in tongues—here, understood as a foreign language—without interpretation:

> For St. Paul writes of the office of preaching in the congregation, to which it is to listen and to learn from it, when he says: Whoever comes forward [*auftreten*], and wants to read, teach, or preach, and yet speaks in tongues [*redet doch mit Zungen*], that is, speaks Latin instead of German, or some unknown language, he is to be silent and preach to himself alone. For no one can hear it or understand it, and no one can get any benefit from it.[4]

In contrast, according to Luther, von Karlstadt

> will allow no singing or Latin words, and applies the teaching of St. Paul about speaking in tongues [*von dem Zungenreden*] not to the office of preaching alone, but to all external forms. . . . Not that I would oppose using nothing but German in the Mass, but I will not endure that someone without God's Word and out of arrogance and wantonness forbids the reading of the Latin gospel and makes sin where none exists.[5]

In the early nineteenth century, debates emerged among German theologians over the best translation and interpretation of *Zungenreden* in 1 Corinthians 14. These debates responded to a controversial thesis of the German philosopher Christoph Gottfried Bardili, published in Latin half a century earlier in 1786.[6] The thesis departed from earlier understandings by, for example, Luther or Herder, who had different ideologies of language but similarly thought of the gift of tongues as referring to earthly patterned regularities of speaking correlated with regional populations. As the Scottish Congregational minister

Ebenezer Henderson explained in a book of lectures on divine inspiration, published in 1836:

> [It] was reserved for modern times to present it under aspects totally at variance with the generally received opinion. The first who excited public notice by the novelty of his hypothesis was C. G. Bardili, of the University of Tübingen, in a small tract on the primitive signification of the word προφήτης as used by Plato, which he applies to the interpretation of the fourteenth chapter of the first epistle to the Corinthians. Conceiving that there is a difference between the phrases γλώσση λαλεῖν, "to speak with a tongue," and ἑτέραις γλώσσαις λαλεῖν, "to speak with other tongues," while he explains the latter according to the common interpretation, he considers the former to signify nothing more than the employment of the tongue as an organ of unknown sounds. The gift, which he represents to have been supernatural, excited those who possessed it to such a pitch of enthusiasm, that they were utterly deprived of consciousness; so that becoming passive instruments of the Spirit, they discoursed or prayed in loud, broken, and half articulated tones, under convulsive affections of the body, resembling those to which the heathen priests were subject, when delivering the oracles of the gods.[7]

Henderson then turned to the work of the Protestant theologian and biblical scholar Johann Gottfried Eichhorn, who, in the very first volume of his ten-volume *Allgemeine Bibliothek der Biblischen Litteratur* (initially published in 1787 and then as a series of publications thereafter), expanded and disseminated Bardili's thesis and set up the exegetical debate that would take place in the 1830s.[8] Eichhorn argued that Paul's references to *glossa* were not to language proper (*die Sprache*) but rather to the tool or instrument of speech (*das Sprachwerkzeug*)—i.e., the anatomical tongue (*die Zunge*)—and that all of Paul's references to speaking in tongues could be understood as "the habit of merely producing incomprehensible tones with the movement of the tongue."[9] He further speculated that the stand-alone use of *glossa* had, as an abbreviation of a full expression, taken on the new meaning of "sound that is unintelligible to humans," interchangeable with "speaking in a tongue" or "speaking in tongues."[10] As Henderson explained:

> The view of the subject thus advanced by Bardili was adopted by Eichhorn in his review of the work: —only with this difference, that he rejected the distinction which had been made between γλῶσσα "tongue," and γλῶσσαι "tongues"; and, agreeably to his well-known rationalistic principle, denying that there was any thing supernatural in the case, he resolved it entirely into the effects of bodily distemper, a heated imagination, or pagan habits, which many of the Corinthians had contracted, while frequenting the temples prior to their conversion to Christianity.[11]

Henderson rejected both Bardili's and Eichhorn's theses on speaking in tongues, but within his distillation of the problem we can find the attributional matrix that would shape biblical hermeneutics, theological debates, and social-scientific perspectives on speaking in tongues for the next two centuries. Along one axis was the form of "tongues": exhibiting the ideological core of language (denotation) or existing at the ideological limits of language (mere sounds). And along an intersecting axis was the function of "tongues": a supernatural, miraculous, divine charism (spiritual), or the effect of earthly, sociohistorically accountable causes (cultural-psychological). The various perduring questions of heresy and superstition, ecstasy and rationality, would be pursued along these lines.

It is no surprise, then, that the first published instance of the neologism *die Glossolalie* I have located should state:

> *Ob die Glossolalie, von welcher die Urgeschichte des Christenthums erzählt, eine natürliche oder eine übernatürliche war, ist nicht dieses Orts zu untersuchen. Vor allen Dingen bedürfte aber wohl das Thatsachliche in dieser Beziehung noch einer genauren Erforschung.*
>
> This is not the place to investigate whether the glossolalia reported in the prehistory of Christianity was natural or supernatural. Above all, the actual facts in this respect would need even more precise research.[12]

These lines were written not by a theologian, however. They were written by Wilhelm Traugott Krug, a professor of philosophy at the University of Leipzig. Krug moved to Leipzig after succeeding Immanuel Kant in the chair of logic and metaphysics at the University of Königsberg (Prussia). The passage above is the final statement in an entry titled "Glossolalie und Glossomanie," with reference to the Greek lexical sources of derivation, from the final supplement of Krug's multivolume general dictionary of the philosophical sciences published in 1829.[13]

For Krug (like Luther), *Glossolalie* meant to speak a foreign tongue, i.e., a language (rather than, perhaps, just to read one). He explained that speaking a foreign language is not to be admonished (*tadeln*) when done by necessity, but that it may develop into an infatuation or even obsession with the foreign language, such that someone finds something "better or more distinguished" (*besser oder vornehmer*) in the foreign language and applies it everywhere, no matter how poorly one speaks it. He considered *glossomanie* to be an extreme case of this and suggested that it is a form of a broader affliction with a "mania" (*die Wuth*) for the foreign, such as *Gallomanie* (Francomania) or *Unglomanie* (Anglomania). As Krug explained in the preface to the supplement, he had prepared the fifth and final volume to supply both a general register for the complete work, as well as to include completely new articles written, as before, "according to the current standpoint of science." It appears that *Glossolalie* had become worthy of inclusion in the two years between the publication of the second volume in 1827 (containing entries from *F* through *M*) and the supplement in 1829.

Krug introduced *Glossolalie* into a lexical field of related terms. Krug's original 1827 publication included related entries for "Glossen oder Glosseme" as well as "Glossonomie."[14] The former denotes words or expressions that are uncommon, strange, or foreign and require explanation. The latter is a kind of "general [*allgemeine*] grammar," also, he noted, sometimes called "Glossologie," denoting the "legislation [*Gesetzgebung*] for language" (including, for example, logic). Approximately a decade later in 1838, Krug published an additional updated encyclopedic lexicon that included a newer entry, *Glossokratie*, or the "rule by the tongue." The term denotes a political situation where orators of the people (*Volksredner*) lead the people entirely with their eloquence. Krug added that an opposite of the eloquence of *Glossokratie* is the "exuberance or impudence" (*Ausgelassenheit oder Frechheit*) of speech, called *Glossomanie*—a word that, he noted, "has been used with a different meaning" (namely the one he had assigned to it earlier).[15] He concluded the entry by directing the reader to the 1829 entry on *Glossolalie* and *Glossomanie*.

Despite Krug's hedging against theology, and despite the secular lexical field of related terms he established, *die Glossolalie* appears to be an etymological invention of the exegetical debate set up by Bardili and Eichhorn. It is likely a calque of the German compound word *das Zungenreden* or *die Zungenrede* back into Greek. As Krug noted, *-lalie* was a gloss of *die Rede*, hence the feminine article *die*. It is also the Greek root of the German verb *lallen*, meaning "to prattle, babble, or mumble." The likelihood that *Glossolalie* is a back-formation from German into Greek is further strengthened by a paper published the same year as Krug's dictionary in a new German scholarly journal, *Theologische Studien und Kritiken*, published through the University of Heidelberg, where lively debates over *Zungenreden* took place during the first decade of its existence (est. 1828).

In 1829, the theologian Friedrich Bleek at the University of Bonn, who had been a student of Friedrich Schleiermacher and August Neander, published a paper on the gift of *glossais lalein* in the first Christian church. He enumerated three possible meanings of the singular term *glossa*. The first was a *phonic* precondition of language: the tongue as a primary organ of speech. The second was the language itself and its culturally ordered *phonosonic* materialization as speech (*die Sprache*). And the third was a range of speech behaviors at the limits of linguistic intelligibility and *sonic* orientation: "uncommon, archaic, poetic, or provincial expressions."[16] Bleek added a footnote to state that there was a fourth possible meaning, "interpretation" (*auslegung, interpretatio*), but omitted it because it "does not exist in the general linguistic use (*Sprachgebrauch*)" of scripture. Bleek argued that the third of these definitions—uncommon or strange expressions—applies to *glossais lalein*. To advance this thesis, Bleek introduced the phrases *reden in Glossen* (speaking in glosses) and *Glossenredner* (glosses-speaker), replacing the plural *die Zungen* with the plural *die Glossen*. *Die Glossen* is precisely the term and, crucially, corresponds to the definition that Krug had included in his 1827 dictionary: unusual or foreign expressions. As Krug further noted, the word had long been in use also to denote the interpretation or clarification of an uncommon or foreign word.[17]

In the title of the article and throughout its pages, Bleek reproduced the original biblical phrase using the Greek alphabet (γλώσσαις λαλεῖν). After an extended discussion of the various forms of the Greek that appear in the New Testament (including the problem of singular and plural appearances of *glossa*), Bleek concluded:

> *Als der einfachste und angemessene Ausdruck muß uns* γλώσσαις λαλεῖν *erscheinen, ohne weitern Zusatz,* **in Glossen reden***, also die Formel, welche gerade auch am haüfigsten vorkommt.*

> As the simplest and most appropriate expression, γλώσσαις λαλεῖν must appear to us, without further addition, **to speak in glosses**, that is, the formula which appears to be the most frequent.[18]

The plural word *die Glossen* permitted Bleek to lexicalize his domain of inquiry, which he could discuss as a working concept—not merely a quote from scripture—and incorporate into the grammatico-syntactic processes of German. Bleek's thesis initiated a debate with theologian Herman Olshausen over the translation and definition of *glossa*, which Olshausen, contra Bleek, insisted on interpreting literally as "language" (*die Sprache*).[19] Olshausen did not adopt Bleek's use of the German word *die Glossen*.

To produce *Glossolalie* from elements of the Greek phrase *glossais lalein*, German scholars exploited the rich and scholarly sounding stock of Greek compounds built on the connecting omicron (*o*) and united them under the German morphological principle of *das Kompositum*, the compound word. Bleek's 1829 phrase, *reden in Glossen*, appears to be a transitional fossil that captures a moment in the period of back-formation from *das Zungenreden* or *die Zungenrede* into the Greek neologism. Leopold Immanuel Rückert, a theologian at the University of Jena, displayed this lexical principle in an

1836 commentary on Paul's Epistles to the Corinthians. In multiple places, he used *Glossenreden* as a single compound word, including in the context of discussing the debate between Bleek and Olshausen, to which he appended a footnote:

> *Der Ausdrücke: Glossen, Glossenreden, u. dgl. bediene ich mich hier wie schon bisher als bloßer Namen, um doch ein Wort zu haben für den Bedarf, ohne irgend etwas über den Begriff andeuten zu wollen.*
>
> [Regarding] the Expressions: *Glossen, Glossenreden,* and such I use here as before as mere names, in order to have a word for the need of not wanting to imply anything about the concept.[20]

Rückert's note indicates the necessity for a new word—a scholarly, theological term—to translate and comprehend the variations of the Greek phrase in the New Testament and, at the same time, to denote a shifting object of research and debate without imposing an existent conceptualization upon it.

In Krug's secular account of *Glossolalie* and *Glossomanie*, the author implied the phonetic resonance (but not exactly the etymological link) between the Greek *-lalie* of *Glossolalie* and the German verb *lallen* (babble, mumble, prattle). Heinrich August Wilhelm Meyer, in his critical summary of Eichhorn's thesis—that *Zungenreden* refers "merely to babble that was inarticulate and unintelligible to others"—made the connection explicit with the hyphenated phrase *Zungen-Lallen*.[21] The theologian Ferdinand Christian Baur of Tübingen also criticized it, agreeing with some of Bleek's points but also chastising him (thus siding with Olshausen) for "going too far" in thinking of *glossais lalein* as involving "a babbling of inarticulate sounds" (*ein Lallen unarticulierter Töne*).[22] Rather, Baur concluded, the desire for and practice of *Glossenreden* at Corinth had, as its condition, the mythologized, idealized miracle of *Sprachenreden*—speaking in various languages—at Pentecost.[23]

This transitional role of *reden in Glossen* and *Glossenreden* from the solidly German *reden in Zungen* to the Greek-like *Glossolalie* is displayed in the textual sequencing, and perhaps also compositional timeline, of an 1836 work by David Schulz, a professor of theology in Breslau (Wrocław, present-day Poland), on the spiritual gifts of the first Christians, focusing in particular on the gift of languages.[24] Addressed to Neander and citing Herder, Bleek, Olshausen, and many others, Schulz's commentary of nearly two hundred pages begins, on page 40, to refer to the phenomenon as *reden in Glossen*, citing the debate between Bleek and Olshausen on the proper translation of the terms. But by page 61, Schulz begins to incorporate the word *die Glossolalie*. The final chapter of the book features *die Glossolalie* in its heading.[25] The conceptual bridge that *Glossen* helped establish between *Zungenreden* and *Glossolalie* becomes explicit in the following passage from Carl Wieseler's 1838 contribution to the debate, where all three terms coexist in an unorthodox interpretation of glossolalia as barely audible utterances interpreted by the glossolalists themselves:

> Denn bestand **die Glossolalie** in einem Erguß des aufgeregten religiösen Gefühls und einer Aeußerung desselben durch leise und kaum vernehmliche Worte, Töne und Laute, so ist zuerst klar, wie Niemand weiter, als der **Zungenredner** selbst seine **Glossen** dollmetschen, dann aber auch, wie dieser, zu sehr von seinen Gefühlen beherrscht und überhaupt des Ordnens seiner Gedanken weniger mächtig, selbst zuweilen daß nicht dollmetschen konnte, was ihn in diesem ekstatischen Zustande bewegt hatte.

> For **glossolalia** existed in an outpouring of the excited religious feeling and an expression of it by quiet and barely audible words, tones, and sounds, so it is clear at first how no one else interprets his **glosses** except the **tongues-speaker** himself, and then, like him, too much dominated by his feelings and altogether less capable of organizing his thoughts, even at times unable to interpret what had moved him in this ecstatic state.[26]

Philip Schaff's 1851 history of the Christian church includes a section on speaking in tongues, with a parenthetical gloss in the first line that further highlights the structural connection of the German *Kompositum* to the Greek-derived neologism, but without the feminine gender agreement between *die Rede* and *die Glossolalie*:

> Das Reden mit anderen oder mit neuen Zungen oder einfach **das Zungenreden (Glossolalie)** ist eine der außerordentlichen Geistesgaben, welche die apostolische Kirche vor anderen Perioden mehr ruhiger und naturgemäßer Entwicklung auszeichnen.

> Speaking with other or with new tongues, or simply **speaking [in] tongues (glossolalia)**, is one of the extraordinary gifts of the Spirit, which distinguishes the apostolic church from other periods of more calm and natural development.[27]

By the 1850s, there were at least two German publications with the new word *die Glossolalie* in the title.[28] And the first sentence of an 1851 paper in French by the Swiss theologian Édouard Reuss, *La Glossolalie*, notes that, since the commencement of the nineteenth century, there had already been fifty-four dissertations in German alone published on the phenomenon of speaking in tongues mentioned in the Acts of the Apostles and Paul's First Epistle to the Corinthians.[29]

The earliest printed English appearance of *glossolalia* that I have located is from 1857, by John William Donaldson, a fellow at Trinity College, Cambridge. In a discussion of the gift of tongues, Donaldson stated that the "most satisfactory view" of glossolalia was Reuss's 1851 characterization: "not a speaking with foreign tongues, but a higher kind of inspiration, which over balanced the ordinary reason, and gave in various degrees an unintelligible exaltation to the language."[30] Similarly, Farrar, two decades later, defined glossolalia in a footnote as "the eloquence of religious transport thrilling with rapture and conviction."[31] Farrar is usually credited with popularizing the term in English. By the turn of the twentieth century, *glossolalia* was in widespread use across scholarly discourses in European languages.

This new lexicalization coincided with a rise in interest among nineteenth-century theologians regarding the relation between speaking in tongues and heightened psychological states, even ecstasy.[32] The broader modernist social-theoretical preoccupation with deviant mental states and the unruly excitement of crowds, in relation to which the coinage and new distinctively psychological definition of glossolalia would travel, was captured in the distinction made by Reverend Arthur Wright of Queens College, Cambridge, in 1898, between rival "ancient" and "modern" interpretations of tongues. The former, based on Luke, describes the gift of languages witnessed in the Acts of the Apostles. The latter, based on Paul, describes the emotional frenzy, unintelligibility, and untranslatability of speech among the Corinthians.[33] These two accounts and their interpretations structured the theological debates of the nineteenth century and continue to structure glossolalia's problematic relation to language today.

The invention of *die Glossolalie* as an etymological back-formation from German into Greek was a metalinguistic irony stimulated by two intersecting problems. The first was the pursuit of the true denotation of *glossais lalein* in the New Testament. The second was the question of whether *glossais lalein* denoted vocalizations that were, themselves, denotational. The present study has been an ethnographic investigation of what the term, two centuries after its coinage, purports to denote.

Notes

Introduction

1. Richard McClintock is credited with tracing *lorem ipsum*'s source to Cicero's *De finibus bonorum et malorum*.

2. For recent analyses of racialization and mock speech, see Chun 2009, Chun 2016, Hill 2008, and Rosa 2019.

3. As the theologian Mark Cartledge (2000) explains, there are quite a few, often contradictory, ways of interpreting references to speaking in tongues in the New Testament (especially Acts 2:4; Mark 16:17; 1 Corinthians 12:8–10; and 1 Corinthians 14:2, 13–15, 20–28; also Romans 12:6–8; and 1 Peter 4:11). For a lexicographic survey, see Harrisville 1976. For a history of glossolalia in Christianity, see Williams and Waldvogel 1975, Cutten 1927, and Shumway 1919. For recent theologies of glossolalia, see Macchia 1992, Macchia 1993, Yong 1998, Esler 1994, and Smith 2010, 123–50. Charles Sullivan's (2010–18) online "Gift of Tongues" project provides a careful collection and treatment of many sources within the ecclesiastical tradition. Despite scholarly concerns over the quality of the translation of the New International Version since its first release in 1973, I have used the NIV for Bible passages in English throughout this book, since Protestants in Korea normally use the NIV when referring to an English-language Bible.

4. See the appendix, "The Nineteenth-Century Invention of *Glossolalia*; an Etymological Reconstruction."

5. For a brief history of speaking in tongues across Christian communities, see Williams and Waldvogel 1975.

6. Farrar 1879, 99–100. Although Farrar's 1879 work is listed first in the *Oxford English Dictionary* entry for *glossolalia*, the earliest English record that I have identified is a theological essay by John William Donaldson (1857, 89–90) published more than two decades earlier. See the appendix in this volume.

7. Ko, Kang, and Cho (2019, 85) estimate that, in 2015, just under half of the population of 49,052,389 claimed a religion, including 9,675,761 Protestants, 3,890,311 Catholics, and 7,619,332 Buddhists (excluding Wŏn Buddhists). The authors admit that the amounts could be exaggerated, since these numbers were collected directly from the religious organizations themselves (98). For the self-reported membership numbers of Pentecostal churches, see *Kukmin Ilbo* 2014.

8. The most well-known of these was Mary Rumsey, who spent 1928–1939 working with local Koreans to establish Pentecostalism in Korea (I.-J. Kim 2003, 56–71). On the history of Pentecostalism in Korea, see also Yoo 1987 and Sin Ho Kim 2009.

9. For Korean Christian scholarship on the introduction of glossolalia into South Korean Protestantism, and various movements against the practice, see Bay 2006, Bay 2004, Bay 2016, and I.-J. Kim 2003. Both authors are associated with Korean Pentecostalism and view Cho's Full Gospel Theology as part of a spiritual movement in a specifically Korean context. By contrast, the Presbyterian Minjung theologian Kwangsŏn Sŏ's (1982) earlier account of the rise of glossolalia specifically, and the Holy Spirit and Revival movements in the 1960s and 1970s more generally, treats them as a kind of underdeveloped or incomplete Minjung theology, not of the politically progressive sort, but rather of a more consumerist, syncretic-shamanistic, and even "antisocial" (*pansahoejŏk*) religion of the everyday, which emphasizes the "Holy Spirit without God" (*Hananim ŏmnŭn Sŏngnyŏng*). Sŏ's account draws extensively on the writings of Cho Yonggi as well as on a master's thesis on the glossolalia "phenomenon" (*hyŏnsang*) by Yi Kwangsu (1970), a student in the Graduate School of Education at Yonsei University who surveyed practitioners of glossolalia and ministers in Seoul.

10. The question regarding how widely the gift is or should be distributed is a perennial problem for practitioners. See, e.g., Bosworth (1917) 2006.

11. Glossolalia is institutionally widespread, not exceptional among Korean Protestants. The exceptions tend to lie at the extremes of doctrinal conservatism or progressive politics. For example, glossolalia is rare within the small, doctrinally conservative Presbyterian *Kosin* subdenomination as well as among the progressive Protestant churches that have inherited the political legacy of Minjung theology and South Korea's democracy movement.

12. Although I have found that Korean speakers sometimes assume that the *pang* in *pangŏn*'s denotation of glossolalia has a Sinographic root that is different from the word for dialect, the translation as "dialect" is confirmed in the *Dictionnaire Coréen-Français* (Missions Étrangères de Paris 1880, 301, which also includes *pangŏ*, 方語), James Scarth Gale's (1897, 386) Korean-English dictionary, as well as throughout Acts and 1 Corinthians in John Ross's (1883) Korean-Han'gŭl translation of the New Testament. One usually "receives" or "prays in" *pangŏn*. The Korean translation of Acts 2:3 does portray the likeness of tongues of fire branching (*mach'i pul ŭi hyŏ chŏrŏm*) and landing upon each apostle (and, by extension, each of their tongues flickering like the red tip of single branching flame), but the metonymic tongue-as-language is not used for the unintelligible verbal behavior described later in Acts (10:46), throughout I Corinthians, or anywhere else (Korean Bible Society 1998). Paul's famous phrase, "the tongues of men and of angels" (I Corinthians 13:1) is glossed in Korean as "the dialect of people and the speech/language of angels" (*saram ŭi pangŏn kwa chŏnsa ŭi mal*). Occasionally, one encounters the word *iŏn* (from *i*, 異, different) as a Korean gloss for the term *glossolalia*.

13. The Korean word for "the gospel," *pogŭm*, is based on the characters for "blessing" (福) and "sound" (音). This is different from the loan word *kasŭp'el*, which refers specifically to gospel music. The Korean word for "bible," *Sŏnggyŏng*, is based on the characters for "holy" (聖) and "scripture" (經).

14. On early Pentecostals in the United States, see R. Anderson 1979. On the significance of the distinction between glossolalia and xenolalia for an analysis of tongues in Black Pentecostalism, see Crawley 2017, 197–250. On speaking in tongues and the pursuit of santification by women in the Church of God in Christ, see Butler 2012.

15. Samarin 1972, 227.

16. As Keane (2007, 56–58, 188–193) has pointed out, glossolalia exemplifies the coupling of two foundational paradoxes of Protestant Christianity: the necessity of dealing with materialized signs of transcendent signification, and the emphasis on sincere individual volition that is inevitably produced by socialization to action.

17. The process can be seen as a kind of exaggerated form of Brøndal's Law of Compensation (Brøndal 1940), which posits the probability of an inverse proportion between the degree of complexity and the differentiation of a linguistic category.

18. On heterglossia, see Bakhtin 1981.

19. On the relation between "voice" as a nexus of the phonic engagement with, and sonic modes of orientation within, cultural frameworks of value and "voicing" as a higher-order semiotic alignment to a recognizable perspective or social identity, see Harkness 2014.

20. On register, see Irvine 2005 and Agha 2005.

21. On primary and secondary speech genres, see Bakhtin 1986. For an important exception to the nonreplicability glossolalic utterances, see chapter 2 in this volume.

22. On the sociology of "self-talk," see Goffman 1978.

23. T. S. Lee 2010 and S.-D. Oak 2012.

24. Samarin 1972, xii.

25. Samarin 1972, 2. Samarin was also writing well before a generation of anthropologists of religion imposed what Danilyn Rutherford (2009) aptly characterized as a "no-fly zone" over belief. With Rutherford, I expect that the problem of belief in anthropology is not easily extinguished by merely banishing the lexeme. (On a similar problem with "culture," see Brightman 1995; Trouillot 2003.)

26. See Silverstein 1976. In Charles Peirce's well-known terms, a symbol is a sign relation of convention, to be distinguished from sign relations of contiguity (index) and of similarity (icon). In twentieth-century linguistics, two crucial dimensions of language (specifically, *langue* in the Saussurean mode) were elevated as unique and definitional of the medium. These are phonology, that part of language "which is composed of elements which are signifiers and yet signify nothing" (Jakobson 1978, 66–67), and syntax, which, in the Chomskyian paradigm, has been treated as autonomous and non-reducible to other planes of analysis. However, as Silverstein has repeatedly pointed out (e.g., Silverstein 2012), these "deeper" planes of analysis are discoverable, isolable, and analyzable only by first passing through (and eliminating) the denotational (semantico-referential); and, moreover, the denotational is isolable and analyzable only by first passing through (and eliminating) the pragmatics of language use (i.e., *parole* in the Saussurean mode). For much of linguistics, it is this passage from the broad domain of pragmatics into the narrower one of denotation that serves to "mark" the ideological passage into language. Metasemantics, or the denotational capacity of language to form metalinguistic equivalences, tends to serve as the exemplar of language's "true symbolic mode" and, not surprisingly, the methodological basis for much of linguistic theory.

27. Saussure (1916) 2011; cf. Benveniste (1939) 1971 and Aarsleff 1978.

28. Silverstein 1976, 54. On language ideology, see also Silverstein 1979, Woolard and Schieffelin 1994, Irvine and Gal 2000, Kroskrity 2000, Schieffelin, Woolard, and Kroskrity 1998, and Nakassis 2016. For a brief distillation of the general problem and its semiotic solution, see Harkness 2016. For a comparative account of the ideological force of the language/non-language distinction, see Inoue 2006, 37–74.

29. Samarin 1973, 85.

30. Samarin 1973, 79.

31. Samarin discussed Jakobson's (1968) structuralist theory of the phonology of child language, as well as his writings on glossolalia and poetry (Jakobson 1966).

32. Joseph 1996, Flournoy (1900) 1994, Henry (1901) 2001, Todorov (1977) 1982, Certeau 1996, Pfister 1917, and Feshchenko and Lao 2013. See also Jakobson and Waugh (1979) 2002, 214ff.

33. On nineteenth-century spiritualism and the semiotics of animation, see Manning 2018; Jones 2018, 96–114.

34. James 1896.

35. For James, Mr. Le Baron's "automatic," everyday speech processes—a socialized motor capacity analogous to what Sapir ([1927] 1949) called, through cultural lens, the "unconscious patterning of behavior in society"—were the psychological mechanism responsible for both the utterance forms and the loss of control that Mr. Le Baron felt as he uttered them. For James, the "automatism" was a "lower" psychological dimension to be contrasted with the "upper" reflective, intellectual faculties. Elsewhere, James asserted that "Beliefs are strengthened wherever automatisms corroborate them" ([1902] 2002, 369). See also Samarin 1972, 22–26, and Bateson 1975.

36. For a brilliantly simple example of how this can work, see Sapir ([1933] 1949) on "overhearing" the glottal stop in English. On the analytical difference among different levels of unintelligibility—phonological, syntactic, semantic, pragmatic—see Kuipers 2007 and Y. Kang 2007.

37. Certeau 1996, 41.

38. Certeau 2015, 142–43.

39. On the theology of glossolalia as a form of linguistic freedom, see also Poythress 1980.

40. Goodman 1972, 8.

41. See, e.g., the copula in the following statement: "Glossolalia (or 'speaking in tongues') **is** an unusual mental state that has great personal and religious meaning." This is the first sentence of the abstract of an article by Newberg et al. (2006), "The Measurement of Regional Cerebral Blood Flow during Glossolalia."

42. Samarin 1974, 209 (emphasis in original). Cf. Goodman 1972.

43. Farrar 1879, 101–2.

44. On this question for spirit mediumship, possession, and divination, see Irvine 1982a and Wirtz 2018.

Chapter One

1. See Luhrmann 2012 on the way charismatic forms of Christianity have become middle class and mainstream in the US. See K.-O. Kim 1993 on middle-class ideology and urban religiosity in Seoul.

2. On English language learning as a site of competition, value, and class aspiration, see J. S.-Y. Park and Lo 2012. See also the ethnographic accounts of the "melodrama" of class mobility expressed by Korean women like Hyejin's mother in Abelmann 2003.

3. On the discourse of Korean Christians' spiritual "abundance" among South Korean missionaries to the United States, see R. Y. Kim 2015.

4. See Chong 2008 on Korean women's description of fervent prayer as refreshing, releasing, and therapeutic, and the functional role these sensuous feelings have in the gendering of spiritual space and the re-domestication of women's labor inside the church and the home.

5. On Pentecostalism and Neoliberalism in South Korea, see Sung Gun Kim 2007. See Cumings 2005 for social-historical accounts of postwar South Korea.

6. World Bank Development Indicators, http://databank.worldbank.org/data/views/reports/tableview.aspx#.

7. T. S. Lee 2010, 88.

8. World Bank Development Indicators, http://databank.worldbank.orgfdatafviewsfreport sftableview.aspx#.

9. The common term in Korean studies for this breakneck transformation of politics, economy, and society is "compressed modernity" (K.-S. Chang 1999).

10. Jung (2012, 13) notes that there was an overall increase in the number of religious adherents during this time.

11. See Baker 2006, 283–84; Grayson 2006, 13–20; and T. S. Lee 2010, 85. Growth estimates differ widely. For example, W. G. Lee 1999 (238) found that the number of Protestant Christian church members jumped from around 625,000 in 1960 to around 3.2 million in 1970—an increase of more than 400 percent in just one decade. By contrast, Grayson (2006, 20) gives a more modest estimate of 1,900,000 adherents by the late 1960s.

12. For a critical discussion of these estimates, see J. H. J. Han 2009.

13. T. S. Lee (2010, 90) argues that intensive and extensive evangelistic campaigns from 1953 to 1988 played a "decisive role in evangelicalism's outpacing other Korean religions in this period."

14. Hyejin's criticism of her mother fits within a broader prejudice against a certain generation of middle-aged women striving for social mobility in South Korea. See H. Cho 2002 and Abelmann 2003.

15. E.g., a phonetic register such as "received pronunciation" (Agha 2003) or a lexical one such as "wine talk" (Silverstein 2006).

16. On the influence of Protestant missionaries on Korean language modernization, see King 2004. On the ambivalence of English in South Korea, see J. S.-Y. Park 2009 and J. S.-Y. Park and Lo 2012.

17. Malinowski 1935, Wirtz 2007, Wirtz 2005.

18. Bloomfield (1933) 1984, 50.

19. Along with the postwar growth of Christianity, Korea also saw the emergence of what Christian traditionalists have understood to be heretical cults or sects, which are usually presented as new forms of Protestantism, where the head pastor claims to be an incarnation of the Messiah or at least to have some personalized salvific or revelatory powers (see Jang 2004, 119–20, 132, and D. W. Kim and Bang 2019).

20. See K.-O. Kim 1998.

21. Harkness 2015c. A Catholic performer and teacher of Korean traditional music asserted to me that Protestant Christianity was self-perpetuating in part because of the way the church building materialized as evidence of a congregation's popularity and success. Once a church building goes up, the congregation must maintain it. Maintenance requires members, for which the church has to compete aggressively with other churches for recruitment. The person joked that church buildings were like cosmetic surgery, because in both cases people had to live with the durable materialization of the trend.

22. See Harkness 2015a.

23. See T. S. Lee 2006, 341, on the overgrowth of seminaries and oversupply of missionaries in South Korea.

24. For an account of this from the perspective of a Christian in Seoul in the 1960s, see Harkness 2015c.

25. On the significance of cleanliness for expressive forms in Korean Christianity, see Harkness 2014.

26. On Christian modernity elsewhere, see van der Veer 1996 and Keane 2007.

27. See T. S. Lee 2010, 111–12, for a similar statement made by a Korean preacher during the 1988 crusade, which took place the same year as South Korea hosted the summer Olympics. See also R. Y. Kim 2015.

28. See J. H. J. Han 2015a on the way Korean missionaries characterize the targets of their missions as resembling their own country's past.

29. Ha 2004, 124.

30. Kim Davis 2011.

31. E.g., Niebuhr 1929, Glock 1964, and R. Anderson 1979.

32. Sin Ho Kim 2009, 184.

33. Yoido Full Gospel Church website, http://yfgc.fgtv.com/y1/04_01.asp (accessed November 1, 2013).

34. Y. Cho 1973, 7, August 26.

35. See Schmid 2002, 122, and Ryang 1997, 151, on white clothes and a long pipe as a sign of Korean backwardness.

36. The advertisement was followed by a number of related articles, including a full testimony from Cho ("When Buddha didn't answer, Jesus did"), a profile of the Assemblies of God Deaf Orphanage in Jeonju ("They too shall know Jesus"), and a report on the work of the Christian Servicemen's Home, operated by the Assemblies of God, to help American soldiers resist the temptations of drugs, liquor, and prostitution in Korea ("An oasis in a desert of ungodliness").

37. The church experienced a growing membership as well as a growing purse of lucrative urban real estate. See Harkness 2015c.

38. In the area of corruption and scandal, Cho's church is like many other Protestant megachurches in South Korea (T. S. Lee 2010, 342–45). In February 2014, as I was conducting fieldwork in Seoul, Cho and his eldest son were convicted of embezzlement and tax evasion. For a critical Christian perspective on money in the Korean church, see G.-S. Han, Han, and Kim 2009.

39. Chong 2008, Jung 2012.

40. Bay 2006. See chapter 5 in this volume for the profound influence of Choi Jashil on Cho Yonggi. Choi Jashil cofounded the church with Cho and eventually become his mother-in-law.

41. S.-D. Oak 2012, A. Kim and Choi 2015.

42. T. S. Lee 2010.

43. See Kendall 2009 on the labeling of shamanism as superstition in South Korea. See van der Veer 2013 for comparative ethnographic examples from Mumbai and Singapore that counter the notion that cities are necessarily sites of secularization. See Stewart and Shaw 1994, 1; McIntosh 2009; and Rutherford 2002 for critical perspectives on the notion of syncretism.

44. Cox 1995, 222. As Harvie Cox writes, "To a visitor schooled in comparative religion, the worship at the Yoido Full Gospel Church bears a striking resemblance to what is ordinarily known as 'shamanism'" (224). See Cox's (1993) more celebratory account of spiritual absorption, syncretic admixtures, and localization in his paper, "Jazz and Pentecostalism." See also Yoo 1986, Yoo 1987, Jang 2004, and A. Kim and Choi 2015. For an ethnographic example of the leakiness of these categories in practice, see Kim Harvey 1987. Although the church has often been accused of syncretism, heresy, and fakery, current Pastor Young-hoon Lee called on Korean churches to unite to prevent the "wave of fakery, heresy, homosexuality, Islam, and anti-discrimination laws." He did so in the spring of 2017 after being forced to resign as Executive Director of the Christian Council of Korea due to violations of council regulations on reelection. Lee's erstwhile challenger for the office, Pastor No-a Kim, has also been labeled a heretic. Labels of heresy by more orthodox organizations are not usually applied directly to the practice of glossolalia (which

NOTES TO CHAPTER TWO 191

most certainly would apply to far too many Korean Protestants), but rather to individual churches and sects where glossolalia is part of broader ensemble of problematic doctrines and practices that contaminate it, e.g., as "unbiblical" (*pisŏnggyŏngjŏk*) or "undulating and shamanic" (*kibok musokchŏk*).

45. I.-J. Kim 2003, 198. See also Kim Harvey 1987.

46. Jang 2004.

47. On the historical precedent for this in the role of the "Bible women" or colporteurs who distributed Christian materials in the early mission period, see C. S. Chang 2008. On Choi Jashil's role in this regard in building the church, see chapter 5 as well as Choi (1978) 2010.

48. Yoo 1986, 74.

49. I.-J. Kim 2003, 23–24. This point was also made for Minjung theology, or 'people's theology,' which the 1970s was conceived as 'a development of the 'political hermeneutics" of the gospel in terms of the Korean reality' (Suh 1983, 17). On Minjung theology, see also W. Kim 2006 and P. Y. Chang 2006.

50. Y. Cho (1979) 1986, 45.

51. Y. Cho (1979) 1986, 36–42.

52. Y. Cho (1979) 1986, 131.

53. I.-J. Kim 2003, 94.

54. I.-J. Kim 2003, 194.

55. I.-J. Kim 2003, 195.

56. I.-J. Kim 2003, 209. Cho explains in multiple places that his faith and theology stem from his own experience with spiritual healing. At 18 years old, Cho, who was said to be sick and frail since childhood, was diagnosed with tuberculosis and was given three months to live. According to the story he tells in sermons and various publications, he prayed repeatedly to Buddha, but nothing happened. Then a girl from school brought him a Bible and convinced him to pray to Jesus. Shortly thereafter he was healed. He explains that this event, followed by training at the Full Gospel Theological seminary and personal experiences of glossolalia, formed the foundation for his personal theology. The theology is based on two central pillars: a fivefold gospel and a threefold blessing. The five gospels include: regeneration (through repentance and faith), the fullness of the Holy Spirit (filling Christians with power), divine healing (through prayers that remove the three sources of our ills: Satan, sin, and curses), blessings (abundance and generosity), and the advent (the second coming of Christ). The threefold blessing is intended to make the five gospels practical, resulting in health, wealth, and wellbeing (or freedom sin, both psychical and physical). As Yoo (1986) explains, the threefold blessing is based on John 1:2: "Beloved, I pray that all may go well with you and that you may be in health; I know that it is well with your soul": (a) "all may go well with you" means business or material prosperity; (b) "that you may be in health" means good health or longevity; (c) "well with your soul" means protection from evil spirits.

57. On voice, scripture, and the "problem of presence," see Engelke 2007.

58. The "full" (*ch'ungman* [充滿] repletion, abundance) in this phrase is not the "full" of the Yoido Full Gospel Church (*Yŏŭido Sun Pogŭm Kyohoe*, where *sun* [純] is "pure," "sheer," "utter").

Chapter Two

1. Chong 2008 and Yoon 2005. For a comparable non-Korean account of this genre of prayer, see Handman 2014, 178–84.

2. Blair 1910, 45.

3. Blair 1910, 47.

4. G. Lee 1907. See also H. K. H. Chang 2014, 13–63. On the place of the 1907 Revival within a longer movement of revivalism beginning in 1903, see S.-D. Oak 2012 and S.-D. Oak 2013.

5. S.-D. Oak 2012, 287–88.

6. Bay 2006, Bay 2004, and Bay 2016. See, however, chapter 5 on cofounder Choi Jashil's influence on the church specifically through glossolalia.

7. Lawless 1982 and Maltz 1985.

8. Samarin 1972, 228.

9. If the Saussurean structuralist conceptualization of signification was indebted to a chemical analogy for understanding the stable combination of signifying elements (on Saussure's "valeur" and Mendeleev's "valence," see Silverstein 2016), then glossolalia is a thoroughly alchemical semiotics in the structuralist mode.

10. Jakobson 1978, 96, invoking Saussure.

11. It is worth remembering that the negative, differential function of the phoneme formed the explicit analogy for twentieth-century structuralism, and that the conceptual fullness of the lexeme (and denotation more generally) formed the basic, if unacknowledged, analogy for twentieth-century "symbolic" anthropology.

12. Chilton 1979.

13. Another option for bypassing grammar is to take a denotationally iconic (i.e., "sound symbolic" or "mimetic") approach, which treats the vocables not as semantically empty phonemes, but rather as speech sounds that, segmentable among themselves, are already pregnant with semantico-spiritual meaning. Korean happens to have an especially rich lexical stock of denotational iconicity (Harkness 2012). See also chapter 6 on the problem of forms.

14. Duranti and Goodwin 1992, Malinowski 1935, McIntosh 2009, Tambiah 1985, and Wirtz 2007.

15. Keane 1997, 58. See also Silverstein 1981. On semiotic overdeterminacy in forms of Quaker address, see Bauman 1983, 43–62. On underdeterminacy and the problem of "meaning" in ritual, see Engelke and Tomlinson 2006.

16. Engelke 2007. On spiritual presence in semantic absence, see Tomlinson 2012.

17. See, e.g., Goodman 1972, Csordas 1990, Bialecki 2011, Luhrmann 2004, and Luhrmann 2012.

18. Sapir 1928, 74–75. Like others, Sapir relied on the concept of "intensity" to characterize the religion: "A religious sentiment" is "typically unconscious, intense, and bound up with a compulsive sense of values" (79). Also, Durkheim's theory of primitive religion, and in particular his evocative if murky notion of "collective effervescence" produced by religious ritual, rested on a concept of "intensity" as a site where members, in whatever cultural ontology of personhood, are made to feel connected to others and contiguous with the social, whatever mystical force these persons might assert that they are encountering (Durkheim [1912] 1995, 226–27 and passim). And it was precisely in response to Durkheim's use of the concept of collective "intensity" that Evans-Pritchard (1965, 1981) critiqued Durkheim for "eliciting a social fact from crowd psychology" (1965, 68; 1981, 153). For Evans-Pritchard, Durkheim had not really dealt with "intensity" as belonging to the subjective-psychological dimensions of religion. By comparison, the methodologically individualist William James (whom Durkheim called an "apologist of religion") wrote: "The essence of religious experiences, the thing by which we finally must judge them, must be that element or quality in them which we can meet nowhere else. And such a

quality will be of course most prominent and easy to notice in those religious experiences which are most one-sided, exaggerated, and intense" (James [1902] 2002, 51).

19. Samarin 1972, 227.

20. See Parmentier 1994 for a technical explanation of these Peircean categories. Some theologians (Smith 2010, Hilborn 2006) have turned to Austinian speech act theory, Gricean linguistic pragmatics, and even continental phenomenology for help justifying glossolalia as speech without having to hold it up to scrutiny as the realization of a symbolic code. The irony is that the theories of both Austin and Grice are constructed as secondary supplements to a conception of language that proceeds from the primacy of literal denotation. Entirely dependent on denotation for their existence, Austinian performativity ("doing things with words") and Gricean pragmatics (supplementing communicative meaning via "implicature" when literal denotation is not enough) have no theoretical power without it to anchor the exceptions they identify.

21. Silverstein 1976, 220. See now Silverstein 2013.

22. This example, using the allophonic rounding of the English phoneme /h/, is adapted from Sapir (1925, 37–40). Sapir compared the sound of the candle being extinguished to the phoneme /w/ at the onset of the word *when*, the allophone of which, in Sapir's time and place, would have been pre-aspirated and voiceless (hence its potential identification with the sound of blowing out a candle).

23. See Harkness 2010, 143–48, and chapters 3 and 4 in this volume.

24. See e.g., Macchia 1992 and Macchia 1993.

25. Engelke 2007, 200–204; Corten and Marshall 2001, 5.

26. On the relation of shamanism to the early Korean church, see S.-D. Oak 2013, 141–87. On shamanism and spirit possession in Korea, see Bruno 2002, Kendall 2009, Seong Nae Kim 2005, Seong Nae Kim 2018, Kim Harvey 1980, Kim Harvey 1987, and D. J. Kim 2013.

27. Whorf 1956, 83. See also Harkness 2015b.

28. Harkness 2015a.

29. Coleridge 1882, 125. It was precisely the distinction between subjective concentration and objective range that provoked Henri Bergson to assert that "intensity is quality and not quantity or magnitude"; "If magnitude, outside you, is never intensive, intensity, within you, is never magnitude. It is through having overlooked this that philosophers have been compelled to distinguish two kinds of quantity, the one extensive, the other intensive, without ever succeeding in explaining what they had in common or how the same words "increase" and "decrease" could be used for things so unlike" (Bergson 1913, 224–25).

30. I want to carefully stress, with Wataru Koyama, that my characterization is not simply "oscillating between the poles of reference-and-modalized-predication (representation) and non-referential praxeology" (Koyama 1997, 4). Both denotation and contact are "praxeological." Within the language ideology of the Word, however, there is a theological tendency to pose the propositional and the phatic as a polarity or gap that needs to be transcended (by, e.g., the work of the Holy Spirit).

31. In Charles Peirce's terms, "a virtual X (where X is a common noun) is something, not an X, which has the efficiency (*virtus*) of an X," whereas "potential" is "almost its contrary," that is, "the potential X is of the nature of X, but is without actual efficiency" (Peirce 1902, 763).

32. *Sh* corresponds to the allophonic palatalization of /s/ when followed by /i/ (i.e., [si*] becomes [ɕi]) or some semivowels (e.g., [syʌ*] becomes [ɕʌ]). Cho is known for palatalization beyond these standard phonological mutations, e.g., pronouncing *mitsŭmnida* ("believe") as *mitshŭmnida*. Cho comes from South Kyŏngsang Province, which is known among regional

variants of Korean for extensive palatalization. However, this palatalization has also developed into an identifiable shibboleth for a whole evangelical phonetic register of Korean (e.g., the intercessor discussed later in the chapter did precisely this). Some like to speculate that this enregisterment is the result of Korean Christians appropriating the evangelical authority of some American missionaries from the Southern and Midwestern states by copying their pronunciation; their "bunched" (or "molar") /r/ and more general rhotacized speech (as in the phonological trope "Amurrica") is said to have led them to palatalize /s/ when speaking in Korean.

33. Martin 1951, 525. See also Kim-Renaud 1977.

34. Some Korean-speaking listeners, noticing the frequency of aspirated consonants, a complete avoidance of tensed consonants, and an almost complete avoidance of the markedly Korean "Yin" or "dark" vowel ŏ [ʌ], likened Cho's glossolalia to a kind of faux or odd-sounding Japanese. Japanese was experienced as a language of power in the early years of Cho's church, and Japan continued for decades to be treated by Cho and other Christians as a source of demonic activity.

35. A video recording was available on YouTube (https://youtu.be/7SnqycbsjLo) but has been removed through a copyright claim by Cho Yonggi. Online discussions of Cho's glossolalia contain both praise and critical doubt, with many users simply posting the Han'gŭl shorthand for laughter (ㅋㅋ or ㅎㅎ). Others have posted their own videos in response, e.g., to espouse, explain, demonstrate, or debunk. For example, a member of Grace Road Church (*Ŭnhye ro Kyohoe*) is featured in a tearful video confessional, where she tells of her past attendance at the Yoido Full Gospel Church, her forty years of fascination with the "lie" (*kŏjinmal*) of glossolalia, and her realization that the simple syllables that are now so widespread are the "sound of demons" or "ghosts" (*kwisin ŭi sori*). Grace Road Church has been called a cult, and its founder and head pastor, Shin Ok-ju, was arrested in August 2018 for "imprisoning" (*kamgŭm hada*) approximately four hundred members on the church's compound in Fiji and forcing them to undergo ritualized collective violence as a means of exorcising demons and removing impurities (see chapter 6).

36. Some of glossolalia's sacred character leaked into the interpretation in lines 6, 8, and 9 when Cho spoke with a trilled [r] and used the archaic exclamatory verb ending *–toda* (instead of the more familiar *–kuna*).

37. In line 11, Cho's own perspective broke through into his recitation of God's message in the interpretation. Using a fixed pattern, he substituted the honorific verb *kye* (to be) and obligatory honorific infix *–si* in the phrase *sara kyesin nŭngnyŏk* (living power). God, it seems, is referring to his own "living power." Normally, a speaker does not raise oneself with honorifics, suggesting that this honorification is a momentary leakage of voicing, as Cho's personal perspective permeates the Word of God rather than the other way around.

38. The phrase *ttŭt taero* in line 12 is translated as "according to [someone's] will," whereas *ttŭt* in line 13 is glossed "meaning" according to its more common semantic equivalent. In line 12, Cho does not specify whose will is being referred to. The implication is that God is doing something for the supplicant, according to the prayerful person's will (as in answering a prayer), but it could also be an assertion of the ultimate authority of God pronouncing and acting according to divine will.

39. See Harkness 2012.

40. An audio recording for this transcript is available on the blog, *Ch'ŏn'guk ŭi yŏlsoe* (Key of Heaven), http://blog.daum.net/rks7533/198, accessed November 1, 2018.

41. Here, as in line 11 in the previous transcript, Cho's perspective as interpreter breaks through into the reported speech of the deity when he uses the honorific form *kyesida*.

42. Here again, Cho's perspective as interpreter breaks through into the reported speech of the deity when he attaches an honorific infix -si- to the verb puruda, "to call." The subject is nŏhŭi, a nonraised second person plural address, which would correspond to the nonhonorific verb form. The honorific form seems to be the accidental use of the phrase, purŭsinŭn Hananim, "God who calls" [e.g., me, you, us, etc.], which circulates in relatively fixed form.

43. Cho's wife, Pastor Kim Sŏnghye (2005), published a book of "faith essays" under the title of this line of scripture. See the conclusion to this volume for a discussion of this psalm.

44. For examples of the murky boundary between music and language, see Feld 1994, Feld and Fox 1994, Graham 1993, Monson 1996, Samuels 2004, and Faudree 2012.

45. Goffman 1979.

46. Bakhtin 1986, 163.

47. I pursue the theme of secrets, and of secrecy more generally, in chapter 6.

48. Agha 2015b and Harkness 2015b. See chapter 5.

49. Brown 2011, Wang 1990, Wang 1984, and Wang et al. 2005. For a comparative view of this dimension of language, see Agha 2007, 301–39.

50. Although I have translated chŏndosa as "evangelist" here (from the verb chŏndo hada, to missionize, evangelize), it refers to an official institutional role within the Korean Protestant church, assigned to theological graduates who have not yet been ordained as pastors.

51. For an ethnographic treatment of the Korean cultural concept of the heart-mind (*maŭm*) in the Christian context, see Harkness 2014, 201–25.

52. Harkness 2010, 151.

53. See Martin 1992, 855.

54. On this methodological and analytic approach to "ethnopoetics," see Moore 2013.

55. This could also be translated as "[You, Jesus] please earnestly desire [for our sake].

56. (?) indicates uncertain speech.

57. For comparative examples, see Feld 1994, 113, 119; and Monson 1996, 133–91. Technically, this collaborative intensification can be understood as the pragmatic-poetic layering of action, co-metricalized across multiple modalities that "intensifies features common to human activity at large" (Stasch 2011, 162). Paradoxically, this phenomenon involves both "condensation" and "redundancy" as "dialectically related processes that produce intensification of meaning as well as the decline of meaning" (Tambiah 1985, 137). The very semiotic function of ritual that produces feelings of "intensity" (in whatever modality or experiential domain) also leads to ritual involution (Yelle 2013b, 117–19). In the ritual socialization of affect, the effects of collaborative intensification are produced through intersecting planes of overt and covert communication (see Urban 1988). On the semiotics of religion, emotion, and sonic atompsheres, see Eisenlohr 2018.

58. See Ball 2014 on "dicentiztion" and the semiotics of presence via the ritual production of perceptions of contiguity and connection.

Chapter Three

1. Hebrews 4:12 and 2 Timothy 3:16–17. For the theological perspectives, see Roberts 2005, 33ff, esp. 40–43, 57–60, on metaphors for conceptualizing the Holy Spirit (e.g., as fluid), especially the fact that "To think about the spirit, you have to think materially, because, in Christian terms, the Spirit has befriended matter" (58). See also Hauerwas 2015, 32–52 and Roberts 2009. As discussed below, Korean Christians commonly personify the Holy Spirit and address the being with the honorific appellation *Sŏngnyŏngnim*.

2. See, e.g., Engelke 2007, Keane 2007, Yelle 2013b, Bialecki and Hoenes del Pinal 2011, and Yelle 2013a.

3. Boas 1887, 589.

4. OpenHeaven.com, accessed November 8, 2008.

5. The Great Faith Church (*K'ŭn Midŭm Kyhoe*) experienced a widely broadcast scandal on November 6, 2015, when one of its associate pastors was caught in a shopping center in Kangnam using a hidden camera (*molk'a*) to record women's bodies. Upon the apprehension of the "*molk'a moksa*" (hidden camera pastor) by police, the man claimed to be his own twin brother. The church was already the object of suspicion among Christians for its controversial doctrine of spiritual phenomena, gifts, and revelations. By 2014, it had been placed on watchlists and accused of heresy (*idan*) by more mainline protestant organizations due to its heterodox theology. (Earlier that same year, in March, I myself attended a prophecy training session at the church, where prophecy teams practiced receiving spiritual messages and prophesying for others. I also received a personal prophecy.) By the end of December 2015, the church had changed its name. The original Korean name of the church was K'ŭn Midŭm Kyohoe, but the English, Great Faith Church, yielded the widely used abbreviation of GFC. GFC is a simple rearrangement of the widely used abbreviation for the Yoido Full Gospel Church (Sun Pogŭm Kyohoe), FGC. Great Faith Church had attracted many members of the Yoido Full Gospel Church for the more extreme pneumatology that it offered. The new church name is Sarang hanŭn Kyohoe, the official translation for which is Beloved Church but could also be rendered "loving church" or "church that loves." The name is now strikingly similar to one of the most prominent, powerful, not to mention scandal-ridden Presbyterian Churches, Sarang ŭi Kyohoe or the Church of Love, discussed in the present chapter. Finally, on September 5, 2016, the founding pastor of the church, Byun Seung Woo (author of charmingly titled books like *Christians Going to Hell*), issued a public apology for having overemphasized spiritual gifts and phenomena and for criticizing other Korean churches and pastors. Specifically, he promised to stop using the word *kyesi* (the biblical term for "revelation") and instead to use *kkaedarŭm* (closer to "realization," "comprehension," even "enlightenment"). One of the two dominant Presbyterian denominations (T'onghap) issued an acknowledgment of Byun's apology and welcomed Sarang hanŭn Kyohoe into the broader denomination. Incidentally, the original Sarang ŭi Kyohoe, discussed in this chapter, belongs to the rival Presbyterian denomination (Haptong).

6. Jansen 2008.

7. For an ethnographic example, see Mellquist Lehto 2017. These practices are merely a recent iteration on Oral Roberts's broadcast sermons, when he would ask the audience to touch their radios or place their hands on their televisions, extending the conduit of the Holy Spirit from the human vessel, beyond the inscriptive, circulating technology of the book, to the electronic broadcast media of phonosonic and eventually visual transmission (Blanton 2015). On mediation and immediacy in worship settings, see Eisenlohr 2009.

8. For formulations of the concept of semiotic ideology, extending from language or linguistic ideology, see Parmentier 1994, 142, and Keane 2018.

9. Bauman and Briggs 1990; Silverstein 2005.

10. Silverstein 2005, 9. See Silverstein 2005, 2, 18, on the analytical danger of using terms like "circulation" or "movement" to describe interdiscursive relations between events of semiotic production, and makes clear the distinction between the text as "a completely socio-spatiotemporal entity" and the text artifact "with its 'thingy' quality of potential physical movement through

NOTES TO CHAPTER THREE 197

time and space in its own regime of circulation, for example, in the commodity form." The two pastors dealt with in this article display resistance to this distinction.

11. Bauman and Briggs (1990, 73) defined entextualization as the process of "rendering discourse extractable, of making a stretch of linguistic production into a unit—a text—that can be lifted out of its interactional setting." Silverstein and Urban (1996, 1) elaborated this definition, stating, "to turn something into a text is to seem to give it a decontextualized structure and meaning, that is, a form and meaning that are imaginable apart from the spatiotemporal and other frames in which they can be said to occur."

12. For example, on the "movement" and recontextualization of feminist discourse, see Gal 2003.

13. Bauman and Briggs 1990, 73. See also Silverstein 1996, 81–105, for an analysis of "interactional residue" alongside repeated entextualizations.

14. For a comparative ethnographic account of the concept of fire and its variant manifestations in charismatic Christian ritual in the United States, see Bialecki 2017.

15. See J. H. J. Han 2015b.

16. See, e.g., H.-H. Oak 2003 and H.-H. Oak 2006.

17. Conn 1966, 29.

18. Baker 2006, 290, and W. Kim 2006, 325.

19. On rumors and gossip among Christian communities, see chapter 5.

20. Oh used this definition of selective textual criticism to make one of his frequent attacks on homosexuality. On South Korea's Christian formations of homophobic bigotry, see J. H. J. Han 2016.

21. Oh closed this sermon with a request that the wives in the audience trust their husbands enough to fall backward into their husbands' arms, just as everyone should trust God enough to fall backward into His arms with their "whole bodies completely stiff" [onmom i wanjŏnhi ttakttakhada]. Once again, Christians' relationships with one another, with God, and, reflexively, with their "whole selves" depend on the Word. The experience of fire as evidence of healing comes in the form of Christ-like relations among Christians and is secured by spoken evidence of the movement and circulation of the Word among members of the group.

22. Baker 2006 and Grayson 2006. In 1984, Pope John Paul II canonized 103 of the estimated 10,000 who died during the Catholic executions of the nineteenth century, raising Korea's rank to fourth in the world in number of Roman Catholic saints. In 1882, Korea and the United States signed a Treaty of Amity and Trade, which protected Christian missionaries from government interference.

23. In Berlin, I have often visited a Korean restaurant called Ixthys, near Winterfeldplatz in the Schöneberg neighborhood of Berlin, which explicitly replicates this scene. The Korean owner, herself a devout and outspoken missionizing Christian, has wallpapered the entire restaurant with Bible verses handwritten in German.

24. Grayson 1999.

25. Y. Cho (1979) 1986, 90–91. On the role of "rhematic" signs—in the semiotic, not theological sense—in the decomposition of speech into glossolalia, see Harkness 2020a.

26. Y. Cho (1979) 1986, 96–97.

27. Y. Cho (1979) 1986, 105.

28. "The Blessing of the Descent of the Holy Spirit."

29. This quote comes from Cho's 1999 sermon "Hŏsang kwa silsang" [Illusion and reality].

30. Y. Cho 1995, 47. This statement was directed at entrepreneurs and others who wished to achieve material prosperity.

31. Cho, "Hŏsang kwa silsang" [Illusion and reality]. I have translated the phrase *malssŭm ŭl mit[-ta]* as "believe the Word" to parallel the adjacent verb phrases ("think" and "speak") in the sequence; however, it could also be translated as "believe in the Word," with the corresponding difference in valence in English. On the verb "to believe" (*croire* in French), see Pouillon 1982.

32. Y. Cho (1979) 1986, 81.
33. Y. Cho (1979) 1986, 81.
34. Y. Cho (1979) 1986, 67.
35. Y. Cho 1995, 69.
36. Y. Cho (1971) 1980.
37. Y. Cho 1979, 177ff.
38. Y. Cho (1979) 1986.
39. Y. Cho 1993.
40. Y. Cho (1979) 1986, 84.
41. I.-J. Kim 2003, 314–15.
42. This quote comes from Cho's 2006 sermon "Hananim ŭl midŭra" [Believe in God].
43. Y. Cho (1979) 1986, 51. See also Y. Cho 2004.

Chapter Four

1. In 1973, construction was also underway for the National Assembly building, which was completed in 1975.

2. Monitors estimated the size of the crowd by determining the density of people within rectangular sections of the asphalt plaza. See Pollack 1979, 54–62.

3. The crusade organized a training program in the nearby Full Gospel Church building (Pollack 1979, 57).

4. As they sought out an interpreter from Graham, the organizers worried that a Presbyterian preacher, while representing the largest denomination in South Korea, would "miss Graham's power" of oratory (Pollack 1979, 51). In 1973, Billy Jang Hwan Kim was not merely a self-identified Christian but also an up-and-coming Baptist preacher. Born in 1934 to a poor family, Kim received a position as a houseboy for the US military. A sergeant helped Kim move to the United States in 1951 and enroll in the Bob Jones Academy in South Carolina. Kim returned to South Korea in 1959 and became a minister at the Suwŏn Baptist Church and eventually went on to be president of the World Baptist Alliance (2000–2005). Kim's biography easily becomes a metaphor for the more general postwar, Cold War, transpacific evangelical Christian relation between the United States and South Korea. For an anthropological contextualization of some religious aspects of the Cold War at its geopolitical peripheries, including on the Korean Peninsula, see Heo and Kormina 2019. For a longer transpacific genealogy of the modern Korean voice through the singing and praying practices of early Christian converts, see H. K. H. Chang 2019, 2020.

5. Far Eastern Broadcasting Company (hereafter FEBC) 2013.
6. FEBC 2013.
7. Pollack 1979, 56.
8. Merriman 2006.
9. Billy Graham Evangelistic Association (hereafter BGEA) 1973.
10. J. B. Kim 2015, 77. Kim compared these preparations to the time and effort he spent as a youth practicing to clearly distinguish his [r] and [l] liquid consonants in order to win an English

speech contest. He also recounted the painful emotional conflict he experienced when agreeing to interpret for Graham, because of the ban his fundamentalist alma mater, the Bob Jones Academy, had placed on associating with Graham. The original Korean autobiography (J. B. Kim 2012) is written as a first-person account. The English translation is written as a third-person account.

11. BGEA 1973.
12. FEBC 2013.
13. BGEA 1973.
14. BGEA 1973.
15. Semiotic transduction, broadly conceived, takes into account the problem of indexicality and the co-constitutive processes of entextualization and contextualization, highlighting the varying degrees of contextualization implicit in all denotational texts, verbally uttered or graphically inscribed, complete or partial. See Doležel 1988 and Silverstein 2003. See also Bauman and Briggs 1990 and Silverstein and Urban 1996. For a more expansive notion of transduction across semiotic modalities, see Keane 2013.
16. In other Christian settings, the term "interpretation" (*t'ongyŏk hada*) is used to describe the act of "translating" glossolalia ("speaking in tongues") into an intelligible code. Of course, every act of translation is also an act of cultural description and interpretation. See Handman 2010 and Webster 2016.
17. On the historical emergence of the genre and its characteristic features, see Warner 2010.
18. FEBC 2013 and BGEA 1973.
19. Barthes (1957) 2012, 110.
20. Billy Graham, quoted in the *Chicago Tribune* (1955).
21. *Chicago Tribune* 1955. On the "delegation" of voice, see Keane 1991.
22. See chapter 3. On language, evangelism, and Christian cultures of circulation, see Handman 2018. On anthropological theories of translation and textual fidelity more generally, see Gal 2015 and Inoue 2018.
23. Silverstein 2005; Ball 2012, 205–6; and Tomlinson 2014. For semiotic perspectives on metaphors of movement in the analysis of culture, see B. Lee and LiPuma 2002, Silverstein 2013, and Urban 2018.
24. Keane 2007. On the problem of sincerity and affect in speech, see Irvine 1982b.
25. See, e.g., MacLochlainn 2015.
26. Harding 2000, 24.
27. Keane 2007, 216.
28. See T. S. Lee 2010.
29. Many of the largest Protestant congregations in the world are located in Seoul, and it is regularly reported that more than twenty thousand South Koreans are carrying out missions abroad (Center for the Study of Global Christianity 2013, 76; see also J. H. J. Han 2010 and J. H. J. Han 2015a).
30. Goffman 1979.
31. On chronotope and chronotopic formulations, see Bakhtin 1981 and Agha 2015a.
32. On voicing and the authoritative word, see Bakhtin 1986, 163.
33. On the poetic "metaforces" of oratory, see Silverstein 1981.
34. Kim uses the verb stem *ir*- (to lose) rather than *ij*- (to forget), which is a common lexical deviation from standard Korean.
35. Here, Kim does not technically—grammatically—complete the Korean sentence. There would normally be a quotative construction after the directive to love (*sarang hara*) followed

by a final verb. Kim's translation seems to approximate somewhat the syntactic structure of Graham's English utterance, which leaves the quoted phrase somewhat raw-sounding in Korean by not "closing" the sentence with a verb. Moreover, Kim uses the present honorific tense of the modifying verb (*chu-ta*), effectively transforming Graham's "said" into "saying." This subtle shift in voicing will be developed into an operational logic of transduction as the sermon proceeds.

36. On indexicality in gesture and linguistic deixis, see Haviland 2004 and Hanks 1992.

37. The Korean term is *panmal*, literally "half-speech," which is normatively (but not exclusively) used reciprocally among intimates or asymmetrically when directed to subordinates, inferiors, juniors, etc.

38. Honorific and deferential forms are standard for the formal address of a group, regardless of the social status of the group being addressed. However, Kim's blunt-style quotations of Jesus's command to "love one another" (*sŏro sarang hara*) suggest that a nonhonorific, nondeferential form of intimate, loving group command is also linguistically imaginable.

39. Robbins 2004b.

40. On qualia as "facts of firstness" in the Peircean idiom, see Harkness 2015d and Chumley and Harkness 2013. The crucial problem presented by qualia is their semiotics of de-signification, i.e., the way sign processes generate the experience of sensuous non-signs, which are taken to be the raw materials constituting the very character and features of experience. For a recent analytical reformulation and methodological demonstration, see Harkness 2017b and Harkness 2020b.

41. Kim pronounced the name "Eve" as *Haewa* rather than the standard *Hawa*.

42. Irvine 2005, 75. See also Agha 2005.

43. Hastings and Manning 2004.

44. See Harkness 2015a.

45. Graham uses the verb stem *karik'i-* (to point, indicate), rather than *karŭch'i-* (to teach), which is a common lexical deviation from standard Korean.

46. Barthes (1957) 2012, 111.

47. I should stress that I am not rehearsing the familiar Austinian point, which treats denotation as logically prior to the indexical processes of social action and therefore is forced to explain how a "locutionary" utterance can take on extra "illocutionary" force. Linguistic and semiotic anthropologists have long maintained that the indexical dimensions of interaction—the "neglected situation" in Goffman's terms—are logically and empirically prior to denotation. From this methodological position, they have shown not only that utterances always "do" and "perform" social things in context but also that under saturated ritual conditions like the ones described here, the semiotic values of ongoing social action can be focused, condensed, and brought to awareness by coinciding with a description of that action—in effect explicitly "saying" what they already implicitly "do." See Silverstein 1979, B. Lee 1997, Harkness 2016.

48. As discussed in n35 above, Kim's approximation of Graham's English syntax produces a technically unfinished sentence in Korean, in which the quoted utterance is left "open" or "raw," effectively contributing to the higher-order voicing transfer of the Word that is taking place through transduction of Graham's sermon into Korean by Kim.

Chapter Five

1. For a review of literature on publics, see Cody 2011.

2. See chapter 4 in this volume, as well as Warner 2010 and Bauman 2016.

3. See chapter 3 in this volume for an evangelical conceptualization of the travels of the Word across media and code. The process of public formation through print circulation was emphasized and illuminated for its political capacities in the now-classic account by B. Anderson 1983.

4. E.g., Habermas (1962) 1989. Cf. Gal and Woolard 2001, Cody 2011, and Lempert 2012.

5. On "hearsay publics" see Yeh 2017. On the relation between gossip and scandal, and the political capacities of this union, see Gluckman 1963 and Merry 1984. For ethnographic investigations into the politics of rumor and gossip, see Haviland 1977, Brenneis 1984, Besnier 2009, and Paz 2018, 111–35.

6. See Sells 1994.

7. See Esler 1994.

8. See Harkness 2015b, 500–503, as well as Labov 1966, Trudgill 1972, and Agha 2015b.

9. As in English, Korean uses the verb "to exchange" (*kyohwan hada*) or "to share" (*nanuda*), in addition to "to tell" (*mal hada, iyagi hada*) and "to disclose/to divulge" (*p'ongno hada*) to describe the management of secrets. This conception of secrecy as a mode of exchange was a central theme in Simmel's "The Secret and Secret Societies": "Every relationship between two individuals or two groups will be characterized by the ratio of secrecy that is involved in it" (1906, 462). He goes on to connect individual and group-level modes of secrecy by viewing the complementary functions of social relation-internal "intimacy" and social relation-external "exclusion." He further develops this in the essay "The Quantitative Determination of the Group," where he writes that the groups, like interpersonal dyads, "easily make their specific content, that is shared only by the members, not by outsiders, their center and real fulfillment. Here we have the form of intimacy" (Simmel [1908] 1950, 126). However, he provides an important qualification: "The reciprocal knowledge, which is the positive condition of social relationships, is not the sole condition. On the contrary, such as those relationships are, they actually presuppose also a certain nescience, a ratio, that is immeasurably variable to be sure, of reciprocal concealment" (Simmel 1906, 448). For ethnographic and programmatic accounts of secrecy in anthropology, see Jones 2014. For recent ethnographic analyses that examine the role of secrecy in producing social groups by policing communicative boundaries, see Debenport 2015; Heo 2013; Herzfeld 2009; D. Lee 2016, 25–56; and Piliavsky 2011.

10. Choi (1978) 2010, 322.

11. On Yi Sŏngbong, see S. Chŏng 1986, 165–72.

12. Choi (1978) 2010, 83.

13. Choi 2009, 102, and Choi (1978) 2010, 92.

14. On the role of prayer mountains as a first "back door" of Pentecostal spirituality in postwar South Korea, see Ma 2014.

15. In 1969, this would have meant that the church had the equivalent of only $3,470.28 USD toward a project estimated to cost $2,776,224 USD. In contemporary dollars, it would be roughly $24 thousand toward a cost of about $19.5 million. Y. Cho ([1979] 1986, 131–51) gives an account of the role of boldness of faith, forcefulness of speech, and thinking in terms of miracles in managing the questionable financing for the construction of the Yoido Full Gospel Church.

16. Choi (1978) 2010, 361.

17. Choi 2009, 355. Emphasis mine.

18. These various derivations of *morŭda* to describe secrecy often appear in literature or song lyrics, e.g., the pop song "*mollae mollae*" by Kpop group I.B.I., or the Korean translation of the tenor aria "Una Furtiva Lagrima" (a furtive tear) from Donizetti's *L'elesir d'amore* as *Nammollae hŭrŭnŭn nunmul*. The Korean coinage, *molk'a*, for a hidden camera, is a combination of

mollae and *k'amera* (see chapter 3, n5, above). The recent discovery of widespread *molk'a* planted in bathrooms and bedrooms throughout Seoul has catalyzed awareness campaigns to protect women's privacy.

19. *Ŭnmilhada* is used to translate Mathew 6:6 into Korean: "But when you pray, go into your room, close the door and pray to your Father, who is unseen. Then your Father, who sees what is done **in secret**, will reward you."

20. On the difficult linguistic problem of defining the very category of the adjective in Korean, see M.-J. Kim 2002.

21. The analysis in this section draws in part on interviews conducted by Yookyeong Im and Yeon-ju Bae in Seoul in 2013 and 2014.

22. Again, e.g., see Simmel 1906: "Secrecy is a universal sociological form, which, as such, has, nothing to do with the moral valuations of its contents. On the one hand, secrecy may embrace the highest values: the refined shame of the lofty spirit, which covers up precisely its best, that it may not seem to seek its reward in praise or wage; for after such payment one retains the reward, but no longer the real value itself. On the other hand, secrecy is not in immediate interdependence with evil, but evil with secrecy" (463).

23. For accounts by Korean American college students about social surveillance and control in Korean churches in the United States, see Abelmann 2009. This feeling of surveillance is continuous with both the explicit forms of state surveillance (*kamsi*) and monitoring (e.g., CCTV) that are the legacy of the cold war military dictatorship, as well as the more subtle everyday cultural forms of consciousness about being observed and judged, which are made explicit in terminologized cultural concepts like *ch'emyŏn* (face) or *nunch'i* (the awareness of, social sensitivity to, and ability to anticipate and adapt to others' moods, desires, and presuppositions about social roles and relations).

24. See Goffman 2009.

25. On the banality of confession, which revolves around reports of anger as sin, see Robbins 2004a, 232–46.

26. The seminarian was a student at the Presbyterian University and Theological Seminary (*Changnohoe Sinhak Taehakkyo*), a prominent seminary that emerged from the missionary education efforts of the missionary Samuel Moffett in 1901.

27. See chapter 6, where the danger of glossolalia is compared to the danger of a knife, not to be placed in the hands of a child.

28. Many churches encouraged their congregants to pray for Lee Myung Bak (in office 2008–2013), Park's conservative Christian presidential predecessor and elder at Somang Presbyterian Church. See Harkness 2014, 48–79.

29. E.g., "*Midŭl su innŭn saram*" or "*silloe hal su innŭn saram.*" The Korean gloss for the English word *faith* is usually *sinang*.

30. On Protestant suspicion of repetition, see Yelle 2013a. The combination of participation and withholding at play in group prayer, and the careful attempts to control what is allowed to circulate and what is kept out of circulation, bear a resemblance to enhanced personal forms of value created through processes of "keeping while giving" in the exchange strategies described by Weiner 1994. See Chumley 2016, 126–51, for a contrastive account of the value of semiotic ambiguity and functional gradients of conventional meaning for pedagogies of personal "creativity" in Chinese Art Schools.

31. Pastor Chŏng Wŏn, founder of Heaven Church (*Hebŭn Kyohoe*), published a series of books titled "Crying Out Prayer" (*Purŭjinnŭn Kido*), which encouraged and justified loud, rapid,

fervent prayer as the privileged method for bringing individuals closer the deity and bringing "heat" and revival to Korean churches (W. Chŏng 2005). The books stress the primacy of the Korean church's tradition of t'ongsŏng kido, prioritize the production of powerful vocal sounds over specific utterances, and, like the informants in this chapter, chart the direct practical continuity between "crying aloud prayer" and glossolalia (developed in W. Chŏng 2012). Like other churches of this sort, Heaven Church and its founder have regularly been accused of heresy (*idan*).

32. In fact, such words would fit well within Paul Feine's (1908) detailed encyclopedia entry in German, which defines glossolalia as ecstatic speech that is organized in a hierarchy from sighing, groaning, exalting, yelling, and babbling to incoherent and strange words (e.g., Abba, Hosanna, Hallelujah, Maranatha) to coherent speech in strange-sounding rejoicing words which make the impression of rapturous prayer and "psalmodic" glorification of God.

33. She also described the prayer style that was encouraged for fervent group worship as praying with the "feeling of metal." With the loan word *met'al*, she was referring to the rapid, strident genre of rock music, but it is worth noting that the "metallic" or "iron" voice (*chŏlsŏng*), along with the "husky" voice (*surisŏng*), is a core aesthetic technique of the Korean sung performance genre *p'ansori* (C. E. Park 2003, 192; cf. Harkness 2014).

34. Paul Grice's ([1968] 1989) maxims of conversation, based on what he called the "cooperative principle," include quantity, quality, relation, and manner. For an ethnographically based critique, see Ochs 1976.

35. On tie signs, see Goffman 1971.

36. They used the English loan word *p'ŭraibŏsi*. Whereas *p'ŭraibŏsi* has a connotation closer to "security" (e.g., one must ensure privacy in public bathrooms, for bank accounts, etc.), the terms for privacy derived from the sinographic character *sa* (私) tend toward the legal (e.g., private property, private school, nonstate enterprises, etc.) or the personal, even sensitive, which, in Korean, can suggest secretive, even shameful or illicit activities (e.g., the kinds of things one does in private but not in public). For a semiotic treatment of the public/private distinction, see Gal 2005.

37. See Harkness 2015a.

Chapter Six

1. From the gospel song, "In the Garden," composed by Charles Austin Miles in 1912.

2. The term *kŭlcha* can refer to individual letters or to a syllabic block. Both *nim* (님) and *nam* (남) are words formed from a single syllabic block, differing by a single stroke or "dot." The line is from the Korean popular song, "*Toronam*," composed by Cho Unp'a. After a career as a popular song writer (and after he composed this song), Cho converted to Christianity and eventually became a deacon at *Sarang ŭi Kyohoe*, the Church of Love.

3. Different rooms, called *chamosil*, are designed for parents and their children to worship together.

4. In more technical semiotic terms, this is a process of identifying, characterizing, and classifying qualia as "facts of firstness" according to lexicalized qualisigns that are themselves structured according to higher-order frameworks of value (see Harkness 2017b, 2020a, 2020b).

5. For a striking parallel in the literature on witchcraft in various African contexts, where sites of trust and intimacy are also the most threatening, see Geschiere 2013.

6. See chapter 2, n50, on the meaning of *chŏndosa* in the Korean church.

7. The *kwŏnsa* position is specific to Korean churches, where women traditionally were not allowed to become elders (*changno*). The *kwŏnsa* or "exhorting deaconess" is an honorary,

nonordained position, often without specific institutional responsibilities, assigned to older women within the church. The term "exhorter," of which *kwŏnsa* is a Korean gloss, was originally a Methodist term for "lay preachers," now called "lay speakers," who evangelized, encouraged, and admonished but were not ordained (see Brekus 1998).

8. The analysis in this section draws in part on interviews conducted by Yookyeong Im and Yeon-ju Bae in Seoul in 2013 and 2014.

9. J. Kang 2012, 212.

10. J. Kang 2012, 213–16.

11. On discernment, emotion, and the semiotics of feeling in glossolalia see Harkness 2020a.

12. Cf. Cartledge 2002 on beauty as a desirable feature of glossolalia.

13. See Taves 1999.

14. The full name of the church is New Heaven and Earth, Church of Jesus, the Temple of the Tabernacle of the Testimony (Sinchŏnji Yesugyo Chŭnggŏjangmaksŏngjŏn). The church gained special notoriety in 2020 when the COVID-19 pandemic in South Korea was exacerbated by the rapid spread of the virus among church members in Daegu.

15. T. Kim 2016.

16. H. Kim 2017.

17. Doucette 2017 and S. Park 2017.

18. On charges of fraud and superstition leveled against shamanic practice in South Korea, especially as it relates to the economics of ritual and the transactional aspects of spiritual practice, see Kendall 2009 and Yun 2019.

Conclusion

1. Darwin 1859, 191, Lieberman 2007, Manning 2012, 1–2.

Appendix

1. von Herder 1794, 63–64.

2. von Herder 1794, 64–65.

3. The exact phrase was "Auch verstehet der Narr St. Pauli Wort nicht recht, da er von Zungenreden schreibt"; "Also the fool does not understand St. Paul's words correctly when he writes of speaking [in] tongues (1 Cor. 14[:2–29]) (Luther [1525] 2015, 101). On Luther's, Calvin's, and early Anabaptists' perspectives on tongues, see Williams and Waldvogel 1975, 70–75.

4. Luther (1525) 2015, 101.

5. Luther (1525) 2015, 101.

6. Bardili 1786.

7. Henderson 1836, 184–85.

8. Eichhorn 1787.

9. Eichhorn 1790: "Die Gewohnheit . . . bloß mit Bewegung der Zunge unverständliche Töne hervorzustoßen" (800).

10. Eichhorn 1790: "Die Bedeutung eines für Menschen unverständlichen Schalles" (801).

11. Henderson 1836, 185–86.

12. Krug 1829, 114 (German spelling in original).

13. In the same dictionary, Krug would also contribute to other now-naturalized lexical forms corresponding to foundational concepts in religion. As Johannes Zachhuber (2018)

explains in his account of the emergence and establishment of the duality of "transcendence" and "immanence" in nineteenth-century German theology and philosophy, Krug, a Kantian, laid out an early conceptual distinction between and coupling of immanence as that which can be known through reason and transcendence as that which surpasses the limits of reason. Like *die Glossolalie*, this conceptual binary motivated theological and philosophical debates in the 1830s and became entrenched by the 1840s, eventually shaping commitments to religious and secular epistemologies for the nearly two centuries, i.e., to the present.

14. Krug 1827, 260–61.

15. Krug 1838, 473.

16. Bleek 1829, 4. On the translation of *glossa*, cf. Cartledge 2000, Turner 2006.

17. See Grimm and Grimm (1854–1961) 1971.

18. Bleek 1829, 44.

19. See Olshausen 1829 and Olshausen 1830. In Bleek's (1830) response to Oslhausen, Bleek also uses the phrase *in einem Glossematischen Reden* (49). "Glossematics" was the name of a twentieth-century mode of structuralist analysis (Hjelmslev and Uldall 1957).

20. Rückert 1836, 356.

21. "Ein *unarticulirtes und für andere unverständliches Lallen*" (Meyer 1835, 154; emphasis in original).

22. Baur 1838, 693.

23. Baur 1838, 698–702.

24. Schulz 1836.

25. "Übersetzung und kurze Erläuterung der die Glossolalie betreffenden Stellen" (Translation and Brief Explanation of the [New Testament] Sections relating to Glossolalia) (Schulz 1836, 162–89).

26. Wieseler 1838, 733.

27. Schaff 1851, 134–39. Schaff's discussion of glossolalia includes an explicit rejection of Bleek's theory with the statement that "language" is grammatically the simplest and most common meaning for the word *Glosse*.

28. Hilgenfeld 1850 and Maier 1855.

29. Reuss 1851, 65.

30. Donaldson 1857, 89–90.

31. Farrar 1879, 101n2.

32. Just around the time the word *die Glossolalie* emerged and spread in German theological discourse, sensational reports were circulating in Europe of the ecstatic gatherings and miraculous gifts of tongues and prophecy among the followers of Scottish Reverend Edward Irving (1832a, 1832b, 1832c), which carried over into the establishment of the Catholic Apostolic Church. Ernst Adolf Rossteuscher, an ordained member of the Catholic Apostolic Church, produced a study of the gift of languages in the Apostolic era, which includes a sustained treatment of the relation between *Glossen* and *Glossolalie* (Rossteuscher 1850). All of this lends support to Charles Sullivan's claim that the emphasis on ecstasy and trance in glossolalia is largely the product of the late eighteenth and nineteenth centuries, before which time "critical debates focused on whether it was a miracle of hearing or speaking, or whether the language constructed itself in the mind or converted at the last moment on the lips" (Sullivan 2010–2018, https://charlesasullivan.com/1896/introduction-history-glossolalia/).

33. Wright 1898, 277–302. Wright also insisted that "we have no scriptural warrant for the contrast between the gift of Pentecost and the confusion of Babel" (278; cf. Macchia 2006).

Bibliography

Aarsleff, Hans. 1978. "Taine and Saussure." *Yale Review* 68 (1): 71–81.
Abelmann, Nancy. 2003. *Melodrama of Mobility: Women, Talk, and Class in Contemporary South Korea.* Honolulu: University of Hawai'i Press.
Abelmann, Nancy. 2009. *The Intimate University: Korean American Students and the Problems of Segregation.* Durham, NC: Duke University Press.
Agha, Asif. 2003. "The Social Life of Cultural Value." *Language & Communciation* 23:231–73.
———. 2005. "Voice, Footing, Enregisterment." *Journal of Linguistic Anthropology* 15 (1): 38–59.
———. 2007. *Language and Social Relations.* Cambridge: Cambridge University Press.
———. 2015a. "Chronotopic Formulations in Kinship Behavior and History." *Anthropological Quarterly* 88 (2): 401–15.
———. 2015b. "Tropes of Slang." *Signs and Society* 3 (2): 306–30.
Anderson, Benedict R. O'G. 1983. *Imagined Communities: Reflections on the Origin and Spread of Nationalism.* London: Verso.
Anderson, Robert M. 1979. *Vision of the Disinherited: The Making of American Pentecostalism.* Peabody, MA: Hendrickson.
Bae, Yeon-ju. 2013. "'Hananim Malssŭm e sunjong hasipsio': Han'guk Kyohoe esŏ ŭi ŏnŏ sayong yuhyŏng mit kach'igwan" ["Obey God's words"]: Patterns and values of speaking in a Korean Protestant church]. Master's thesis, Department of Anthropology, Seoul National University.
Baker, Donald. 2006. "Sibling Rivalry in Twentieth-Century Korea: Comparative Growth Rates of Catholic and Protestant Communities." In *Christianity in Korea*, edited by Robert E. Buswell and Timothy S. Lee, 283–308. Honolulu: University of Hawai'i Press.
Bakhtin, Mikhail M. 1981. *The Dialogic Imagination: Four Essays.* Austin: University of Texas Press.
———. 1986. *Speech Genres and Other Late Essays.* Translated by Vern W. McGee. Austin: University of Texas Press.
Ball, Christopher. 2012. "Boasian Legacies in Linguistic Anthropology: A Centenary Review of 2011." *American Anthropologist* 114 (2): 203–16.
———. 2014. "On Dicentization." *Journal of Linguistic Anthropology* 24 (2): 151–73.
Bardili, Christoph Gottfried. 1786. *Significatus primitivus vocis προφήτης ex Platone erutus, cum novo tentamine interpretandi I. Cor. Cap. XIV.* Gottinga: I. C. Dieterich.

Barthes, Roland. (1957) 2012. "Billy Graham at the Vel' d'Hiv." In *Mythologies*, 109–15. New York: Hill and Wang.

Bateson, Gregory. 1975. "Some Components of Socialization for Trance." *Ethos* 3 (2):143–55.

Bauman, Richard. 1983. *Let Your Words Be Few: Symbolism and Silence among Seventeenth-Century Quakers*. Cambridge: Cambridge University Press.

———. 2016. "Projecting Presence: Aura and Oratory in William Jennings Bryan's Presidential Races." In *Scale: Discourses and Dimensions of Social Life*, edited by E. Summerson Carr and Michael Lempert, 25–51. Berkeley: University of California Press.

Bauman, Richard, and Charles Briggs. 1990. "Poetics and Performance as Critical Perspectives on Language and Social Life." *Annual Review of Anthropology* 19:59–88.

Baur, Ferdinand Christian. 1838. "Kritische Übersicht über die neuesten, das γλώσσαις λαλεῖν [Glossais Lalein] in der estern christlichen Kirche betreffenden Untersuchungen (mit besonderer Rücksicht auf der Schrift: die Geistesgaben der ersten Christen, insbesondere die sogennante Gabe der Sprachen. Eine exegetische Entwicklung von Dr. David Schulz. Breslau 1836." *Theologische Studien und Kritiken* 11 (3): 618–702.

Bay, Bonjour [Bae Bon Chul]. 2004. "Han'guk kyohoesa sok ŭi pangŏn munje" [The problem of speaking in tongues in Korean church history]. *Hanse Sŏn'gyŏl Sinhak Nondan* 1:31–50.

———. 2006. "Glossolalia in Korean Christianity: An Historical Survey." *Evangelical Review of Theology* 30 (3): 237–48.

———. 2016. "Yŏngsan Cho Yong-gi Moksa ŭi sŏngnyŏng serye kyori: 1970–80—yŏndae Han'guk kyohoe sŏngnyŏngnon nonjaeng ŭi p'yojŏk" [Spirit baptism of Rev. David Yonggi Cho: Target of the pneumatological controversy in 1970–80s Korean Christianity]. *Yŏngsan Journal of Theology (Yŏngsan Sinhak Chŏnŏl)* 36:7–50.

Benveniste, Émile. (1939) 1971. "The Nature of the Linguistic Sign." In *Problems in General Linguistics*, 43–48. Coral Gables, FL: University of Miami Press.

Bergson, Henri. 1913. *Time and Free Will: An Essay on the Immediate Data of Consciousness*. Translated by F. L. Pogson. London: George Allen.

Besnier, Niko. 2009. *Gossip and the Everyday Production of Politics*. Honolulu: University of Hawai'i Press.

BGEA (Billy Graham Evangelistic Association). 1973. Billy Graham Crusade in Seoul, South Korea, 1973. Charlotte, NC: Billy Graham Evangelistic Association.

Bialecki, Jon. 2011. "No Caller ID for the Soul: Demonization, Charisms, and the Unstable Subject of Protestant Language Ideology." *Anthropological Quarterly* 84 (3): 679–704.

———. 2017. *A Diagram for Fire: Miracles and Variation in an American Charismatic Movement*. Berkeley, CA: University of California Press.

Bialecki, Jon, and Eric Hoenes del Pinal. 2011. "Beyond Logos: Extensions of the Language Ideology Paradigm in the Study of Global Christianity(-ies)." *Anthropological Quarterly* 84 (3): 575–94.

Blair, William Newton. 1910. *The Korea Pentecost: And Other Experiences on the Mission Field*. New York: Board of Foreign Missions of the Presbyterian Church in the U.S.A.

Blanton, Anderson. 2015. *Hittin' the Prayer Bones: Materiality of Spirit in the Pentecostal South*. Chapel Hill: University of North Carolina Press.

Bleek, Friedrich. 1829. "Über die Gabe des γλώσσαις λαλεῖν [Glossais Lalein] in der Ersten Christlichen Kirche." *Theologische Studien und Kritiken* 2:3–79.

———. 1830. "Noch ein paar Worte über die Gabe des γλώσσαις λαλεῖν [Glossais Lalein]." *Theologische Studien und Kritiken* 3:45–64.

Bloomfield, Leonard. (1933) 1984. *Language*. Chicago: University of Chicago Press.
Boas, Franz. 1887. "Museums of Ethnology and their Classification." *Science* 9 (228): 587–89.
Bosworth, Fred Francis. (1917) 2006. "Do All Speak in Tongues?" In *A Reader in Pentecostal Theology: Voices from the First Generation*, edited by Douglas Jacobsen, 137–48. Bloomington: Indiana University Press.
Brekus, Catherine. 1998. *Strangers and Pilgrims: Female Preaching in America, 1740–1845*. Chapel Hill: University of North Carolina Press.
Brenneis, Donald. 1984. "Grog and Gossip in Bhatgaon: Style and Substance in Fiji Indian Conversation." *American Ethnologist* 11 (3): 487–506.
Brightman, Robert. 1995. "Forget Culture: Replacement, Transcendance, Relexification." *Cultural Anthropology* 10 (4): 509–46.
Brøndal, Viggo. 1940. "Compensation et Variation: Deux Principes de Linguistique Générale." *Scientia* 61:101–9.
Brown, Lucien. 2011. *Korean Honorifics and Politeness in Second Language Learning*. Philadelphia: John Benjamins.
Bruno, Antonetta Lucia. 2002. *The Gate of Words: Language in the Rituals of Korean Shamans*. Leiden: Research School of Asian, African, and Amerindian Studies, Universiteit Leiden.
Butler, Anthea. 2012. *Women in the Church of God in Christ: Making a Sanctified World*. Chapel Hill: University of North Carolina Press.
Cartledge, Mark J. 2000. "The Nature and Function of New Testament Glossolalia." *The Evangelical Quarterly* 72 (2): 135–50.
———. 2002. *Charismatic Glossolalia: An Empirical-Theological Study*. Burlington, VT: Ashgate.
Center for the Study of Global Christianity. 2013. *Christianity in Its Global Context, 1970–2020: Society, Religion, and Mission*. South Hampton, MA: Gordon-Conwell Theological Seminary.
Certeau, Michel de. 1996. "Vocal Utopias: Glossolalias." *Representations* 56: 29–47.
———. 2015. *The Sixteenth and Seventeenth Centuries*. Vol. 2 of *The Mystic Fable*, translated by Michael B. Smith and edited by Luce Giard. Chicago: University of Chicago Press.
Chang, Christine Sungjin. 2008. "Hidden but Real: The Vital Contribution of Biblewomen to the Rapid Growth of Korean Protestantism, 1892–1945." *Women's History Review* 17 (4): 575–95.
Chang, Hyun Kyong Hannah. 2014. "Musical Encounters in Korean Christianity: A Trans-Pacific Narrative." PhD diss., Department of Music, University of California, Los Angeles.
———. 2019. "Singing and Praying among Korean Christian Converts (1896–1915): A Trans-Pacific Genealogy of the Modern Korean Voice." In *The Oxford Handbook of Voice Studies*, edited by Nina Sun Eidsheim and Kaktherine Meizel, 457–74. New York: Oxford University Press.
———. 2020. "A Fugitive Christian Public: Singing, Sentiment, and Socialization in Colonial Korea." *Journal of Korean Studies* 25 (2) 291–323.
Chang, Kyung-Sup. 1999. "Compressed Modernity and Its Discontents: South Korean Society in Transition." *Economy and Society* 28 (1): 30–55.
Chang, Paul Y. 2006. "Carrying the Torch in the Darkest Hours: the Socio-Political Origins of Minjung Protestant Movements." In *Christianity in Korea*, edited by Robert Buswell Jr. and Timothy Lee, 195–220. Honolulu: University of Hawai'i Press.
Chicago Tribune. 1955. "Interpreted, Billy Graham Wins One of 13." *Chicago Tribune*, June 6, 2. http://archives.chicagotribune.com/1955/06/06/page/2/article/display-ad-56-no-title.
Chilton, Paul. 1979. "The Sounds and Sound-Changes of Pseudolanguage: A Case Study." *Anthropological Linguistics* 21 (3): 124–46.

Cho, Haejoang. 2002. "Living with Conflicting Subjectivies: Mother, Motherly Wife, and Sexy Woman in the Transition from Colonial-Modern to Postmodern Korea." In *Under Construction: The Gendering of Modernity, Class, and Consumption in the Republic of Korea*, edited by Laurell Kendall, 165–95. Honolulu: University of Hawai'i Press.

Cho, Yonggi. 1973. "Pray for Korea." *Pentecostal Evangel*, August 26, 7.

———. (1971) 1980. *Sŏngnyŏngnon* [Pneumatology]. Seoul: Sŏul Sŏjŏk.

———. (1979) 1986. *The Fourth Dimension*. Vol. 1. Gainesville, FL: Bridge-Logos.

———. 1979. *Sun pogŭm ŭi chilli* [The truth of full gospel]. 2 vols. Seoul: Yŏngsan Ch'ulp'ansa.

———. 1993. *Dr. Cho's Patterns of Prayer*. Seoul: Seoul Book Center.

———. 1995. *Great Business Men*. Seoul: Seoul Book Publishing Company.

———. 2004. *3-ch'awŏn ŭi insaeng ŭl chibae hanŭn 4-ch'awŏn ŭi yŏngsŏng: '4-ch'awŏn ŭi yŏngjŏk segye' chŏgyong p'yŏn* [The fourth-dimensional spirituality that controls the three-dimensional life: Application of the world of the fourth-dimensional spirituality]. Seoul: Kyohoe Sŏngjang Yŏn'guso.

Choi, Jashil [Ch'oe, Cha-sil]. 2009. *Hallelujah Lady*. Translated by Jonny Neung H. Lee and Junhee Kim. Seoul: KIATS Press.

———. (1978) 2010. *Na nŭn Hallelluya Ajumma yŏtta* [I was the Hallelujah Lady]. Seoul: Sŏul Malssŭmsa.

Chong, Kelly. 2008. *Deliverance and Submission: Evangelical Women and the Negotiation of Patriarchy in South Korea*. Cambridge: Harvard University Press.

Chŏng, Sŏng-gu. 1986. *Han'guk kyohoe sŏlgyosa* [A history of preaching in the Korean church]. Seoul: Ch'ongsin Taehak Ch'ulp'ansa.

Chŏng, Wŏn. 2005. *Hanŭl ŭi kwŏnnŭng i imhanŭn purŭjinnŭn kido* [Crying aloud prayer which makes the power of heaven present]. Vol. 1. Seoul: Yŏngsŏng ŭi Sup

———. 2012. *Pangŏn kido ŭi ŭnhye wa nŭngnyŏk* [The grace and power of praying in tongues]. Vol. 1. Seoul: Yŏngsŏng ŭi Sup.

Chumley, Lily Hope. 2016. *Creativity Class: Art School and Culture Work in Postsocialist China*. Princeton: Princeton University Press.

Chumley, Lily Hope, and Nicholas Harkness. 2013. "Introduction: QUALIA." *Anthropological Theory* 13 (1/2): 3–11.

Chun, Elaine. 2009. "Ideologies of Legitimate Mockery: Margaret Cho's Revoicings of Mock Asian." In *Beyond Yellow English: Toward a Linguistic Anthropology of Asian Pacific America*, edited by Angela Reyes and Adrienne Lo, 261–87. Oxford: Oxford University Press.

———. 2016. "The Meaning of Ching-Chong: Language, Racism, and Response in New Media." In *Raciolinguistics: How Language Shapes Our Ideas about Race*, edited by H. Samy Alim, John R. Rickford, and Arnetha F. Ball, 81–96. New York: Oxford University Press.

Cody, Francis. 2011. "Publics and Politics." *Annual Review of Anthropology* 40:37–52.

Coleridge, Samuel Taylor. 1882. "Coleridge Marginalia, Hitherto Unpublished." *Blackwood's Edinburgh Magazine* 131:107–25.

Conn, Harvie H. 1966. "Studies in the Theology of the Korean Presbyterian Church: A Historical Outline, I." *Westminster Theological Journal* 29: 24–57.

Corten, Andre, and Ruth Marshall, eds. 2001. *Between Babel and Pentecost: Transnational Pentecostalism in Africa and Latin America*. Bloomington: Indiana University Press.

Cox, Harvey. 1993. "Jazz and Pentecostalism." *Archives de Sciences Sociales des Religions* 84:181–88.

———. 1995. *Fire from Heaven: The Rise of Pentecostal Spirituality and the Reshaping of Religion in the Twenty-First Century*. Cambridge: Da Capo Press.

Crawley, Ashon T. 2017. *Blackpentecostal Breath: The Aesthetics of Possibility*. New York: Fordham University Press.
Csordas, Thomas. 1990. "Embodiment as a Paradigm for Anthropology." *Ethos* 18 (1): 5–47.
Cumings, Bruce. 2005. *Korea's Place in the Sun: A Modern History (Updated Edition)*. New York: W. W. Norton.
Cutten, George Barton. 1927. *Speaking with Tongues: Historically and Psychologically Considered*. New Haven, CT: Yale University Press.
Darwin, Charles. 1859. *On the Origin of Species*. London: John Murray.
Debenport, Erin. 2015. *Fixing the Books: Secrecy, Literacy, and Perfectibility in Indigenous New Mexico*. Santa Fe, NM: School for Advanced Research.
Doležel, Lubomír. 1988. "Literary Transduction: A Prague School Approach." In *The Prague School and Its Legacy in Linguistics, Literature, Semiotics, Folklore, and the Arts*, edited by Yishai Tobin, 165–76. Amsterdam: John Benjamins.
Donaldson, John William. 1857. *Christian Orthodoxy Reconciled with the Conclusions of Modern Biblical Learning: A Theological Essay, with Critical and Controversial Supplements*. London: Williams and Norgate.
Doucette, Jamie. 2017. "The Occult of Personality: Korea's Candlelight Protests and the Impeachment of Park Geun-hye." *Journal of Asian Studies* 76 (4): 851–60.
Duranti, Alessandro, and Charles Goodwin. 1992. *Rethinking Context: Language as an Interactive Phenomenon*. Cambridge: Cambridge University Press.
Durkheim, Émile. (1912) 1995. *The Elementary Forms of Religious Life*. Translated by Karen Fields. New York: Free Press.
Eichhorn, Johann Gottfried. 1787. "Significatus primitivus vocis προφήτης ex Platone erutus cum novo tentamine interpretandi I Corinth Cap. XIV. a. C. Bardili Phil. M. et stipendi theolog. Tubingens. fodali. Goettingae ap. I. C. Dieterich 1786. 56. S. in 8." In *Allgemeine Bibliothek der Biblischen Litteratur*, edited by Johann Gottfried Eichhorn, Part 1, 91–108. Leipzig: Weidmanns Erben und Reich.
———. 1790. "Ueber die Giestes-Gaben der ersten Christen." In *Eichhorn's Allgemeine Bibliothek der Biblischen Litteratur*, edited by Johann Gottfried Eichhorn, 757–859. Leipzig: Weidmannschen Buchhandlung.
Eisenlohr, Patrick. 2009. "Technologies of the Spirit: Devotional Islam, Sound Reproduction and the Dialectics of Mediation and Immediacy in Mauritius." *Anthropological Theory* 9 (3): 273–96.
———. 2018. *Sounding Islam: Voice, Media, and Sonic Atmospheres in an Indian Ocean World*. Berkeley: University of California Press.
Engelke, Matthew. 2007. *A Problem of Presence: Beyond Scripture in an African Church*. Berkeley: University of California Press.
Engelke, Matthew, and Matt Tomlinson, eds. 2006. *The Limits of Meaning: Case Studies in the Anthropology of Christianity*. New York: Berghahn.
Esler, Philip. 1994. "Glossolalia and the Admission of Gentiles into the Early Christian Community." In *The First Christians in Their Social Worlds: Social-Scientific Approaches to New Testament Interpretation*, 37–51. London: Routledge.
Evans-Pritchard, E. E. 1965. *Theories of Primitive Religion*. Oxford: Oxford University Press.
———. 1981. "Durkheim (1858–1917)." *Journal of the Anthropological Society of Oxford* 12 (3): 150–64.
Farrar, Frederic William. 1879. *The Life and Work of St. Paul*. London: Casell.

Faudree, Paja. 2012. "Music, Language, and Texts: Sound and Semiotic Ethnography." *Annual Review of Anthropology* 41:519–36.

FEBC (Far Eastern Broadcasting Company). 2013. Chisang ch'oedae ŭi sŏngnyŏng k'onsŏt'ŭ, ajik kkŭnnaji anŭn yŏksa [The greatest Holy Spirit concert on earth, an unfinished history]. Far Eastern Broadcasting Company.

Feine, Paul. 1908. "Zungenreden." In *Realencyklopädie für Protestantische Theologie und Kirche*, edited by Albert Hauck, 749–59. Leipzig: J. C. Hinrichs'sche Buchhandlung.

Feld, Steven. 1994. "'Aesthetics as Iconicity of Style' (uptown title); or, (downtown title) 'Lift-up-over Sounding': Getting into the Kaluli Groove." In *Music Grooves: Essays and Dialogues*, edited by Charles Keil and Steven Feld, 109–50. Chicago: University of Chicago Press.

Feld, Steven, and Aaron Fox. 1994. "Music and Language." *Annual Review of Anthropology* 23: 25–53.

Feshchenko, Vladimir, and Newman Lao. 2013. "From the History of Glossolalia Studies: The Case of Hélène Smith on the Borderlines of Linguistics, Psychology, and Religion." *Cahiers Ferdinand de Saussure* 66:67–79.

Flournoy, Théodore. (1900) 1994. *From India to the Planet Mars: A Case of Multiple Personality with Imaginary Languages*. Translated by Daniel B. Vermilye. Princeton, NJ: Princeton University Press.

Gal, Susan. 2003. "Movements of Feminism: The Circulation of Discourses about Women." In *Recognition Struggles and Social Movements: Contested Identities, Power and Agency*, edited by Barbara Hobson, 93–120. Cambridge: Cambridge University Press.

———. 2005. "Language Ideologies Compared: Metaphors and Circulations of Public and Private." *Journal of Linguistic Anthropology* 15 (1): 23–37.

———. 2015. "The Politics of Translation." *Annual Review of Anthropology* 44: 225–40.

Gal, Susan, and Kathryn Woolard, eds. 2001. *Languages and Publics: The Making of Authority*. Manchester, UK: St. Jerome.

Gale, James Scarth. 1897. *A Korean-English Dictionary*. Yokohama: Kelly & Walsh.

Geschiere, Peter. 2013. *Witchcraft, Intimacy, and Trust: Africa in Comparison*. Chicago: University of Chicago Press.

Glock, Charles Y. 1964. "The Role of Deprivation in the Origin and Evolution of Religious Groups." In *Religion and Social Conflict*, edited by Robert Lee and Marty Martin, 24–36. New York: Oxford University Press.

Gluckman, Max. 1963. "Gossip and Scandal." *Current Anthropology* 4:307–15.

Goffman, Erving. 1971. *Relations in Public: Microstudies of the Public Order*. New York: Harper and Row.

———. 1978. "Response Cries." *Language* 54 (4): 787–815.

———. 1979. "Footing." *Semiotica* 25 (1–2): 1–29.

———. 2009. *Stigma: Notes on the Management of Spoiled Identity*. New York: Simon and Schuster.

Goodman, Felicitas. 1972. *Speaking in Tongues: A Cross-Cultural Study in Glossolalia*. Chicago: University of Chicago Press.

Graham, Laura. 1993. "A Public Sphere in Amazonia? The Depersonalized Collaborative Construction of Discourse in Xavante." *American Ethnologist* 20 (4): 717–41.

Grayson, James Huntley. 1999. "The Legacy of John Ross; A Neglected Chapter in the History of Pan-East Asian Missions." *International Bulletin of Missionary Research* 23 (4): 167–72.

———. 2006. "A Quarter-Millennium of Christianity in Korea." In *Christianity in Korea*, edited by Robert E. Buswell and Timothy S. Lee, 7–25. Honolulu: University of Hawai'i Press.

Grice, Paul. (1968) 1989. *Studies in the Way of Words*. Cambridge: Harvard University Press.

Grimm, Jacob, and Wilhelm Grimm. (1854–1961) 1971. "Glosse." In *Deutsches Wörterbuch von Jacob und Wilhelm Grimm*. Leipzig: S. Hirzel / Universität Trier Center for Digital Humanities.

Ha, Seong-Kyu. 2004. "New Shantytowns and the Urban Marginalized in Seoul Metropolitan Region." *Habitat International* 29:123–41.

Habermas, Jürgen. (1962) 1989. *The Structural Transformation of the Public Sphere: An Inquiry into a Category of Bourgeois Society*. Translated by Thomas Burger and Frederick Lawrence. Cambridge, MA: MIT Press.

Han, Gil-Soo, Joy J. Han, and Andrew Eungi Kim. 2009. "'Serving Two Masters': Protestant Churches in Korea and Money." *International Journal for the Study of the Christian Church* 9 (4): 333–60.

Han, Ju Hui Judy. 2009. "Contemporary Korean/American Evangelical Missions: Politics of Space, Gender, and Difference." PhD diss., Geography, Unviersity of California, Berkeley.

———. 2010. "Reaching the Unreached in the 10/40 Window: The Missionary Geoscience of Race, Difference and Distance." In *Mapping the End Times: American Evangelical Geopolitics and Apocalyptic Visions*, edited by Jason Dittmer and Tristan Sturm, 183–207. Hampshire, UK: Ashgate.

———. 2015a. "Our Past, Your Future: Evangelical Missionaries and the Script of Prosperity." In *Territories of Poverty: Rethinking North and South*, edited by Ananya Roy and Emma Shaw, 178–94. Athens: University of Georgia Press.

———. 2015b. "Urban Megachurches and Contentious Religious Politics in Seoul." In *Handbook of Religion and the Asian City: Aspiration and Urbanization in the Twenty-First Century*, edited by Peter van der Veer, 133–51. Berkeley: University of California Press.

———. 2016. "The Politics of Homophobia in South Korea." *East Asia Forum* 8 (2): 6–7.

Handman, Courtney. 2010. "Events of Translation: Intertextuality and Christian Ethnotheologies of Change among Guhu-Samane, Papua New Guinea." *American Anthropologist* 112 (4): 576–88.

———. 2014. *Critical Christianity: Translation and Denominational Conflict in Papua New Guinea*. Berkeley: University of California Press.

———. 2018. "The Language of Evangelism: Christian Cultures of Circulation beyond the Missionary Prologue." *Annual Review of Anthropology* 47:149–65.

Hanks, William. 1992. "The Indexical Ground of Deictic Reference." In *Rethinking Context: Language as Interactive Phenomenon*, edited by Charles Goodwin and Alessandro Duranti. Boulder, CO: Westview.

Harding, Susan. 2000. *The Book of Jerry Falwell: Fundamentalist Language and Politics*. Princeton, NJ: Princeton University Press.

Harkness, Nicholas. 2010. "Words in Motion and the Semiotics of the Unseen in Two Korean Churches." *Language & Communication* 30 (2): 139–58.

———. 2012. "Vowel Harmony Redux: Correct Sounds, English Loan Words, and the Sociocultural Life of a Phonological Structure in Korean." *Journal of Sociolinguistics* 16 (3): 358–81.

———. 2014. *Songs of Seoul: An Ethnography of Voice and Voicing in Christian South Korea*. Berkeley: University of California Press.

———. 2015a. "Basic Kinship Terms: Christian Relations, Chronotopic Formulations, and a Korean Confrontation of Language." *Anthropological Quarterly* 88 (2): 305–36.

———. 2015b. "Linguistic Emblems of South Korean Society." In *The Handbook of Korean Linguistics*, edited by Lucien Brown and Jaehoon Yeon, 492–508. Hoboken, NJ: Wiley-Blackwell.

———. 2015c. "Other Christians as Christian Others: Signs of New Christian Populations and the Urban Expansion of Seoul." In *Handbook of Religion and the Asian City: Aspiration and Urbanization in the Twenty-First Century*, edited by Peter van der Veer, 333–50. Berkeley: University of California Press.

———. 2015d. "The Pragmatics of Qualia in Practice." *Annual Review of Anthropology* 44: 573–89.

———. 2016. "A Bottleneck in the Plenum." Comment on "Ethical Life: Its Natural and Social Histories," by Webb Keane. *HAU: Journal of Ethnographic Theory* 6 (1): 463–67.

———. 2017a. "Glossolalia and Cacpohony in South Korea: Cultural Semiosis at the Limits of Language." *American Ethnologist* 44 (3): 476–89.

———. 2017b. "The Open Throat: Deceptive Sounds, Facts of Firstness, and the Interactional Emergence of Voice." *Signs and Society* 5 (S1): 21–52.

———. 2017c. "Transducing a Sermon, Inducing Conversion: Billy Graham, Billy Kim, and the 1973 Crusade in Seoul." *Representations* 137:112–43.

———. 2020a. "La Glossolalia, i Qualia e la Semiotica del Sentimento (Glossolalia, Qualia, and the Semiotics of Feeling)." Translated by Franciscu Sedda. *Rivista Italiana di Filosofia del Lingguaggio* 13 (2): 26–41.

———. 2020b. "Qualia." In *The International Encyclopedia of Linguistic Anthropology*, edited by James Stanlaw. Hoboken, NJ: Wiley-Blackwell.

Harrisville, Roy A. 1976. "Speaking in Tongues: A Lexicographic Study." *Catholic Biblical Quarterly* 38 (1): 35–48.

Hastings, Adi, and Paul Manning. 2004. "Introduction: Acts of Alterity." *Language & Communciation* 24 (4): 291–311.

Hauerwas, Stanley. 2015. *The Work of Theology*. Grand Rapids, MI: William B. Eerdmans.

Haviland, John. 1977. *Gossip, Reputation, and Knowledge in Zinacantan*. Chicago: University of Chicago Press.

———. 2004. "Gesture." In *Companion to Linguistic Anthropology*, edited by Alessandro Duranti, 197–221. Malden, MA: Blackwell.

Henderson, Ebenezer. 1836. *Divine inspiration; or, The Supernatural Influence Exerted in the Communication of Divine Truth; and Its Special Bearing on the Composition of the Sacred Scriptures*. London: Jackson and Walford.

Henry, Victor. (1901) 2001. *Antinomies Linguistiques; Le Langage Martien: études*. Paris: Didier Erudition.

Heo, Angie. 2013. "The Bodily Threat of Miracles: Security, Sacramentality, and the Egyptian Politics of Public Order." *American Ethnologist* 40 (1): 149–64.

Heo, Angie, and Jeanne Kormina. 2019. "Introduction: Religion and Borders in (Post-) Cold War Peripheries." *Journal of Religion* 99 (1): 1–17.

Herder, Johann Gottfried von. 1794. *Von der Gabe der Sprachen am ersten christlichen Pfingstfest*. Riga: Johann Friedrich Hartknoch.

Herzfeld, Michael. 2009. "The Performance of Secrecy: Domesticity and Privacy in Public Spaces." *Semiotica* 175:133–62.

Hilborn, David. 2006. "Glossolalia as Communication—a Linguistic-Pragmatic Perspective." In *Speaking in Tongues: Multi-disciplinary Perspectives*, edited by Mark J. Cartledge, 111–46. Eugene: Wipf and Stock.

Hilgenfeld, Adolf. 1850. *Die Glossolalie in der alten Kirche: in dem Zusammenhang der Geistesgaben und des Geisteslebens des alten Christenthums: eine exegetische-historische Untersuchung.* Leipzig: Breitkopf and Härtel.

Hill, Jane. 2008. *The Everyday Language of White Racism.* Malden, MA: Wiley-Blackwell

Hjelmslev, Louis, and Hans Jørgen Uldall. 1957. *Outline of Glossematics: A Study in the Methodology of the Humanities with Special Reference to Linguistics.* Copenhagen: Nordisk Sprog- og Kulturforlag.

Im, Yookyeong. 2015. "Modu ŭi sŏngch'an: Sŏng sosuja chiji kyohoe ŭi sarye ro pon k'wiŏ Kidokkyoin simin'kwŏn" [Communion for all: Queer Christian citizenship in an LGBTQ-affirming church]. Master's thesis, Department of Anthropology, Seoul National University.

Inoue, Miyako. 2006. *Vicarious Language: Gender and Linguistic Modernity in Japan.* Berkeley: University of California Press. Inoue, Miyako. 2018. "Word for Word: Verbatim as Political Technologies." *Annual Review of Anthropology* 47:217–32.

Irvine, Judith. 1982a. "The Creation of Identity in Spirit Mediumship and Possession." In *Semantic Anthropology*, edited by David Parkin, 241–60. London: Academic.

———. 1982b. "Language and Affect: Some Cross-Cultural Issues." In *Contemporary Perceptions of Language: Interdisciplinary Dimensions*, edited by Heidi Byrnes. Washington, DC: Georgetown Universty Press.

———. 2005. "Commentary: Knots and Tears in the Interdiscursive Fabric." *Journal of Linguistic Anthropology* 15 (1): 72–80.

Irvine, Judith, and Susan Gal. 2000. "Language Ideology and Linguistic Differentiation." In *Regimes of Language*, edited by Paul Kroskrity, 35–83. Santa Fe, NM: School of American Research Press.

Irving, Edward. 1832a. "Facts Connected with Recent Manifestations of Spiritual Gifts." *Fraser's Magazine for Town and Country* 4 (24): 754–61.

———. 1832b. "On Recent Manifestations of Spiritual Gifts." *Fraser's Magazine for Town and Country* 5 (26): 198–205.

———. 1832c. "On Recent Manifestations of Spiritual Gifts (Conclusion)." *Fraser's Magazine for Town and Country* 5 (27): 316–20.

Jakobson, Roman. 1966. "Retrospect." In *Selected Writings, Vol. IV: Slavic Epic Studies*, 637–64. The Hague: Mouton.

———. 1968. *Child Language, Aphasia, and Phonological Universals.* Translated by Allan Keiler. The Hague: Mouton.

———. 1978. *Six Lectures on Sound and Meaning.* Cambridge, MA: MIT Press.

Jakobson, Roman, and Linda R Waugh. (1979) 2002. *The Sound Shape of Language.* Berlin: Mouton de Gruyter.

James, William. 1896. "A Case of Psychic Automatism, Including 'Speaking with Tongues.'" In *Proceedings of the Society for Psychical Research, Volume XII (1896–7)*, 277–97. London: Kegan Paul, Trench, Trubner.

———. (1902) 2002. *The Varieties of Religious Experience: A Study in Human Nature.* New York: Routledge.

Jang, Nam Hyuck. 2004. *Shamanism in Korean Christianity, Korean Studies Dissertation Series No. 4.* Seoul: Jimoondang International.

Jansen, Jan. 2008. "God's Goodness and Power in Seoul, Korea." Kingdom Awakening Portal. http://www.openheaven.com/forums/forum_posts.asp?TID=23303. Accessed November 8, 2008.

Jones, Graham. 2014. "Secrecy." *Annual Review of Anthropology* 43:53–69.

Jones, Graham. 2018. *Magic's Reason: An Anthropology of Analogy.* Chicago: University of Chicago Press.

Joseph, John. 1996. "Undoubtedly a Powerful Influence: Victor Henry's *Antinomies Linguistiques* (1896), with an Annotated Translation of the First Chapter." *Language & Communication* 16 (2): 117–44.

Jung, Jin-heon. 2012. "Some Tears of Religious Aspiration: Dynamics of Korean Suffering in Post-War Seoul, South Korea." *Max Planck Institute MMG Working Papers* 12 (19): 1–31.

Kang, Josep. 2012. *Pangŏn kido e sumŭn pimil* [The hidden secret to praying in tongues]. Seoul: Tosŏ Ch'ulpan Sŏngnyŏng.

Kang, Yoonhee. 2007. "Unintelligibility and Imaginative Inerpretation in a Petalangan Healing Ritual." *Text & Talk* 27 (4): 409–33.

Keane, Webb. 1991. "Delegated Voice: Ritual Speech, Risk, and the Making of Marriage Alliances in Anakalang." *American Ethnologist* 18 (2): 311–30.

———. 1997. "Religious Language." *Annual Review of Anthropology* 26:47–71.

———. 2007. *Christian Moderns: Freedom and Fetish in the Mission Encounter*. Berkeley: University of California Press.

———. 2013. "On Spirit Writing: Materialities of Language and the Religious Work of Transduction." *Journal of the Royal Anthropological Institute* 19 (1): 1–17.

———. 2018. "On Semiotic Ideology." *Signs and Society* 6 (1): 64–87.

Kendall, Laurel. 2009. *Shamans, Nostalgias, and the IMF: Korean Popular Religion in Motion*. Honolulu: University of Hawai'i Press.

Kim, Andrew Eungi, and Joon-sik Choi. 2015. *Contemporary Korean Culture: The Persistence of Shamanistic and Confucian Values and Practice*. Seoul: Korea University Press.

Kim, David J. 2013. "Critical Mediations: Haewŏn Chinhon Kut, a Shamanic Ritual for Korean 'Comfort Women.'" *Positions: East Asia Cultures Critique* 21 (3): 725–54.

Kim, David W., and Won-il Bang. 2019. "Guwonpa, WMSCOG, and Shincheonji: Three Dynamic Grassroots Groups in Contemporary Korean Christian NRM History." *Religions* 10 (3). https://www.mdpi.com/2077-1444/10/3/212.

Kim, Hyejin. 2017. "'Spoon Theory' and the Fall of a Populist Princess in Seoul." *Journal of Asian Studies* 76 (4): 839–49.

Kim, Ig-Jin. 2003. *History and Theology of Korean Pentecostalism: Sunbogeum (Pure Gospel) Pentecostalism. An Attempt to Research the History of the Largest Congregation in Church History and the Theology of Its Pastor Yonggi Cho*. No. 35 in the Mission Series (Missiological Research in the Netherlands). Zoetermeer: Uitgeverij Boekencentrum.

Kim, Jang-hwan Billy. 2012. *Sŏmgimyŏ sanŭn kippŭm* [The joy of living a serving life]. Seoul: Nach'imban.

———. 2015. *The Life of Billy Kim: From Houseboy to World Evangelist*. Chicago, IL: Moody.

Kim, Kwang-Ok. 1993. "The Religious Life of the Urban Middle Class." *Korea Journal* 33 (4): 5–33.

———. 1998. "The Communal Ideology and Its Reality: With Reference to the Emergence of Neo-Tribalism." *Korea Journal* 38 (3): 5–44.

Kim, Min-Joo. 2002. "The Absence of the Adjective Category in Korean." In *Proceedings of the 2002 International Conference on Korean Linguistics*, 596–612. Seoul: Hankook Munhwasa.

Kim, Rebecca Y. 2015. *The Spirit Moves West: Korean Missionaries in America*. Oxford: Oxford University Press.

Kim, Seong Nae. 2005. "The Psychology and Aesthetics of Spirit Possession." *Korean Shamanism (Han'guk Musokhak)* 9 (2): 181–209.

———. 2018. *Han'guk Mugyo ŭi Munhwa Illyuhak* [Cultural anthropology of Korean shamanism]. Seoul: Sonamu.

Kim, Sin Ho. 2009. "Korean Pentecostalism and the Reconstruction of the Holy Spirit Movement." PhD diss., Department of Religion, Drew University.
Kim, Sŏnghye. 2005. *Ne ip ŭl nŏlke yŏlla* [Open your mouth wide]. Seoul: Sŏul Malssŭmsa.
Kim, Sung Gun. 2007. "Korean Protestant Christianity in the Midst of Globalization: Neoliberalism and the Pentecostalization of Korean Churches." *Korea Journal* 47 (4): 147–70.
Kim, T'aeyŏng. 2016. "Palp'yo chŏn padŭn '44 kae yŏnsŏlmun' . . . kŭkpi Tŭresŭdŏn kkaji" ["Forty-four speeches" received before official presentations . . . even including the highly classified Dresden address]. *JBTC*, October 24, 2016. https://news.joins.com/article/20772736.
Kim, Wonil. 2006. "Minjung Theology's Biblical Hermeneutics: An Examination of Minjung Theology's Appropriation of the Exodus Account." In *Christianity in Korea*, edited by Robert E. Buswell and Timothy S. Lee, 221–37. Honolulu: University of Hawai'i Press.
Kim Davis, Lisa. 2011. "International Events and Mass Evictions: A Longer View." *International Journal of Urban and Regional Research* 35 (3): 582–99.
Kim Harvey, Youngsook. 1980. "Possession Sickness and Women Shamans in Korea." In *Unspoken Worlds: Women's Religious Lives in Non-Western Cultures*, edited by Nancy Auer Falk and Rita M Gross, 41–52. New York: Harper and Row.
———. 1987. "The Korean Shaman and Deaconess: Sisters in Different Guises." In *Religion and Ritual in Korean Society*, edited by Laurel Kendall and Griffin Dix, 149–70. Berkeley: University of California Press.
Kim-Renaud, Young-Key. 1977. "Syllable-Boundary Phenomena in Korean." *Korean Studies* 1:243–73.
King, Ross. 2004. "Western Protestant Missionaries and the Origins of Korean Language Modernization." *Journal of International and Area Studies* 11(3): 7–38.
Ko, Byŏngchŏl, Ton'gu Kang, and Hyŏnbŏm Cho. 2019. 2018 nyŏn Han'guk ŭi chonggyo hyŏnhwang [2018 state of religion of Korea]. Seoul: Ministry of Culture, Sports and Tourism.
Koyama, Wataru. 1997. "Desemanticizing Pragmatics." *Journal of Pragmatics* 28:1–28.
Kroskrity, Paul, ed. 2000. *Regimes of Language: Ideologies, Polities, and Identities*. Santa Fe, NM: School of American Research Press.
Krug, Wilhelm Traugott. 1827. *Allgemeines Handwörterbuch der Philosophischen Wissenschaften, nebst ihrer Literatur und Geschichte*. Vol. 2 of 5. Vol. 2. Leipzig: F. A. Brockhaus.
———. 1829. *Allgemeines Handwörterbuch der Philosophischen Wissenschaften, nebst ihrer Literatur und Geschichte*. Vol. 5 of 5. Leipzig: F. A. Brockhaus.
———. 1838. *Encyklopäedisches Lexikon in Bezug auf die neuste Literatur und Geschichte der Philosophie*. Vol. 1 of 2. Leipzig: F. A. Brockhaus.
Kuipers, Joel. 2007. "Comments on Ritual Unintelligibility." *Text & Talk* 27 (4): 559–66.
Kukmin Ilbo. 2014. "Kihasŏng Yŏŭido Sun Pogŭm Sosok Kyohoe Kungnaeoe 3102 kae, kyoin 115 manyŏmyŏng" [3,102 churches, 1,150,000 members, domestic and international, belong to the Assembly of God Korea Yoido Full Gospel Church]. *Kukmin Ilbo*, October 9.
Labov, William. 1966. *The Social Stratification of English in New York City*. Washington, DC: Center for Applied Linguistics.
Lawless, Elaine. 1982. "Make a Joyful Noise: An Ethnography of Communication in the Pentecostal Religious Service." *Southern Folklore Quarterly* 44–45:1–21.
Lee, Benjamin. 1997. *Talking Heads: Language, Metalanguage, and the Semiotics of Subjectivity*. Durham, NC: Duke University Press.
Lee, Benjamin, and Edward LiPuma. 2002. "Cultures of Circulation: The Imaginations of Modernity." *Public Culture* 14 (1): 191–213.

Lee, Doreen. 2016. *Activist Archives: Youth Culture and the Political Past in Indonesia*. Durham: Duke University Press.

Lee, Graham. 1907. "How the Spirit Came to Pyeng Yang." *Korea Mission Field* 3 (3): 33–37.

Lee, Timothy S. 2006. "Beleaguered Success: Korean Evangelicalism in the Last Decade of the Twentieth Century." In *Christianity in Korea*, edited by Robert E. Buswell and Timothy S. Lee, 330–50. Honolulu: University of Hawai'i Press.

———. 2010. *Born Again: Evangelicalism in Korea*. Honolulu: University of Hawai'i Press.

Lee, Won Gue. 1999. "A Sociological Study on the Factors of Church Growth and Decline in Korea." *Korea Journal* 39 (4): 235–69.

Lempert, Michael. 2012. *Discipline and Debate: The Language of Violence in a Tibetan Buddhist Monastery*. Berkeley: University of California Press.

Lieberman, Philip. 2007. "The Evolution of Human Speech: Its Anatomical and Neural Bases." *Current Anthropology* 48 (1): 39–66.

Luhrmann, Tanya. 2004. "Metakinesis: How God Becomes Intimate in Contemporary US Christianity." *American Anthropologist* 106 (3): 518–28.

———. 2012. *When God Talks Back: Understanding the American Evangelical Relationship with God*. New York: Alfred A. Knopf.

Luther, Martin. (1525) 1589. *Wider die Himlischen Propheten, Von den Bildern, vnnd Sacrament*. Laugingen: Leonhart Reinmichel.

———. (1525) 1833. "Wider die himlischen Propheten von den bildern und Sacrament." In *Dr. Martin Luther's sämmtliche Werke: Dr. Martin Luther's polemische deutsche Schriften*, edited by Johann Konrad Irmischer, 134–297. Erlangen: Verlag Carl Heyder.

———. (1525) 2015. "Against the Heavenly Prophets in the Matter of Images and Sacraments." In *The Annotated Luther: Word and Faith*, edited by Kirsi I. Stjerna and Hans J. Hillerbrand, 50–125. Minneapolis: Augsburg Fortress.

Ma, Wonsuk. 2014. "Asian Pentecostalism in Context: A Challenging Portrait." In *The Cambridge Companion to Pentecostalism*, edited by Cecil M. Robeck Jr. and Amos Yong, 152–71. New York: Cambridge University Press.

Macchia, Frank. 1992. "Sighs Too Deep for Words: Toward a Theology of Glossolalia." *Journal of Pentecostal Theology* 1 (1): 47–73.

———. 1993. "Tongues as a Sign: Towards a Sacramental Understanding of Pentecostal Experience." *PNEUMA: The Journal of the Society for Pentecostal Studies* 15 (1): 61–76.

———. 2006. "Babel and the Tongues of Pentecost: Reversal or Fulfillment?—A Theological Perspective." In *Speaking in Tongues: Multi-disciplinary Perspectives*, edited by Mark J. Cartledge, 34–51. Eugene, OR: Wipf and Stock.

MacLochlainn, Scott. 2015. "Divinely Generic: Bible Translation and the Semiotics of Circulation." *Signs and Society* 3 (2): 234–60.

Maier, Adalbert. 1855. *Glossolalie des apostolischen Zeitalters exegetisch-kritisch beleuchtet*. Freiburg: Universitaets-Buchdruckerei von Hermann M. Poppen.

Malinowski, Bronislaw. 1935. "An Ethnographic Theory of the Magical Word." In *Coral Gardens and Their Magic*, 2:213–50. New York: Dover.

Maltz, Daniel. 1985. "Joyful Noise and Reverent Silence: The Significance of Noise in Pentecostal Worship." In *Perspectives on Silence*, edited by Deborah Tannen and Muriel Saville-Troike. Norwood, NJ: Ablex.

Manning, Paul. 2012. *The Semiotics of Drink and Drinking*. London: Continuum.

———. 2018. "Spiritualist Signal and Theosophical Noise." *Journal of Linguistic Anthropology* 28 (1): 67–92.
Martin, Samuel. 1951. "Korean Phonemics." *Language* 27 (4): 519–33.
———. 1992. *A Reference Grammar of Korean: A Complete Guide to the Grammar and History of the Korean Language*. Rutland, VT: Charles E. Tuttle.
McIntosh, Janet. 2009. *The Edge of Islam: Power, Personhood, and Ethnoreligious Boundaries on the Kenya Coast*. Durham, NC: Duke University Press.
Mellquist Lehto, Heather. 2017. "Screen Christianity: Video Sermons and the Creation of Transnational Korean Churches." *Acta Koreana* 20 (20): 395–421.
Merriman, Michael. 2006. *Billy Graham: God's Ambassador*. Beverly Hills, CA: 20th Century Fox.
Merry, Sally Engle. 1984. "Rethinking Gossip and Scandal." In *Toward a General Theory of Social Control*, edited by Donald J. Black, 271–302. New York: Academic.
Meyer, Heinrich August Wilhelm. 1835. *Kritisch Exegetisches Handbuch über die Apostelgeschichte, Das Neue Testament griechisch nach den besten hülfsmitteln kritisch revidirt mit einer neuen deutschen übersetzung und einem kritischen und exegetischen kommentar; 3 Abt*. Göttingen: Vandenhoek und Ruprecht.
Missions Étrangères de Paris. 1880. *Dictionnaire Coréen-Français*. Yokohama: C. Lévy.
Monson, Ingrid. 1996. *Saying Something: Jazz Improvisation and Interaction*. Chicago: University of Chicago Press.
Moore, Robert. 2013. "Reinventing Ethnopoetics." *Journal of Folklore Research* 50 (1–3): 13–39.
Nakassis, Constantine. 2016. "Linguistic Anthropology in 2015: Not the Study of Language." *American Anthropologist* 118 (2): 340–45.
Newberg, Andrew B., Nancy A. Wintering, Donna Morgan, and Mark R. Waldman. 2006. "The Measurement of Regional Cerebral Blood Flow during Glossolalia: A Preliminary SPECT Study." *Psychiatry Research: Neuroimaging* 148: 67–71.
Niebuhr, H. Richard. 1929. *The Social Sources of Denominationalism*. New York: H. Holt.
Oak, Han-Hŭm. 2003. *Healthy Christians Make a Healthy Church*. Fearn, Ross-shire, Scotland: Christian Focus.
———. 2006. *Called to Awaken the Laity*. Fearn, Ross-shire, Scotland: Christian Focus.
Oak, Seung-Deuk. 2012. "Major Protestant Revivals in Korea, 1903–35." *Studies in World Christianity* 18 (3): 269–90.
———. 2013. *The Making of Korean Christianity: Protestant Encounters with Korean Religions, 1876–1915*. Waco, TX: Baylor University Press.
Ochs, Elinor. 1976. "The Universality of Conversational Postulates." *Language in Society* 5 (1): 67–80.
Olshausen, Hermann. 1829. "Nachträgliche Bemerkungen über das Charisma des γλώσσαις λαλεῖν [Glossais Lalein], in Beziehung auf die Abhandlung darüber vom Herrn Prof. Bleek." *Theologische Studien und Kritiken* 3: 538–49.
———. 1830. "Kurze Bemerkung über denselben Gegenstand." *Theologische Studien und Kritiken* 3:64–66.
Park, Chan E. 2003. *Voices from the Straw Mat: Toward and Ethnography of Korean Story Singing*. Honolulu: University of Hawai'i Press.
Park, Joseph Sung-Yul. 2009. *The Local Construction of a Global Language: Ideologies of English in South Korea*. Berlin: Mouton de Gruyter.

Park, Joseph Sung-Yul, and Adrienne Lo. 2012. "Transnational South Korea as a Site for a Sociolinguistics of Globalization: Markets, Timescales, Neoliberalism." *Journal of Sociolinguistics* 16 (2): 147–64.

Park, Shalon. 2017. "The Politics of Impeaching Shamanism: Regulating Religions in the Korean Public Sphere." *Journal of Church and State* 60 (4): 636–60.

Parmentier, Richard. 1994. *Signs in Society: Studies in Semiotic Anthropology*. Bloomington: Indiana University Press.

Paz, Alejandro. 2018. *Latinos in Israel: Language and Unexpected Citizenship*. Bloomington: Indiana University Press.

Peirce, Charles S. 1902. "Virtual." In *Dictionary of Philosophy and Psychology*, edited by James M. Baldwin, 763–64. New York: Macmillan.

Pfister, Oskar. 1917. *The Psychoanalytic Method*. Translated by Charles Rockwell Payne. New York: Moffat, Yard.

Piliavsky, Anastasia. 2011. "A Secret in the Oxford Sense: Thieves and the Rhetoric of Mystification in Western India." *Comparative Studies in Society and History* 53 (2): 290–313.

Pollack, John. 1979. *Billy Graham: Evangelist to the World. An Authorized Biography of the Decisive Years*. New York: Harper and Row.

Pouillon, Jean. 1982. "Remarks on the Verb 'to Believe.'" In *In Between Belief and Transgression: Structuralist Essays in Religion, History, and Myth*, edited by Michel Izard and Pierre Smith, 1–8. Chicago: University of Chicago Press.

Poythress, Vern S. 1980. "Linguistic and Sociological Analyses of Modern Tongues-Speaking: Their Contributions and Limitations." *Westminster Theological Journal* 42 (2): 367–88.

Reuss, Édouard. 1851. "La Glossolalie: Chapitre de Psychologie Évangélique." *Revue de Théologie et de Philosophie Chrétienne* 3:65–97.

Robbins, Joel. 2004a. *Becoming Sinners: Christianity and Moral Torment in a Papua New Guinea Society*. Berkeley: University of California Press.

———. 2004b. "The Globalization of Pentecostal and Charismatic Christianity." *Annual Review of Anthropology* 33:117–43.

Roberts, Eugene. 2005. *After the Spirit: A Constructive Pneumatology from Resources outside the Modern West*. Grand Rapids, MI: William B. Eerdmans.

———, ed. 2009. *The Holy Spirit: Classic and Contemporary Readgins*. Malden, MA: Wiley-Blackwell.

Rosa, Jonathan. 2019. *Looking Like a Language, Sounding Like a Race: Raciolinguistic Ideologies and the Learning of Latinidad*. New York: Oxford University Press.

Ross, John. 1883. "Corean New Testament." *Chinese Recorder and Missionary Journal* 14 (6): 491–97.

Rossteuscher, Ernst. 1850. *Die Gabe der Sprachen in apostolischen Zeitalter*. Marburg: Elwert'sche Universitäts-Buchhandlung.

Rückert, Leopold Immanuel. 1836. *Die Briefe Pauli an die Korinther*. Vol. 1 of 2. Leipzig: K. F. Köhler.

Rutherford, Danilyn. 2002. "After Syncretism: The Anthropology of Islam and Christianity in Southeast Asia. A Review Article." *Comparative Studies in Society and History* 44 (1): 196–205.

———. 2009. "An Absence of Belief?" *The Immanent Frame*, December 1, 2009. https://tif.ssrc.org/2009/12/01/an-absence-of-belief/.

Ryang, Sonia. 1997. "Japanese Travelers in Korea." *East Asian History* 13/14:133–52.

Samarin, William. 1972. *Tongues of Men and Angels: The Religious Language of Pentecostalism*. New York: Macmillan.

BIBLIOGRAPHY

———. 1973. "Glossolalia as Regressive Speech." *Language and Speech* 16 (1): 77–89.
———. 1974. Review of *Speaking in Tongues: A Cross-Cultural Study of Glossolalia*, by Felicitas Goodman (Chicago: University of Chicago Press, 1972). *Language* 50 (1): 207–12.
Samuels, David. 2004. "Language, Meaning, Modernity, and Doowop." *Semiotica* 149 (1): 297–323.
Sapir, Edward. 1925. "Sound Patterns in Language." *Language* 1 (2): 37–51.
———. (1927) 1949. "The Unconscious Patterning of Behavior in Society." In *Selected Writings in Language, Culture, and Personality*, edited by David G. Mandelbaum, 544–59. Berkeley: University of California Press.
———. 1928. "The Meaning of Religion." *American Mercury* (36): 72–79.
———. (1933) 1949. "The Psychological Reality of Phonemes." In *Selected Writings in Language, Culture, and Personality*, edited by David G. Mandelbaum, 46–60. Berkeley: University of California Press.
Saussure, Ferdinand de. (1916) 2011. *Course in General Linguistics*. Edited by Perry Meisel and Haun Saussy. Translated by Wade Baksin. New York: Columbia University Press.
Schaff, Philipp. 1851. *Geschichte der Christlichen Kirche von iherer Gründung bis auf die Gegenwart*. Mercersberg, PA: Self-published.
Schieffelin, Bambi, Kathryn Woolard, and Paul Kroskrity, eds. 1998. *Language Ideologies: Practice and Theory*. New York: Oxford University Press.
Schmid, Andre. 2002. *Korea between Empires, 1895–1919*. New York: Columbia University Press.
Schulz, David. 1836. *Die Geistesgaben der ersten Christen insbesondere die sogenannte Gabe der Sprachen: Eine exegetische Entwicklung*. Breslau: A. Gosohorsky.
Sells, Michael A. 1994. *Mystical Languages of Unsaying*. Chicago: University of Chicago Press.
Shumway, Charles William. 1919. "A Critical History of Glossolalia." PhD diss., Boston University.
Silverstein, Michael. 1976. "Shifters, Linguistic Categories, and Cultural Description." In *Meaning in Anthropology*, edited by Keith Basso and Keith Selby, 11–55. Albuquerque: University of New Mexico Press.
———. 1979. "Language Structure and Linguistic Ideology." In *The Elements: A Parasession on Linguistic Units and Levels*, edited by Paul Cline, William Hanks, and Charles Hofbauer, 193–247. Chicago: Chicago Linguistic Society.
———. 1981. "The Limits of Awareness." *Working Papers in Sociolinguistics*, no. 84. Austin, TX: Southwestern Educational Laboratory.
———. 1996. "The Secret Life of Texts." In *Natural Histories of Discourse*, edited by Michael Silverstein and Greg Urban, 81–105. Chicago: University of Chicago Press.
———. 2003. "Translation, Transduction, Transformation: Skating "Glossondo" on Thin Semiotic Ice." In *Translating Cultures: Perspectives on Translation and Anthropology*, edited by Paula Rubel and Abraham Rosman, 75–105. Oxford: Berg.
———. 2005. "Axes of Evals: Token versus Type Interdiscursivity." *Journal of Linguistic Anthropology* 15 (1): 6–22.
———. 2006. "Old Wine, New Ethnographic Lexicography." *Annual Review of Anthropology* 25:481–96.
———. 2012. "Does the Autonomy of Linguistics Rest on the Autonomy of Syntax? An Alternative Framing of Our Object of Study." In *Pragmaticizing Understanding: Studies for Jef Verschueren*, edited by Michael Meeuwis and Jan-Ola Östman, 15–38. Amsterdam: John Benjamins.
———. 2013. "Discourse and the No-Thing-Ness of Culture." *Signs and Society* 1 (2): 327–66.
———. 2016. "Postscript: Thinking about the 'Teleologies of Structuralism.'" *Hau: Journal of Ethnographic Theory* 6 (3): 79–84.

Silverstein, Michael, and Greg Urban. 1996. *Natural Histories of Discourse*. Chicago: University of Chicago Press.

Simmel, Georg. 1906. "The Sociology of Secrecy and of Secret Societies." *American Journal of Sociology* 11 (4): 441–98.

———. (1908) 1950. "Quantitative Aspects of the Group." In *The Sociology of Georg Simmel*, edited by Kurt H. Wolff, 87–180. New York: Free Press.

Smith, James K. A. 2010. *Thinking in Tongues: Pentecostal Contributions to Christian Theology*. Grand Rapids, MI: William B. Eerdmans.

Sŏ, Kwangsŏn. 1982. "Han'guk kyohoe sŏngnyŏng undong kwa puhŭng undong ŭi sinhak ihae" [Understanding the theology of the Korean church Holy Spirit movement and Revival movement]. In *Han'guk kyohoe sŏngnyŏng undong ŭi hyŏnsang kwa kujo: Sun Pogŭm Chungang Kyohoe rŭl chungsim ŭro*, edited by Kwangsŏn Sŏ, 23–99. Seoul: K'ŭrisŭch'yan Ak'ademi.

Stasch, Rupert. 2011. "Ritual and Oratory Revisited: The Semiotics of Effective Action." *Annual Review of Anthropology* 40: 159–74.

Stewart, Charles, and Rosalind Shaw, eds. 1994. *Syncretism/Anti-Syncretism: The Politics of Religious Synthesis*. London: Routledge.

Suh, Kwang-Sun David. 1983. "A Biographical Sketch of an Asian Theological Consultation." In *Minjung Theology: People as the Subjects of History*, edited by Commission on Theological Concerns of the Christian Conference of Asia, 15–38. Maryknoll, NY: Orbis.

Sullivan, Charles A. 2010–2018. "Gift of Tongues Project." https://charlesasullivan.com/special-projects/gift-tongues-project/. Accessed August 1, 2018.

Tambiah, Stanley. 1985. *Culture, Thought, and Social Action: An Anthropological Perspective*. Cambridge: Harvard University Press.

Taves, Ann. 1999. *Fits, Trances, and Visions: Experiencing Religion and Explaining Experience from Wesley to James*. Princeton, NJ: Princeton University Press.

Todorov, Tzvetan. (1977) 1982. "Saussure's Semiotics." In *Theories of the Symbol*, 255–70. Oxford: Basil Blackwell.

Tomlinson, Matt. 2012. "God Speaking to God: Translation and Unintelligibility at a Fijian Pentecostal Crusade." *Australian Journal of Anthropology* 23:274–89.

———. 2014. *Ritual Textuality: Pattern and Motion in Performance*. New York: Oxford.

Trouillot, Michel-Rolph. 2003. "Adieu, Culture: A New Duty Arises." In *Global Transformations: Anthropology and the Modern World*, 97–116. London: Palgrave MacMillan.

Trudgill, Peter. 1972. "Sex, Covert Prestige and Linguistic Change in the Urban British English of Norwich." *Language in Society* 1 (2): 179–95.

Turner, Max. 2006. "Early Christian Experience and Theology of 'Tongues'—a New Testament Perspective." In *Speaking in Tongues: Multi-Disciplinary Perspectives*, edited by Mark J. Cartledge, 1–33. Eugene, OR: Wipf and Stock.

Urban, Greg. 1988. "Ritual Wailing in Amerindian Brazil." *American Anthropologist* 90 (2): 385–400.

———. 2018. "The Role of Metaforces in Cultural Motion." *Signs and Society* 6 (1): 256–80.

van der Veer, Peter, ed. 1996. *Conversion to Modernities: The Globalization of Christianity*. New York: Routledge.

———. 2013. "Urban Aspirations in Mumbai and Singapore." In *Topographies of Faith: Religion in Urban Spaces*, edited by Irene Becci, Marian Burchardt, and José Casanova, 61–71. Leiden: Brill.

Wang, Hahn-sok. 1984. "Honorific Speech Behavior in a Rural Korean Village: Structure and Use." PhD diss., University of California, Los Angeles.

———. 1990. "Toward a Description of the Organization of Korean Speech Levels." *International Journal of the Sociology of Language* 82:25–39.
Wang, Hahn-sok, et al. 2005. *Hanguk Sahoe wa Hoch'ingŏ* [Korean society and terms of address]. Seoul: Yŏngnak.
Warner, Michael. 2010. "The Preacher's Footing." In *This Is Enlightenment*, edited by Clifford Siskin and William Warner, 368–83. Chicago: University of Chicago Press.
Webster, Anthony. 2016. "The Art of Failure in Translating a Navajo Poem." *Journal de la Société des Américanistes* 102 (1): 9–41.
Weiner, Annette. 1994. "Cultural Difference and the Density of Objects." *American Ethnologist* 21 (2): 391–403.
Whorf, Benjamin Lee. 1956. *Language, Thought, and Reality: Selected Writings of Benjamin Lee Whorf*. Cambridge, MA: MIT Press.
Wieseler, Carl. 1838. "Über das γλώσσαις λαλεῖν [Glossais Lalein] im neuen Testament. Neur kritisch-exegetischer Besuch über 1 Kor. 14 in Verbindung mit Ap. Gesch. 2." *Theologische Studien und Kritiken* 11 (3): 703–72.
Williams, George H., and Edith Waldvogel. 1975. "A History of Speaking in Tongues and Related Gifts." In *The Charismatic Movement*, edited by Michael P. Hamilton, 61–113. Grand Rapids, MI: William B. Eerdmans.
Wirtz, Kristina. 2005. " 'Where Obscurity Is a Virtue': The Mystique of Unintelligibility in Santería Ritual." *Language & Communication* 25 (4): 351–75.
———, ed. 2007. "Ritual Unintelligibility." Special issue, *Text & Talk* 27 (4).
———. 2018. "Materializations of Oricha Voice through Divinations in Cuban Santería." *Journal de la Société des Américanistes* 104 (1): 149–77.
Woolard, Kathryn, and Bambi Schieffelin. 1994. "Language Ideology." *Annual Review of Anthropology* 23: 55–82.
Wright, Arthur. 1898. *Some New Testament Problems*. London: Methuen.
Yeh, Rihan. 2017. *Passing: Two Publics in a Mexican Border City*. Chicago: University of Chicago Press.
Yelle, Robert. 2013a. *The Language of Disenchantment: Protestant Literalism and Colonial Discourse in British India*. New York: Oxford.
———. 2013b. *Semiotics of Religion: Signs of the Sacred in History, Bloomsbury Advances in Semiotics*. London: Bloomsbury.
Yi, Kwangsu. 1970. "Pangŏn hyŏnsang yŏn'gu" [Research on the phenomenon of glossolalia]. Master's thesis, Graduate School of Education, Yeonsei University.
Yong, Amos. 1998. " 'Tongues of Fire' in the Pentecostal Imagination: The Truth of Glossolalia in Light of R. C. Neville's Theory of Religious Symbolism." *Journal of Pentecostal Theology* 12:39–65.
Yoo, Boo-Woong. 1986. "Response to Korean Shamanism by the Pentecostal Church." *International Review of Mission* 75 (297): 70–74.
———. 1987. *Korean Pentecostalism: Its History and Theology*. New York: Verlag Peter Lang.
Yoon, Paul Chong-Chul. 2005. "Christian Identity, Ethnic Identity: Music Making and Prayer Practices among 1.5- and Second-Generation Korean American Christians." PhD diss., Department of Music, Columbia University.
Yun, Kyoim. 2019. *The Shaman's Wages: Trading in Ritual on Cheju Island*. Seattle: University of Washington Press.
Zachhuber, Johannes. 2018. "Transcendence and Immanence." In *The Edinburgh Critical History of Nineteenth-Century Christian Theology*, edited by Daniel Whistler, 164–81. Edinburgh: Edinburgh University Press.

Index

"Acting by Faith, Not by Sight" (*Midŭm ŭro haenghago ponŭn kŏt ŭro haji anŭm*) (Cho), 85–86
Against the Heavenly Prophets in the Matter of Images and Sacraments (Luther), 176
agency, 16–17, 66. *See also* denotation
Allgemeine Bibliothek der Biblischen Litteratur (Eichhorn), 177
Anch'al kido (violent laying on of hands), 146, 147–48
ansu kido (laying on of hands), 146, 150
Austin, J. L., 193n20, 200n47
authority, 28–29
Azusa Street revival (1906), 39

Bardili, Christoph Gottfried, 176–77, 178, 179
Barthes, Roland, 93
Bauman, Richard, 197n11
Baur, Ferdinand Christian, 181
belief, 187n25
"Believe in God" (*Hananim ŭl midŭra*) (Cho), 78–80, 86
Bergson, Henri, 193n29
Bible. *See* New Testament; Word, the
biblical interpretation, 3, 185n3
Blair, William, 39
Bleek, Friedrich, 179–80, 181, 205n27
"Blessing of the Descent of the Holy Spirit, The" (*Sŏngnyŏng kangnim ŭi ch'ukpok*) (Cho), 80–81
Blocher, Jacques, 93
Boas, Franz, 66
Bob Jones Academy, 198n4, 199n10
Briggs, Charles, 197n11
broadcast, 122–23. *See also* regimes of revelation
Brøndal, Viggo, 187n17
Buddhism, 44
Byun Seung Woo, 196n5

cacophonic group prayer. *See t'ongsŏng kido*
Calvinism, 73
Cartledge, Mark, 185n3
Catholic Apostolic Church, 205n32
cell phone miracles, 67
Certeau, Michel de, 14
chagŭk (stimulation), 25–26, 147, 157, 158. *See also* fervency
ch'obangŏn (starter tongues), 13–14, 57, 153
Cho, Hyŏnbŏm, 185n7
Choi Jashil, 4, 31, 124–27, 128, 129–31
Choi Soon-sil, 162–63, 164
Choi Tae-min, 163, 164
Chomsky, Noam, 187n26
chŏndosa (evangelist) role, 150, 195n50
Chŏng Wŏn, 202–3n31
Cho Unp'a, 146, 203n2
Cho Yonggi: on benefits of glossolalia, 36–37, 50–51, 191n58; and Choi Jashil, 127, 128; on Christian self-confirmation, 87; on fourth dimension, 35–36, 79, 80–82, 83–84, 85; *Fourth Dimension, The* (*4-Ch'awŏn*), 35–36, 81–82, 83–84; at Full Gospel Seminary, 127–28; on healing, 82–83, 85, 86, 197n30; on Holy Spirit and the Word, 68, 72, 81, 88; "Illusion and Reality," 58; and introduction of glossolalia, 34, 39–40; on mediating function of Holy Spirit, 85–86; vs. Minjung theology, 186n9; on miracles, 79–80, 86–87; personal theology of, 191n56; on personification of Holy Spirit, 84; *Pneumatology* (*Sŏngnyŏng-non*), 84; on positional affirmation prayer, 84–85; on privacy/secrecy, 55, 80–81, 124, 130; and scandal, 190n38; on spiritual contact, 80, 81–82; *Truth of Full Gospel*, 84; on the Word as historical fact, 78–79; and Yoido Full Gospel Church establishment, 31, 32,

Cho Yonggi (cont.)
33–34, 33, 128–29. See also Cho Yonggi's glossolalia; Yoido Full Gospel Church. Sermons: "Acting by Faith, Not by Sight" (*Midŭm ŭro haenghago ponŭn kŏt ŭro haji anŭm*), 85–86; "Believe in God" (*Hananim ŭl midŭra*), 78–80, 86; "Blessing of the Descent of the Holy Spirit, The" (*Sŏngnyŏng kangnim ŭi ch'ukpok*), 80–81; "Grace of Jesus's Cure, The" (*Yesunim ŭi ch'iryo ŭi ŭnhye*), 82–83; "Outer Person and the Inner Person, The" (*Kŏtsaram kwa soksaram*), 52–54
Cho Yonggi's glossolalia: criticisms of, 194n35; examples of, 1, 47–50; interpretation of, 46–51, 194nn36–38, 41, 195n42; and palatalization, 193–94n32; prosody of, 52–54
Christian self-confirmation, 87, 95
Chung Yoo-ra (Chŏng Yura), 163
church community pressure, 10; and cultural value of glossolalia, 28; and glossolalia ubiquity, 23, 27; and learning processes for glossolalia, 57; and privacy/secrecy, 131–34, 135–36, 140, 202nn28, 30; and real glossolalia discernment, 152–53, 155–56; and *t'ongsŏng kido*, 133–34, 135, 203n33
church dialect (*kyohoe sat'uri*), 133–34
Church of Eternal Life, 163
Church of Love. See Sarang Church
circulation, 122, 201n3. See also regimes of revelation
class status, 23, 29, 152
Cold War, 92, 119, 198n4
Coleridge, Samuel Taylor, 45
collaborative intensity, 60–61, 63, 195n57
Corinthians I, 3
COVID-19 pandemic, 204n14
"Crying Out Prayer" (*Purŭjinnŭn Kido*) (Chŏng Wŏn), 202–3n31
cultural semiosis, 11, 12, 42–43, 62, 92, 118–19. See also glossolalia as produced at limits of language

danger. See suspicion of glossolalia
deceptive intimacy, 159–69; and decline of glossolalia, 168–69; and denotation, 164–65; and heterodox churches, 159–61, 204n14; and Park Geun-hye, 161–64; and suspicion of glossolalia, 165–67
deity. See spiritual contact
demonic forces: and fourth dimension, 36; and heterodox churches, 160, 161; and Kim's interpretation of Graham, 104, 106, 108; and privacy/secrecy, 55, 165; and real glossolalia discernment, 159; and the Word as historical fact, 78
denotation: and deceptive intimacy, 164–65; defined, 2; and glossolalia as produced at limits of language, 43, 44, 45, 193n22; and glossolalia as social experience, 58; and Holy Spirit, 65; and iconic mode, 42, 192n13; and inerrancy of the Word, 73; and intercessors, 58; and interpretation, 46–51, 194nn36–38, 41, 195n42; linguistic theories of, 11, 14; and phonemes, 41; and pragmatics (indexical mode), 8, 42, 192n20; and segmentation, 41, 192n11; and social action, 200n47; suppression of, 2, 9, 45–46, 167–68; as symbolic mode, 11, 187n26; and the Word, 70
devil. See demonic forces
discipleship training (*cheja hullyŏn*), 70–71
Donaldson, John William, 183, 185n6
Durkheim, Emile, 39, 192n18

Eichhorn, Johann Gottfried, 177, 178, 179
Elementary Forms of Religious Life (Durkheim), 39
entextualization, 69, 86, 122, 197n11
evangelism: and Choi Jashil, 125–26; and Cold War, 92; and cultural semiosis, 118–19; and inerrancy of the Word, 94, 114; and Kim's interpretation of Graham, 95, 108, 113–19, 115, 116, 200n48; in Korean Protestantism, 10, 27, 34, 95, 189n13, 199n29; Nevius method, 70–71; and voicing, 101, 104; and the Word, 69, 77–78, 88, 93, 94, 197n23; and Yoido Full Gospel Church, 30, 31, 34, 190n27. See also Kim's interpretation of Graham
Evans-Pritchard, E. E., 192n18
exchange, 122, 201n9. See also regimes of revelation

Falwell, Jerry, 94–95
Farrar, Frederic William, 3–4, 15, 183, 185n6
Feine, Paul, 203n32
fervency, 9, 25–26, 188n4
fire metaphor, 69–70, 72, 77, 82–83, 135, 197n21
Flournoy, Théodore, 12
fourth dimension: and interdiscursivity, 85; and shamanism, 35–36; and the Word, 79–80, 81–82, 83–84, 198n31
Fourth Dimension, The (4-Ch'awŏn) (Cho), 35–36, 81–82, 83–84
Full Gospel Church. See Cho Yonggi; Yoido Full Gospel Church
Full Gospel Seminary, 127–28

Garden, the, 139–42
gender. See women
GFC (Great Faith Church) (K'ŭn midŭm kyohoe), 67, 196n5
gifts, earthly (*sŏnmul*) vs. spiritual (*ŭnsa*), 10, 30–31, 34–36, 85
Global Fire Ministries, 67
glossolalia: as alchemical semiotics, 192n9; and *ansu kido*, 151; anthropological theories of, 11,

14–15, 41–42, 43; Certeau on, 14; competition over, 57; cultural value of, 27–28; decline of, 168–69; discernment of real, 50, 150, 152–59; at Full Gospel Seminary, 127, 128; gift distribution, 5, 10, 155, 156, 186n10; James on, 12–13, 188n35; and Kim's interpretation of Graham, 119–20; Korean term for, 5–6, 186nn12–13; Korean ubiquity of, 4, 5, 7, 23, 34, 186n11; learning processes for, 13–14, 39, 50–52, 57–58, 153–55; as linguistic hierarchy, 203n32; phonetics of, 12, 48, 50; as placeholder, 1–2; and prayer centers, 139; and regimes of revelation, 123–24; Samarin's theory of, 11–12, 14–15, 40, 42, 187n31; silent, 135, 136–37; in small-group worship, 138; as sociolinguistic fact, 7, 168–69; as sonorant flow, 51, 54, 119, 149, 158, 165; term origins, 3, 175, 178–83, 185n6, 205nn19, 27, 32; theological theories of, 3–4; as trance phenomenon, 14–16, 42, 188n41; varying experiences of, 21–23; varying linguistic forms of, 156–57; the Word as source of, 66; as *Zungenreden*, 175–78, 204n3. *See also* privacy/secrecy

glossolalia as dangerous. *See* suspicion of glossolalia

glossolalia as produced at limits of language, 40–58; and alchemical semiotics, 192n9; and Cho Yonggi's interpretation, 46–51, 194nn36–38, 41, 195n42; and denotation, 43, 44, 45, 193n22; and desire for language, 42–43; and intensity, 42, 45, 192–93nn18, 29–30; and learning processes for glossolalia, 57–58; overview, 7–8; and palatalization, 193–94n32; and phonetic inventory, 8, 13–14, 46, 187n17, 194n34; and pragmatics, 42, 45, 48; and privacy/secrecy, 55–56; and prosody, 51–54; and Protestant theology, 187n16; and segmentation, 40–42; and semiosis, 42; and social indexicality, 44, 56, 58; and spiritual contact, 43–45, 46, 193n31; and suspicion of glossolalia, 166; and *t'ongsŏng kido*, 45–46; and voicing, 187n19

glossolalia as social experience, 24–25; and authority, 28–29; privacy/secrecy and, 63–64; and social indexicality, 44, 56, 58; and the Word, 58

"God Who Heals" (*Ch'iyu hasinŭn Hananim*) (Oh), 73–76

Goffman, Erving, 95, 101, 200n47

Goodman, Felicitas, 14–15

gospel, 142–43, 186n13. *See also* Word, the

gossip, 56, 71–72, 122–23, 131, 142, 143

"Grace of Jesus's Cure, The" (*Yesunim ŭi ch'iryo ŭi ŭnhye*) (Cho), 82–83

Grace Road Church, 194n35

Graham, Billy, 34, 89, 90, 93. *See also* Kim's interpretation of Graham

grammar, 41, 192n13

Great Faith Church (K'ŭn midŭm kyohoe) (GFC), 67, 196n5

Grice, Paul, 138, 193n20, 203n34

group prayer. *See t'ongsŏng kido*

Han'gŭl, 46

Harding, Susan Friend, 94–95

healing: by Choi Jashil, 128; and Holy Spirit, 82–83, 85, 86, 197n30; Oh Jung-hyun on, 73–77, 83

Heaven Church (Hebŭn Kyohoe), 202–3n31

Henderson, Ebenezer, 177–78

Henry, Victor, 12

Herder, Johann Gottfried von, 175–76, 181

heresy. *See* heterodox churches

heterodox churches, 28, 159–61, 189n19, 204n14

heteroglossia, 8

Hidden Secret to Praying in Tongues, The (*Pangŏn kido e sumŭn pimil*) (Kang), 154–55

Hobbes, Thomas, 87

Hodgson, Richard, 13

Holley, Henry, 91

Holy Spirit: and denotation, 65; and fourth dimension, 84; and healing, 82–83, 85, 86, 197n30; and interpretation, 91–92; and Kim's interpretation of Graham, 119–20; mediating function of, 85–86; and organizational structure of Yoido Full Gospel Church, 85; personification of, 84, 195n1; and real glossolalia discernment, 157; technological transmission of, 67, 196n7; and the Word, 65, 68–69, 72, 79, 81–82, 88. *See also* spiritual contact

homophobia, 73, 197n20

honorifics. *See* social indexicality

"How Do We Tame the Tongue" (*Hyŏ rŭl ŏttŏk'e kildŭlilkka*) (Oh), 71

"Illusion and Reality" (Cho), 58

indexicality. *See* pragmatics; social indexicality

inerrancy of the Word: and evangelism, 94, 114; and fire metaphor, 69–70; and healing, 77; and movement, 72–73, 88; and sermons, 94–95; and sincerity, 94–95; and textual criticism, 73, 197n20; and universalized individuation, 109, 110; and the Word as historical fact, 78–79; and the Word as source of glossolalia, 66

intensity: collaborative, 60–61, 63, 195n57; and glossolalia as produced at limits of language, 42, 45, 192–93nn18, 29–30; and magnitude, 121. *See also* fervency

intercessors, 58–60, 195n55

interdiscursivity, 69, 76, 81–82, 85, 86

interpretation: of Cho Yonggi's glossolalia, 46–51, 194nn36–38, 41, 195n42, 199n15; and the Word, 91–92. *See also* Kim's interpretation of Graham

intertextuality, 69, 85, 86, 196–97nn10–11

InterVarsity Christian Fellowship (Kidok Haksaenghoe), 156
intimacy: and prayer centers, 141–42; and privacy/secrecy, 141–42, 143–44. *See also* deceptive intimacy; privacy/secrecy; spiritual contact
Irving, Edward, 205n32
isolation, 146–49
I Was the Hallelujah Lady (*Na nŭn halleluya ajumma yŏtta*) (Choi), 125

Jakobson, Roman, 187n31
James, William, 12–13, 188n35, 192–93n18
Jansen, Jan, 67
Jansen, Jeff, 67
Japanese speech, 194n34
John Paul II, 197n22

Kang, Tonʼgu, 185n7
Kang Yosep, 154, 157
Keane, Webb, 41–42, 95, 187n16
Kim, Billy Jang Hwan, 89, *90*, 198–99nn4, 10. *See also* Kim's interpretation of Graham
Kim, Ig-Jin, 35
Kim, Kyong Nae, 91
Kim, No-a, 190n44
Kim, Sin Ho, 32
Kim's interpretation of Graham, 89, *90*, 91–96, *98*, *99*, *100*; and cultural semiosis, 92; and evangelism, 95, 108, 113–19, *115*, *116*, 200n48; and glossolalia, 119–20; and Holy Spirit, 91, 92; and inerrancy of the Word, 94; moral chronotope in, 96–101, *101*, 108, 199–200nn34–35, 37–38; and Park Geun-hye, 164; and semiotic transduction, 92–93, 109, 111, 114, 200n48; universalized individuation in, 108–13, *110*, *111*; voicing in, 101, *102*, *103*, 104–8, *105*, *106*, 200n41
Kim Sŏnghye, 195n43
Kingdom Awakening Portal, 66–67
Ko, Byŏngchŏl, 185n7
Korean Pentecost, The (Blair), 39
Korean Protestantism: *chŏndosa* role in, 195n50; church buildings in, 189n20; and congregational membership, 28, 189n21; denominations, 185n7; and economic growth, 26, 31, 34, 189n9, 190n28; fervent quality of, 9; glossolalia ubiquity in, 4, 5, 7, 23, 34, 186n11; and heterodox churches, 28, 189n19; history of, 9–10, 26–27, 77–78, 197nn22–23; importance of *tʼongsŏng kido* in, 39; *kwŏnsa* (deaconess) role in, 150, 203–4n7; magnitude in, 121–22; and missionaries, 27, 78, 194n32; postwar growth of, 9–10, 25, 26–27, 95, 189nn9–11, 199n29; role of evangelism in, 10, 27, 34, 95, 189n13, 199n29; role of prayer centers in, 139; scandals in, 34, 70, 121–22, 123, 190n38, 196n5
Korean speech, 27, 44

Korean War, 96–97, 101
Kosin subdenomination, 186n11
Koyama, Wataru, 193n30
Krug, Wilhelm Traugott, 178–79, 181, 204–5n13
kwŏnsa (deaconess) role, 150, 203–4n7

language, Korean terms for, 5–6, 44
language, limits of. *See* glossolalia as produced at limits of language
Lee, Graham, 39
Lee Man-hee (Yi Manhŭi), 160
Lee Myung-bak (Yi Myŏngbak), 162, 202n28
Lee, T. S., 189n13
Lee, Young-hoon, 38, 190n44
lexemes, 41, 192n11
limits of language. *See* glossolalia as produced at limits of language
Locke, John, 87
logos, 81, 84
"Longing for a Revival of the Word" (*Malssŭm ŭi puhŭng ul kalmangham*) (Oh), 71–73
lorem ipsum placeholder, 1–2, 185n1
Luther, Martin, 176, 178

Manmin Church, 121
Martin, Samuel, 46
megachurches, 26, 27, 28, 121–22, 124, 137, 169. *See also specific churches*
Mendeleev, Dmitri, 192n9
metasemantics, 187n26
Meyer, Heinrich August Wilhelm, 181
Minjung theology, 186nn9, 11, 191n49
miracles, 67, 73–74, 75–76, 79–80, 86–87. *See also* healing
missionaries, 27, 78, 194n32
moral chronotopes, 96–101, *101*, 108, 199–200nn34–35, 37–38
morphemes, 41
Mountain of Fire and Miracles Ministries, 160–61
music, 51–52. *See also* prosody
Myung Sung Church, 121

neurophysiology, 14, 188n41
Nevius method, 70–71
New Testament: and Cho Yonggi's personal theology, 191n56; fire metaphor in, 69–70; and glossolalia as *Zungenreden*, 176–78, 204n3; and glossolalia term origins, 3, 175, 180, 183, 205n33; Korean translations of, 78, 186n12; and regimes of revelation, 124; on spiritual gift (*charism*) distribution, 156; varying interpretations of, 3, 185n3

Oak Han-Heum (Ok Hanhŭm), 70
Oh Jung-hyun (O Chŏnghyŏn), 68; on Christian self-confirmation, 87; on gossip, 71–72; on healing, 73–77, 83; on history of Korean Protestant-

ism, 77; on inerrancy of the Word, 72–73, 77, 88, 92, 197n20; and scandal, 70. *See also* Sarang Church. Sermons: "God Who Heals" (*Ch'iyu hasinŭn Hananim*), 73–76; "How Do We Tame the Tongue" (*Hyŏ rŭl ŏttŏk'e kildŭlilkka*), 71; "Longing for a Revival of the Word" (*Malssŭm ŭi puhŭng ul kalmangham*), 71–73; "Overcoming the Limits of the Flesh" (*Yuksin ŭi han'gye ttwiŏnŏmgi*), 76–77
Old Testament, 50, 78–79, 168, 195n43
Olshausen, Herman, 180, 181
Olukoya, Daniel Kolawole, 160
Osanri Prayer Mountain, 128
"Outer Person and the Inner Person, The" (*Kŏtsaram kwa soksaram*) (Cho), 52–54
"Overcoming the Limits of the Flesh" (*Yuksin ŭi han'gye ttwiŏnŏmgi*) (Oh), 76–77

palatalization, 193–94n32
Pang Chiil, 91
pangŏn (dialect, glossolalia), 5–6, 186n12
Park Chung-hee, 89, 162, 163, 202n28
Park Geun-hye, 161–64
Peirce, Charles, 11, 187n26, 193n31
Pentecostalism: and class, 23, 29, 152; and glossolalia ubiquity, 4, 34; Korean history of, 186n8; and shamanism, 36; and *t'ongsŏng kido*, 39; World Conference (1973), 32–34, 33. *See also* Yoido Full Gospel Church
Pentecostal World Conference, 32–34, 33
peripheral worship, 146–48
Pfister, Oskar, 12
phaticity, 44, 85, 123, 143
phonemes, 40–41, 192n11
phonetic inventory, 8, 13–14, 46, 187n17, 194n34
phonology, 187n26
phonosonic nexus (voice), 8, 60, 108, 133, 179–80, 187n19
pitch, 60
Pneumatology (*Sŏngnyŏng-non*) (Cho), 84
pogŭm (gospel), 186n13
popularity, 27
positional affirmation prayer, 84–85
poststructuralism, 14
pragmatics: and denotation, 8, 42, 192n20; and evangelism, 118, 119; and glossolalia as produced at limits of language, 42, 45, 48; and glossolalia as social experience, 58; and interpretation, 92; and moral chronotopes, 101; and social indexicality, 44, 118; and social mediation, 65; and *t'ongsŏng kido*, 58; and universalized individuation, 111–12
prayer centers (*kidowŏn*), 138–42, 150, 203n36
preaching. *See* sermons
Presbyterianism, 4, 78. *See also* Korean Protestantism; *specific churches*

Presbyterian University and Theological Seminary (*Changnohoe Sinhak Taehakkyo*), 202n26
privacy/secrecy, 24; and Choi Jashil's glossolalia, 127; and church community pressure, 131–34, 135–36, 140, 202nn28, 30; and church dialect (*kyohoe sat'uri*), 133–34; and fourth dimension, 80–81; and glossolalia as produced at limits of language, 55–56; and intimacy, 141–42, 143–44; and Osanri Prayer Mountain, 129, 130–31; and prayer centers, 138–42, 203n36; and regimes of revelation, 124, 142–43, 144–45, 201n9; and scandal, 123; and silent glossolalia, 135, 136–37; and small-group worship, 137–39; and social contact, 63–64; and spiritual contact, 16–17, 55; and surveillance, 55–56, 131–32; and suspicion of glossolalia, 148, 165; terms for, 129–30, 201–2nn18–19; and *t'ongsŏng kido*, 46, 55–56, 133, 134, 202–3n31; and trust, 133, 202n30
prophecy, 59–60, 64, 196n5
prosody, 51–54, 106–7
Psalm 81:10, 50, 195n43
P'yŏngyang Great Revival (1907), 39, 72, 88

qualia, 101, 107–8, 148, 200n40, 203n4

regimes of revelation, 121–24; and privacy/secrecy, 124, 142–43, 144–45, 201n9. *See also* gossip
register, 8–9, 27, 189n15
Reuss, Édouard, 182, 183
revivalism. *See* evangelism; Kim's interpretation of Graham
rhema, 81, 84
Roberts, Oral, 196n7
Ross, John, 78
Rossteuscher, Ernst Adolf, 205n32
Rückert, Leopold Immanuel, 180–81
rumors. *See* gossip
Rumsey, Mary, 186n8
Rutherford, Danilyn, 187n25

Sae Maŭm (new heart-mind) movement, 163
saints, 197n22
Salvation Sect (*Kuwŏnp'a*), 162
Samarin, William, 6, 11–12, 14–15, 40, 42, 187nn25, 31
Samil Church, 121
Sapir, Edward, 42, 192n18, 193n22
Sarang Church (Church of Love) (*Sarang ŭi Kyohoe*), 68, 70–78; and Cho Unp'a, 203n2; organizational structure of, 85; vs. Sarang hanŭn Kyohoe, 196n5; and scandal, 70, 121, 196n5. *See also* Oh Jung-hyun
Satan. *See* demonic forces
Saussure, Ferdinand de, 11, 12, 187n26, 192n9

scales of belonging, 141
scandal: in Great Faith Church, 67, 196n5; and magnitude, 121–22; Park Geun-hye, 162–64; and privacy/secrecy, 123; in Yoido Full Gospel Church, 34, 70, 121, 190n38, 196n5
Schaff, Philip, 182, 205n27
Schulz, David, 181–82
scripture. *See* Word, the
secrecy. *See* privacy/secrecy
segmentation, 40–42
semantics, 42
semiotic transduction, 92–93, 109, 111, 114, 199n15, 200n48
sermons: and inerrancy of the Word, 94–95; and interpretation, 95; in Yoido Full Gospel Church, 61–62. *See also* Kim's interpretation of Graham; sermons *under* Cho Yonggi *and* Oh Jung-hyun
Sewŏl ferry tragedy, 162
shamanism: and deceptive intimacy, 164; and spiritual contact, 44; and suspicion of glossolalia, 26, 29; and Yoido Full Gospel Church, 34–36, 190–91n44
Shincheonji (New Heaven and Earth), 159–60, 161, 204n14
Shin, Ok-ju, 194n35
silent glossolalia, 135, 136–37
Silverstein, Michael, 12, 42, 187n26, 196–97nn10–11
Simmel, Georg, 201n9, 202n22
sincerity, 39, 94–95
slang, 55, 80, 124
small-group (*sogŭrup*) worship, 137–39, 203n34
social indexicality, 44, 56, 58, 118
social mediation, 65, 66, 121–22
sociolinguistics, 11–12
Sŏ, Kwangsŏn, 186n9
Somang Presbyterian Church, 121, 202n28
Speaking in Tongues (Goodman), 14–15
speech, Korean terms for, 5–6, 44
spiritual contact: as dangerous, 149; and denotation, 65; and fire metaphor, 69–70; and fourth dimension, 80, 81–82; and glossolalia as produced at limits of language, 43–45, 46, 193n31; and glossolalia as social experience, 63; and privacy/secrecy, 16–17, 55; and shamanism, 44; and suspicion of glossolalia, 25; and the Word, 65–66, 81–82. *See also* Holy Spirit
starter tongues (*ch'obangŏn*), 13–14, 57, 153
structuralism, 192nn9, 11
Sullivan, Charles, 185n3, 205n32
surveillance, 55–56, 131–32, 137, 139, 202n23
suspicion of glossolalia: and class, 23, 29, 152; and deceptive intimacy, 165–67; and evolution of speech, 167; and fervency, 25–26; and glossolalia as produced at limits of language, 166; and isolation, 148–49; personal reports of, 22–23,

135, 143, 151–52; and privacy/secrecy, 148, 165; and real glossolalia discernment, 150, 158–59; and shamanism, 26, 29; and spiritual danger, 148–49
syllables, 41, 46
syncretism, 35, 44. *See also* shamanism

Tambiah, Stanley, 195n57
textual criticism, 73, 197n20
Thomas, Robert Jermain, 77
throat, 167–68
t'ongsŏng kido (vocalized group prayer): and *ansu kido*, 151; boastful, 57–58; and church community pressure, 133–34, 135, 203n33; and collaborative intensity, 63; glossolalia arising from, 38–39; and glossolalia as produced at limits of language, 45–46; and prayer centers, 139; and privacy/secrecy, 46, 55–56, 133, 134, 202–3n31; and spiritual contact, 65
tongues. *See* glossolalia
Tongues of Men and Angels (Samarin), 11
Toronam (Cho Unp'a), 146, 203n2
trust, 133, 202n30
Truth of Full Gospel (Cho), 84

ulgo pulgo (crying and shouting), 26
Urban, Greg, 197n11

voice and voicing, 101, *102*, *103*, 104–8, *105*, *106*, 187n19, 200nn40–41
von Karlstadt, Andreas Bodenstein, 176

Whorf, Benjamin, 44
Wieseler, Carl, 182
women: and fervency, 188n4; *kwŏnsa* (deaconess) role, 150, 203–4n7; and shamanism, 35; and social mobility, 189n14
Word, the: and agency, 66; and authority, 29; and Cho Yonggi's glossolalia, 54; and Christian self-confirmation, 87; and denotation, 70; and discipleship training, 70–71; and entextualization, 87; and evangelism, 69, 77–78, 88, 93, 94, 197n23; and fire metaphor, 69–70, 72, 77, 82–83, 197n21; and fourth dimension, 79–80, 81–82, 83–84, 198n31; and glossolalia as social experience, 58; and gossip, 71, 122; and healing, 73–76; and history of Korean Protestantism, 77–78; and Holy Spirit, 65, 68–69, 72, 79, 81–82, 88; and interdiscursivity, 69, 76, 81–82; and interpretation, 91–92; and intertextuality, 69, 196–97nn10–11; Korean terms for, 5–6, 44; and logos vs. rhema, 81, 84; movement of, 67–68, 71–73, 88, 94; and prayer centers, 140; and regimes of revelation, 142–43; and social action, 74, 75–77; as source of glossolalia, 66; and spiritual contact, 65–66, 81–82; and theological

theories of glossolalia, 3; and trust in God, 197n21; varying orientations toward, 67–69. *See also* inerrancy of the Word
Wright, Arthur, 183, 205n33

xenolalia/xenoglossia, 3

Yi, Kwangsu, 186n9
Yi, Sŏngbong, 126, 127
Yoido Full Gospel Church, 30–37; church services in, 38, 58–59, 61–62; construction of, 89, 90, 128–29, 201n15; establishment and growth of, 31–34, 33, 125, 190nn27–28, 35–37; and evangelism, 30, 31, 34, 190n27; glossolalia as intrinsic to theology of, 36–37; and Great Faith Church, 196n5; as institutional center for glossolalia, 4, 24, 39–40; vs. Minjung theology, 186n9; organizational structure of, 85; and poverty, 30, 31, 32; scandal in, 34, 70, 121, 190n38, 196n5; sermons in, 61–62; and shamanism, 34–36, 190–91n44; and suspicion of glossolalia, 22, 152. *See also* Cho Yonggi
Yoo, Boo-Woong, 35, 191n56
Yoo Byung-eun (Yu Pyŏngŏn), 162
Youth with a Mission (Yesu Chŏndodan), 156

Zachhuber, Johannes, 204–5n13
Zungenreden (speaking in tongues), 175–78, 204n3

www.ingramcontent.com/pod-product-compliance
Lightning Source LLC
Chambersburg PA
CBHW050302010526
44108CB00040B/2028